Towards Ecological Taxation

Corporate Social Responsibility Series

Series Editors:
Professor Güler Aras, Yildiz Technical University, Istanbul, Turkey
Professor David Crowther, DeMontfort University, Leicester, UK

Presenting applied research from an academic perspective on all aspects of corporate social responsibility, this global interdisciplinary series includes books for all those with an interest in ethics and governance, corporate behaviour and citizenship, regulation, protest, globalization, responsible marketing, social reporting and sustainability.

Recent titles in this series:

Spirituality and Corporate Social Responsibility
David Bubna-Litic
ISBN: 978-0-7546-4763-8

Global Perspectives on Corporate Governance and CSR
Edited by Güler Aras and David Crowther
ISBN: 978-0-566-08830-8

Looking Beyond Profit
Peggy Chiu
ISBN: 978-0-7546-7337-8

Corruption in International Business
Edited by Sharon Eicher
ISBN: 978-0-7546-7137-4

Wealth, Welfare and the Global Free Market
Ibrahim Ozer Ertuna
ISBN: 978-0-566-08905-3

A Handbook of Corporate Governance and Social Responsibility
Edited by Güler Aras and David Crowther
ISBN: 978-0-566-08817-9

Towards Ecological Taxation

The Efficacy of Emissions-Related Motor Taxation

DAVID RUSSELL
DeMontfort University, UK

Routledge
Taylor & Francis Group

LONDON AND NEW YORK

First published 2011 by Gower Publishing

Published 2016 by Routledge
2 Park Square, Milton Park, Abingdon, Oxon OX14 4RN
711 Third Avenue, New York, NY 10017, USA

Routledge is an imprint of the Taylor & Francis Group, an informa business

Gower Applied Business Research
Our programme provides leaders, practitioners, scholars and researchers with thought provoking, cutting edge books that combine conceptual insights, interdisciplinary rigour and practical relevance in key areas of business and management.

British Library Cataloguing in Publication Data
Russell, David.
    Towards ecological taxation : the efficacy of emissions-related motor taxation. – (Corporate social responsibility series)
    1. Automobiles – Motors – Exhaust gas – Environmental aspects. 2. Automobiles, Company – Taxation – Great Britain. 3. Carbon taxes – Great Britain. 4. Carbon dioxide mitigation – Economic aspects – Great Britain.
    I. Title II. Series
    336.2'7836373874'0941 – dc22

Library of Congress Cataloging-in-Publication Data
Russell, David, 1963–
    Towards ecological taxation : the efficacy of emissions-related motor taxation / David Russell.
        p. cm. – (Corporate social responsibility)
    Includes bibliographical references and index.
    ISBN 978-0-566-08979-4 (hbk. : alk. paper)
    1. Environmental impact charges – Great Britain. 2. Carbon taxes – Great Britain. 3. Automobiles, Company – Great Britain. 4. Automobiles – Taxation – Great Britain. 5. Automobiles – Motors – Exhaust gas – Government policy – Great Britain. I. Title.

    HJ5404.Z73R87 2010
    336.2'7833370941 – dc22

                                                                2010034180

ISBN 9780566089794 (hbk)

Contents

Contents

List of Figures

About the Author

Dr. David Russell MSc DBA FCCA FCMA FHEA MCMI MBCS CITP is Head of the Department of Accounting & Finance at De Montfort University, Leicester, UK, where he teaches on a variety of undergraduate, postgraduate, professional and post-experience accounting and management programmes. David has been researching, writing and lecturing on accounting and taxation matters with regard to environmental policy for over ten years and was shortlisted for the International Federation of Accountants, Articles of Merit Award for his work on *Financing Renewable Energy: Creating the Right Package of Incentives for a Level Playing Field for Commercial Electricity Production from Wind Turbines*. More recently David has focused on the issue of carbon emissions and how a broad spectrum of taxation policy measures aligned with an economic framework, based upon the current economic model, could be best suited to curb carbon emissions for society as a whole.

Prior to entering academia, David has worked in engineering, construction, aviation and local government. He has also worked as a freelance consultant providing business specific solutions to a wide variety of clients.

Preface

Environmental policy is becoming an increasing focus of Government as a consequence of mounting environmental awareness and international agreements. Under the Kyoto Agreement on climate change, the United Kingdom is legally committed to the reduction of six greenhouse gases by 12.5% below 1990 emission levels over the period 2008–2012.

As one of the key mechanisms to address this matter, the use of taxation policy to reduce the demand for fossil fuels and encourage a shift towards Carbon Dioxide (CO_2)-neutral energy production has been widely canvassed.

Motorcars are a major source of CO_2 emission. The alterations to road transport taxes, for lead-free petrol and ultra-low sulphur diesel, to promote environmental objectives has already been tried in the UK with good effect. Modifications to the taxation system have also been extended to company cars, where individuals are taxed as a Benefit in Kind (BIK) for the use of a company vehicle.

The changes in company car taxation from 6 April 2002 transformed the way individuals were taxed for their company cars and may as a consequence have a significant impact on CO_2. The previous system of taxation had encouraged drivers of company cars to maximise business mileage beyond certain thresholds to reduce their individual tax burden, with little regard for the levels of emissions produced.

This book considers the efficacy of ecological taxation, with respect to emissions-related taxation, by examining the change to the taxation for company cars to take into account the level of CO_2 emission. It investigates the effect on business mileage and company car selection by individuals and the impact on company car policy of organisations. By utilising empirical evidence based on a survey of company car drivers, this book contributes to a more comprehensive understanding of whether such changes to a principle and method in the UK taxation regime, which is potentially applicable generally for ecological taxation, may contribute to lowering CO_2 emissions.

A research text of this nature often raises as many questions as it points to solutions. The intention of this book is to make specific proposals and recommendations where the evidence permits, but also to permit sufficient discourse and theoretical conjecture to allow the reader to appreciate and contemplate the problem domain.

The book has been written with several different audiences in mind. Firstly, it should provide an introduction to the environmental context for carbon emissions and provide the reader with an insight into the issues facing theorists in devising a conceptual framework which is consistent with our economic model.

Secondly, by focusing on a specific taxation reform relating to carbon emissions, which encompass motor taxation regimes, this book provides the reader with an insight into the efficacy of emissions-related motor taxation regimes. It does this via both a pragmatic viewpoint – in examining the success of a particular reform – and a theoretical perspective – in using the findings to identify the characteristics of a framework required for successful implementation of model for future ecological tax reforms. This model may be consistent with achieving environmental objectives in the form of emissions reductions.

The book may be used in a number of ways. It may be read in its entirety and used to support teaching and research. Alternatively, it may be used as a reference text to address particular issues, or as a text for general guidance on specific matters relating to economics, sustainability, ecological taxation and the efficacy of the latter.

The conclusions have implications for, and would be of interest to, governments, policy makers, particularly those charged with the responsibility of achieving international obligations (for example, Kyoto), and bodies that have a particular interest in the reduction of carbon emissions (United Nations Framework Convention on Climate Change (UNFCCC), United Nations Conference on Trade and Development (UNCTAD), United Nations Commission on Environment and Development (UNCED), Intergovernmental Panel on Climate Change (IPCC), European Union (EU), Department for Transport (DfT) and Department of Environment Transport and the Regions

(DETR). Academics and scholars may also find this book of interest, as may others who wish to gain a better understanding of how taxation could be adapted innovatively within the existing economic status quo to deliver specific and measurable reductions in CO_2. It may also be of relevance to those, whom like the author of this work, have a sincere interest and apprehension for long-term sustainability based upon the current economic model.

Acknowledgements

I would like to take this opportunity to express my sincere gratitude and appreciation to those who have assisted me along the way with this writing. In particular I would like to mention:

Professor David Crowther, for introducing me to this publishing opportunity and providing me with invaluable help and guidance in writing this book.

Helen, Luke, Hayley and Rasc, for their support.

Finally, to everybody else, whose help and cooperation has been appreciated in the completion of this book.

Dedicated to:

Rasc. (our best friend)

List of Abbreviations

BHP	Brake Horsepower
BIK	Benefit in kind
CC	Cubic capacity
CFC	Chlorofluorocarbon
CO_2	Carbon dioxide
CNG	Compressed natural gas
CSR	Corporate Social Responsibility
DEFRA	Department for Environment, Food and Rural Affairs
DETR	Department of Environment Transport and the Regions
DfT	Department for Transport
EC	European Commission
ECU	Electronic Control Unit
EEA	European Environment Agency
EU	European Union
FCA	Full Cost Accounting
GDP	Gross Domestic Product
GHG	Greenhouse gas
IAS	International Accounting Standards
IFAC	International Federation of Accountants
IPCC	Intergovernmental Panel on Climate Change
LPG	Liquid Petroleum Gas
MAC	Marginal Abatement Cost
MDC	Marginal damage cost
MtC	Million tonnes of Carbon
NI	National Insurance
OECD	Organisation for Economic Co-operation & Development
PCP	Personal Contract Purchase
PPMV	Parts per million by volume
REC	Regional Environmental Center for Central and Eastern Europe
SEPA	Swedish Environmental Protection Agency

SMMT	Society of Motor Manufacturers and Traders
SUV	Sports Utility Vehicle
TDM	Total Design Method
UNCED	United Nations Commission of Environment and Development
UNCTAD	United Nations Conference on Trade and Development
UNFCCC	United Nations Framework Convention on Climate Change
USEPA	United States Environmental Protection Agency
VAT	Value Added Tax
VED	Vehicle Excise Duty

1

The Problem of Carbon Dioxide Emissions

In order to consider the efficacy of ecological motor taxation regimes for emission reduction, this introductory chapter lays the foundation for discussion and analysis in the subsequent chapters by introducing the research domain and emphasising the problems associated with Carbon Dioxide (CO_2) emissions within an international context. Moreover, the significance of the research matter considered in this book has been emphasised by reference to the Kyoto Agreement on international obligations for emissions reductions. This treaty, between the majority of Organisation for Economic Co-operation & Development (OECD) countries, provides for the regulation and reduction of emission of Greenhouse Gases (GHGs) from industrialised countries. The mechanisms to achieve these goals are wide ranging and diverse.

Scientific discussion relating to carbon has been introduced to enable better appreciation of the challenges faced by the global society in the management of carbon. The concept of sustainability is introduced, discussed and emphasised from an economic perspective to facilitate the discussion and subsequent examination of a revenue-neutral tax reform, which has both economic and public policy implications. In so doing, the study aims to contribute to a more comprehensive understanding of whether such changes to a principle and method in the UK taxation regime, which is potentially applicable generally, are likely to achieve significant reductions of CO_2 emissions and contribute towards achieving the Kyoto Target.

Accordingly, the concepts and theories underpinning this study are identified in an attempt to explain the current situation and to provide an opportunity for further conceptualising of theory later in the book, once conclusions are drawn from the study and subsequent analysis.

Moreover, it is intended that strategies for and characteristics of an effective ecological tax related to carbon emissions may gain prominence to contribute to an overall framework for ecological taxation to assist the developed economies to meet their environmental obligations.

The post-industrial revolution era has seen an exponential increase in the consumption of finite and non-renewable resources, coupled with substantial destruction of the natural environment. This has, for example, taken the form of deforestation, extinction of species, ozone depletion and pollution which may have had an impact on climate change. Pollution is also recognised as a major international phenomenon, affecting water, air and the soil. Not only was the global energy system 16 times larger in 2000 than in 1900, but the fossil fuels, which have undesirable emission consequences when burnt, provided 84% of global energy (Jaccard 2006).

Weizsacker & Jesinghaus (1992) observed of the *Brundtland Report* (UNCED 1987) that the consequence of further growth in a conventional sense would not be worldwide prosperity, but rather lead to destruction, putting in jeopardy prosperity and indeed the very basis of life. It follows that the continuance of such growth is unsustainable and illogical in the long run.

Traditional environmental policy has focused upon standard setting for environmental quality or a ceiling level of emission per unit of polluting source. Weizsacker & Jesinghaus (1992) argued that this 'end of the pipe' approach has, when evaluated from a global perspective proven essentially inadequate. This observation is based on the additional costs that must be borne for measures of environmental safeguards, with the consequence that there would be a degree of reluctance from the developing economies to develop an environmental policy or sustainability agenda. At the same time such economies envisage sizeable increases in demand for energy that will, in the main, be satisfied from the combustion of fossil fuels, which in turn may contribute to the unabated rise in CO_2 emissions.

Conventional measures have done little to narrow the gap between the current and future world energy demands and achieve the reduction in levels of global energy consumption necessary to stabilise the climate through a sustainable level of CO_2 emissions. The countries in the Northern hemisphere consume on average approximately ten times more natural resources per capita than those in the Southern hemisphere. Reductions in consumption of resources and emissions in the Northern hemisphere are imperative if the countries in the South are to be encouraged to follow a more sustainable agenda.

Concern over sustainability matters has become an area of considerable public policy debate at international, national and local level (Bebbington & Thomson 1996). The problem is very serious, as it is inextricably linked with social issues and has implications for the long-term survival of our society.

The 'greenhouse effect' which refers to the build-up of CO_2 and other GHGs in the earth's atmosphere (Nordhaus 1991) is expected to contribute to global warming and other associated climate changes within the next century. Such a notion was first considered by Tyndall (1863), who hypothesised that changes to the composition of the atmosphere could alter climate. Arrhenius (1896) attempted to quantify such changes and concluded that a doubling of CO_2 would lead to a rise in global (mean) temperature of between 4°C and 6°C.

Evidence of global warming is beginning to emerge. An analysis of the sources of uncertainty concerning future climate change was presented in Nordhaus & Yohe (1983). This review estimated that a doubling of CO_2 or its radiative equivalent would increase global mean surface temperature by 1°C to 5°C. A further study by Nordhaus (1991) provided support for an association between increases in CO_2 and rising temperatures.

However, research has failed to conclusively establish the extent of an association between the human activity relating to the burning of fossil fuels, CO_2 emissions and global atmospheric temperature. This is possibly because of the delayed climate response to radiative inputs, caused by the 'thermal inertia of the oceans' (Nordhaus 1991:922). Estimates of such a delay range from six to 95 years (Nordhaus 1991). However studies of global warming have established very high levels of probability between global warming and climate change (Stott et al. 2004) (Nordhaus 1998). The Intergovernmental Panel on Climate Change (IPCC) estimated that the temperature rise could be in the region of 1.4°C–5.8°C for the next century (IPCC 2001). Nordhaus (1998) estimate of an average increase of 3°C for this period is not inconsistent with the temperature rise suggested by the IPCC.

Retallack (2005) suggested that impacts of global warming become considerable if globally averaged surface temperatures rise above 2°C of the pre-industrial level. Rising global temperatures have a variety of consequences not least the melting of polar ice. World ocean levels are rising at a rate of 2 mm per annum, which is double the increase prior to the mid-nineteenth century (Hawkes 2005).

Retallack (2005) estimated that to prevent the temperature threshold of 2°C being exceeded, CO_2 concentrations should not exceed 400 ppmv. Azar & Rodhe (1997) suggested a similar level of 350 ppmv–450 ppmv, while Alcamo & Kreileman (1996) concurred with a level below 450 ppmv. Eleven studies of climate sensitivity by Meinshausen (2006) suggest the probability of exceeding the 2°C threshold if GHGs stabilised at 450 ppmv is as high as 78% (low 26%). Stern (2007) notes that CO_2 concentrations have now risen to approximately 430 ppmv, compared to a pre-industrial revolution level of 280 ppmv and to stabilise at 450ppmv, global emissions would be required to peak during the next decade, followed by a consistent fall to 70% below current levels by 2050.

The debate concerning climate change has continued with the scientific community remaining divided as to the level of threat posed by global warming. Costanza (1989) devised a pay-off matrix approach to the dilemma, with those who recognise no significant threat to the environment from the burning of fossil fuels and CO_2 emissions described as 'optimists' and those who recognise a significant threat to the environment from this source as 'pessimists'.

If the optimists' assessment of global warming prove to be correct then a response to this is *not* required. If the pessimists assessment of global warming prove to be correct then a response to this *is* required. This may result in further costs being borne by society to react to these environmental problems. However, if the pessimists' assessments of global warming prove to be incorrect, then there could be costs imposed on society that were not necessary. If the pessimists prove to be correct (and the optimists were wrong) and an appropriate response had been taken an ecological disaster would be averted. Contrast this with the optimists' assessment of global warming proving to be incorrect (the pessimists were right) and no appropriate response being taken to avoid this would result in an ecological disaster. In this event, the costs of pursuing the optimistic course of action are immeasurably high and the conclusion probably irreversible. Therefore, the arguments in favour of a risk-averse strategy appear persuasive. The benefits from early responses, in the form of taking action now on possible environmental problems, despite the absence of conclusive proof, are expected to be very high (Pearson & Smith 1990).

Grubb et al. (1999) asserted that, over the last four decades, theories relating to global warming do indicate a consensus that climate change has adverse outcomes and it is likely to be human induced. The authors observed that in 1990, the IPCC first assessment of this matter underpinned the United Nations Framework Convention on Climate Change (UNFCCC) that was considered at the Earth Summit (1992) at Rio.

The Earth Summit sought to debate issues concerning the human influence on global sustainability matters with particular emphasis on the differing needs of the developed and developing world. The Summit was particularly valuable in providing the beginnings for international action. It served to highlight the fact that the existing ecological problems arise largely because of the actions of those countries in the Northern hemisphere.

The Kyoto Protocol to the (UNFCCC) was finalised in Kyoto, Japan, on 11 December 1997. The Protocol was open for signature from 16 March 1998 to 15 March 1999, although the parties that have not yet acceded to the Kyoto Protocol may do so at any time.[1]

The protocol became enforceable on 16 February 2005 and sought to respond to the threat of climate change, by reducing emissions of GHGs, including CO_2 emissions from fossil fuels, by providing a global agreement for a framework to deal with climate change and provides for a series of initially modest economic and environmental commitments from nations.

Under the Kyoto Agreement, all parties listed in Annex B (Figure 1) to the protocol[2] have agreed to reduce GHGs. The commitment is to reduce CO_2 emissions by on average at least 5.2% below 1990 levels for the period 2008–2012. The UK target for this period is 12.5%. (This follows the European Union's (EU) member states agreement to redistribute their target of 8%.)[3]

---

1   See http://unfccc.int/essential_background/kyoto_protocol/status_of_ratification/items/2613.php
2   See www.unfccc.de
3   See http://unfccc.int/essential_background/kyoto_protocol/items/3145.php

Figure 1   **Kyoto Protocol target commitments for Annex B countries**

Party	Target (percentage of base year or period)
Australia	108
Austria	92
Belgium	92
Bulgaria	92
Canada	94
Croatia	95
Czech Republic	92
Denmark	92
Estonia	92
European Community	92
Finland	92
France	92
Germany	92
Greece	92
Hungary	94
Iceland	110
Ireland	92
Italy	92
Japan	94
Latvia	92
Liechtenstein	92
Lithuania	92
Luxembourg	92
Monaco	92
Netherlands	92
New Zealand	100
Norway	101
Poland	94
Portugal	92
Romania	92
Russian Federation	100
Slovakia	92
Slovenia	92
Spain	92
Sweden	92
Switzerland	92
Ukraine	100
United Kingdom	92
United States of America	93

Source: United Nations (1998).

The Kyoto Protocol is significant in that it provides agreement between all OECD countries, with the exception of the United States which has indicated its intention not to ratify the protocol (despite being party to the target setting) for the emission of GHGs from industrialised countries. The mechanisms to achieve this are wide ranging and diverse with more research required to systematically evaluate their efficacy.

The UK Deputy Prime Minister announced at the Kyoto Earth Summit that the UK would be unilaterally reducing its emissions of GHGs by a more ambitious target of 20% by 2010. This pledge has been reiterated in three successive Labour party manifestos (Wintour 2006).

However, the UK Government later conceded that they were not on course to achieve the latter target (DTI 2003). The energy White Paper suggested that further action would be needed in the longer term and proposed a target of reducing CO_2 emissions by 60% by 2050 (DTI 2003). In September 2004, the Government announced a review into its UK Climate Change Programme, culminating in the Climate Change Bill gaining Royal assent in 2008. This legislation requires the UK to cut its GHG emissions by 80% by 2050. The UK is the first country in the world to make GHG reduction targets law and will put Britain at the forefront of accountability for tackling climate change. The legislation includes a provision for a carbon budgeting system to run from 2008–12, 2013–17 and 2018–22, with a requirement for Government to report to Parliament on proposals and policies to meet the targets set out in the budgets. Moreover, the legislation requires the creation of a Committee on Climate Change, a new independent, expert body to advise Government on the carbon budgets and submit annual reports to Parliament on the UK's progress.

During the past three decades, many authors have recognised the damage our actions have on the natural environment and have attempted to develop methods to reduce, or optimistically, eliminate the impact of our activity on the environment. Bebbington et al. (2001:28) suggested that research in this area has questioned fundamental characteristics of our economic system and indeed 'the very tenets of our civilisation: exploitation, over-consumption, growth…and so on' and highlighted the deficiencies in our economic systems, which do not adequately recognise environmental considerations, in so far as the costs of environmental damage or environmental repair are not properly taken into account in costing systems and pricing policy.

The detailed implications arising from such a lack of recognition of environmental matters is, in the absence of a conceptual framework for this, difficult to assess or model with precision. Notwithstanding that it is possible to make assessments of how society may evolve if certain types of reforms were instituted to alleviate or remedy the current situation. Such reforms point to a less comfortable existence for those in the West, where the greatest benefit from our economic systems has been derived and the greatest exploitation of the environment has taken place. The greatest resistance to such reforms is therefore likely to come from those who have to change the most and have the most to lose. There have been issues of justice in climate change negotiations between wealthy and poor countries (Wittneben et al. 2005).

The detailed implications arising from estimating the damage from global warming were considered by Nordhaus (1991). Agricultural yields may decline as a result of higher temperatures, but this may be compensated by higher levels of CO_2, which would have a fertilisation result. Sea levels will rise, although the extent of the rise will be dependent on the rise in global temperatures. Nordhaus (1991) suggested that the rise in sea levels will have consequences of the loss of land and higher value property, because of the increased scarcity of the same and increased coastal protection costs.

The difficulties in quantification, and hence the oversimplification of the intricate mutual relationship between economic and climatic factors, are acknowledged. Nordhaus (1991) when attempting to make an assessment of the effects of global warming on an economy estimated the net economic effect from a 3°C rise in temperature to be approximately 0.25% of national income for the USA. Such estimates of costs may be worthy of consideration in the development of any strategy for the reduction of GHGs.

Sustainable Development

The term sustainable development is a 'contestable concept' (Neumayer 1999) in so far as it is difficult to decipher the term in practice. Neumayer (1999) suggested that there are two very different economic paradigms of sustainable development, based upon weak and strong forms of sustainability and concluded that development may be characterised as that which does not reduce the capacity to provide non-declining per capita utility for infinity. Since the capacity to provide utility arises from stock that potentially provides goods and/or services, it follows that natural capital is 'the totality of nature – resources, plants, species and ecosystems' (Neumayer 1999:9). An appreciation of natural capital is paramount to discriminate between the two differing sustainability paradigms referred to by Neumayer (1999) and is discussed later on in this chapter.

In its weak form, sustainability requires the maintenance of the combined aggregate total of man-made capital and natural capital to be constant as a minimum condition. The weak sustainability paradigm asserts that natural capital may be depleted as long as man-made capital is substituted. Over time, earlier generations may exercise their entitlement to (optimally) draw down the pool so long as they also contribute to the stock of reproducible capital. This suggests that sustainable development is unnecessary provided that man-made capital arises at a rate at least equivalent to or greater than the rate of depletion.

On the other hand, in its strong form, sustainability essentially asserts that natural capital is non-substitutable with other forms of capital. These two potentially conflicting views arising out of these two paradigms may be reconciled if a caveat is added to the definition of weak sustainability of 'the total value of natural capital to remain at least constant'. The differences arise largely from the contrasting views on substitutability of natural capital.

Heuting & Reijnders (1998) maintained that the preservation of the physical stock of all natural capital is paramount for environmental purpose such that their capacity to rejuvenate must not be exceeded. This notion prohibits substitutability between differing forms of natural capital.

Neumayer (1999) highlighted the scientific uncertainty about the consequences of continuing depletion of natural capital and the extent to which such losses are irreversible, coupled with the requirement of some forms of natural capital to provide life itself. This established the case for non-substitutability of man-made capital and natural capital and provided a powerful argument in favour of the strong sustainability paradigm being more viable.

The urgency in addressing environmental problems cannot be offset against an expectancy that a greater economic good could arise from environmental degradation. 'More and more it is [the] remaining natural capital that now plays the role of limiting factor' (Daly 1995:50).

A good deal of the discussion in the next chapter arises from a strong sustainability paradigm, the need to address deficiencies of the economic status quo and the recognition that the fundamental attributes of our economic system are unlikely to change in pursuance of a strong sustainability agenda. There are many vested interests in the status quo. However, not withstanding that, the possibilities of socially and politically acceptable reforms exist which could provide opportunities through incentive for ecological improvement and a move towards a more sustainable environment. Nordhaus (1991) observed that the essential policy question involved how much reduction in consumption should be incurred today to slow the pace of future climate change consequences.

The Research Matter

This research is concerned with the consequences of consumption of natural capital. It attempts to address some of the issues of sustainability, at least in part, by contributing to a more comprehensive understanding of the role that resource pricing (see Figure 2) can take for specific forms of (non-substitutable) natural capital by internalising, through the application of ecological tax reform, to include previously disregarded externalities.

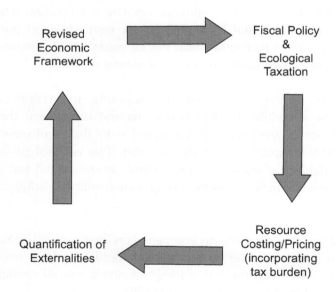

| Revised Economic Framework | → | Fiscal Policy & Ecological Taxation |

Quantification of Externalities ← Resource Costing/Pricing (incorporating tax burden)

Figure 2   **Internalisation of externalities into the economic framework via ecological taxation**

This book considers the efficacy of changes to the principle and method of the company car taxation regime in the UK, with a view to reduce carbon emissions and thus contribute to the Kyoto Target for lowering CO_2 emissions from fossil fuels. The principles underlying such reforms may also be applicable generally in the developed world. The generalisability of the findings may be of interest also. It therefore primarily aimed at the developed world in the hope that research developments applied successfully in the developed world may also serve as a credible model for developing nations.

In doing so this book will also consider scientific, economic and public policy matters that should underpin any strategy for environmental improvement.

The scientific matters relate to validating the causes for environmental concern and to determine their effects together with CO_2 and other pollution abatement strategies.

The economic matters relate to the consideration of the possibilities for quantification of the negative environmental effects of GHGs and CO_2 in particular and how theoretical developments may contribute to an approach, to offer some significant environmental improvement or pollution curtailment, albeit disaggregated or piecemeal, within the context of the existing economic framework (that is, the status quo).

The public policy matters relate largely to issues and implications of implementation of fiscal policy in the form of taxation arising from the desire to reduce or eliminate externalities, in pursuit of both a more efficient allocation of resources from an economic point of view and a more sustainable position from an environmental perspective.

Carbon Emissions

Heavy reliance is currently placed on energy from fossil fuels. Bebbington et al. (2001) suggested that energy lay at the heart of our unsustainable means of economic organisation and suggested that energy was not only considered to be a good indicator of wider resource use, but the relative cheapness of fossil fuels encouraged wastefulness in general consumption. Traditional methods of motor vehicle transportation relying on fossil fuels have satisfied the demand for transport in the United Kingdom at a relatively cheap price. However, considerable amounts of hydrocarbons, nitrogen oxides, carbon monoxide and

CO_2 are produced per litre of fuel consumed. The long-term environmental consequences of this have yet to be assessed fully. However, the GHG effect and its potential impact on global climate, sea levels (Cline 1991) and on the global economy (Nordhaus 1991) have heightened concerns particularly about CO_2 emissions.

Brook (2005) explained that our understanding of long-term human-induced effects on GHG levels in the atmosphere may be gained from air trapped in ice core samples extracted from polar ice sheets. This enables researchers to place modern changes in the context of natural variations over considerable time periods of hundreds of thousands of years. 'The new long records of carbon dioxide, methane, and nitrous oxide from [the] European Project for Ice Coring in Antarctica (EPICA) ... extend the window on greenhouse gas levels to 650,000 years. The results confirm that the modern atmosphere is highly anomalous and reinforce the view that greenhouse gases and climate are intimately related' (Brook 2005:1285).

Cox et al. (2000) noted of anthropogenic emissions, that the continued increase in the atmospheric concentration of CO_2 is likely to lead to significant changes in climate. Bolin et al. (1986) suggested that the release of 'greenhouse gases' into the atmosphere is likely to cause fundamental changes in global climate. CO_2 combines homogeneously within the atmosphere of the planet.

The concentration of CO_2 in the atmosphere depends on the rates of exchange of CO_2 between the atmosphere and the terrestrial biomass, the oceans and the carbon in deposits of fossil fuel and other geological formations. Approximately half of the current carbon emissions are being absorbed by the ocean and by land ecosystems, however this absorption is sensitive to climate change which is difficult to model with precision.

Cox et al. (2000) discussed a three-dimensional carbon-climate model, indicating that carbon-cycle feedbacks would significantly accelerate climate change during the twenty-first century and concluded that under a 'business as usual' scenario, the terrestrial biosphere would act as an overall carbon sink until around 2050, but then turn into a source of emission accelerating the rates of global warming already experienced.

Since the post-industrial revolution, economic growth has greatly increased the input into the atmosphere of carbon from fossil fuel deposits; however the processes that remove carbon from the atmosphere have not increased proportionately. It is estimated that current carbon levels are rising at approximately 2.5ppmv per annum (Stern 2007) from a pre-industrial level of approximately 280ppmv (DETR 1999). In the period 1950 to present, CO_2 emission approximations are based upon energy statistics published by the United Nations (Marland et al. 2006).

CO_2 concentrations may be stabilised by measures that increase rates of removal and storage (sequestration) and also policies which decrease CO_2 emissions into the atmosphere. Both may have a role to play in limiting the accumulation of CO_2 and other GHGs in the atmosphere and to stabilise concentrations at levels that would prevent further damage to the climate system.

Emissions abatement is advocated as a priority by most, but not by all. Wigley et al. (1996) suggested that CO_2 abatement should be delayed for the future. The explanations for this are that, firstly, there are considerable stocks of carbon fuels yet to be used up. Secondly, that technological progress over time will allow for low-carbon substitute fuels to be developed. Thirdly, that capital growth would require fewer resources to be set aside now and, fourthly, that carbon emitted sooner is subjected to a natural removal process for a longer time period than carbon emitted later.

The stabilisation of CO_2 concentrations is of particular international concern and has produced policy responses from the UNFCCC and the Kyoto Protocol. The ratification of the Kyoto Treaty on climate change has resulted in all developed countries (with the exception of the USA) agreeing to legally binding targets to reduce GHGs. These agreements aim to limit the accumulation of CO_2 and other GHGs in the atmosphere, but are not themselves prescriptive as to how they are to be achieved.

Economic Theory

Economic theory may be useful in determining the benefits of lower CO_2 emissions and in identifying such measures as market-based instruments, as opposed to command and control. Economic theory may also prove useful when appraising the introduction of environmental taxation for traditional labour-based taxation, the reappraisal and redrafting of environmental regulation and the removal of inappropriate subsidies linked to emissions to achieve this is further discussed in Chapter 2.

Economic theory is also pertinent to the study in so far as the modifications to the arrangements for company car taxation through an ecological tax reform provides an opportunity to study the price sensitivity of a category of mandatory car users, namely company car drivers. The effect such price sensitivity has on car procurement decisions and distance travelled, both of which have consequences for the level of pollution generally, and in this case CO_2 emissions in particular, can also be addressed.

In order to preserve certain natural capital, the costs incurred may well exceed the benefits, based upon the current methods of quantification for costs and benefits. Decisions to pursue a policy of incurring excessive financial costs for less financial benefits in certain circumstances may be considered to be a political rather than an economic matter. This highlights the need for government to have a clear definition of its environmental objectives with respect to CO_2. Clear trajectory for CO_2 to 2050 is referred to by the Department for Environment, Food and Rural Affairs (DEFRA) with respect to the Climate Change Act (2008) for CO_2 reduction.

However, the UK Government's approach to the achievement of this does not take into account the potential divergence between underlying economic theory which requires everything to have a value and environmental matters, including emissions, where in certain circumstances no value is currently attributed (for example, fresh air).

Research Problem

The research problem under consideration is concerned with the development and implementation of concepts and methodologies for the internalisation of environmental costs into accounting and pricing mechanisms and to study and identify characteristics which contribute to the efficacy of the same specifically through the use of taxation to achieve a specific environmental objective – the reduction of CO_2 emission. In so doing the research recognises that the market will not give proper recognition to environmental considerations unless the costs of environmental damage and the benefits of environmental improvement are accommodated within prices charged for goods and services.

To appraise taxation reform affecting energy consumption and emissions of CO_2, a significant GHG, a single revenue-neutral reform of a change in the company car taxation system has been selected for study. Modifications to the company car taxation system, from April 2002, resulted in individuals being taxed as a BIK for the use of a company vehicle based upon the level of CO_2 emission, rather than solely on the list price. This reform provided an opportunity for an assessment of the costs and benefits of a vehicle with a particular level of CO_2 emission for an individual and may, as a consequence, have a significant impact on individuals' attitudes to company car acquisition and overall levels of CO_2 production from the same.

Individuals with company cars were surveyed about their future procurement intentions and polluting behaviour as a part of the study, to determine whether this revenue-neutral ecological taxation reform improved the prospects for sustainability by determining whether such tax reforms would reduce polluting behaviour and also reduce the consumption of natural capital.

Will the ecological tax reforms have the desired consequences in practice? And does the change in the taxation arrangements affecting company car drivers also have the potential to raise additional revenue to contribute towards clean-up costs for the environmental damage caused?

Such an investigation requires some consideration of price elasticity and behavioural matters affecting company car procurement, to obtain an insight into the magnitude of increase in company car taxation that would be required to encourage individuals' procurement choice of a low-emission vehicle, possibly moderate business mileage travelled and therefore consume less natural resource and pollute less. Technological developments and significant determinants of success of such taxation reform, for example revenue neutrality, have also been contemplated.

To strive for the ambitious targets for reduction of CO_2 emissions below 1990 levels, for the period 2008–2012, the use of taxation to reduce the demand for fossil fuels has been widely promoted. 'A tax (if set at the right level – an important proviso!) will often be more economically efficient than directly stopping polluting behaviour through legal curbs. Taxes are better than regulation in controlling some sorts of pollution because they allow individuals to weigh up the costs and benefits of their behaviour on a case-by-case basis' (Pearson & Smith 1990:2).

This book provides an opportunity to appraise the significance of fiscal and economic instruments in achieving a quantified target, partially through the scrutiny of literature and predominately through the consideration of the research problem. The research problem facilitates measuring the level of CO_2 emission from company cars for pre- and post-taxation reform periods, to determine:

- the extent to which taxation does have an impact on the level of CO_2 emission from company cars;

- whether taxation can effectively internalise some environmental costs, which were previously borne by society as a whole.

Dasgupta et al. (1980) argued that a particular pattern of taxation can produce any required path of resource usage and concluded that taxation provides an adequately broad set of policy tools to manipulate resource depletion according to requirements.

Accordingly, it is hoped that strategies and characteristics for 'green' taxation in the form of a framework for ecological taxation, which is discussed in the penultimate chapter, may contribute to the efficacy of taxation relating to emissions to assist the UK and other similar economies to meet their environmental obligations, with regard to carbon emissions.

Increasingly, environmental factors will be at the forefront of policy at all levels. The difficulties of quantification of such factors have already been alluded to. However, notwithstanding that, there is likely to be greater effort to establish environmental costs of activities and to internalise the same via methods including taxation. Symons et al. (1994) emphasised the significance of economic policies in controlling CO_2 emissions globally.

According to Stern (2007) transport is the third largest source of global emissions, representing 14% of global emissions, with three-quarters of these emissions arising from road transport. Transport is likely to remain a substantial source of pollution, contributing significant amounts of GHGs. Indeed Stern (2007) contends that total CO_2 emissions from transport is expected to double by 2050. An externality from road transport is congestion. Increases in road usage will increase the volume of pollution, which is further compounded by congestion.

The Department of Environment Transport and the Regions (DETR) (2000) implemented measures to promote the advancement and use of more fuel efficient vehicles. Such measures include the graduation of Vehicle Excise Duty (VED) and the reform of company car taxation. In addition, agreements between the European Commission and the European Automobile Manufacturers Association to reduce CO_2 emissions from new cars to at least 25% below existing levels, to an average CO_2 emission figure of 140g/km by 2008, is now supplemented with legislation with targets for car manufacturers of 65% of new cars averaging a 130g/km target by 2012, 75% by 2013, 80% by 2014 and 100% by 2015. Such reductions offer those who wish to procure a new vehicle a lower-emission option than was previously available.

At the time of the company car tax reform, considered for this study, the average new car produced 178g/km of CO_2, which represents a 7% reduction on 1997 levels (SMMT 2002).

The DETR (2000) estimated that its own measures would deliver CO_2 emissions from road traffic in England of 30.8 Million Tonnes of Carbon (MtC) in 2010, which is approximately the same level as for 1996 (30.5 MtC). However this is still in excess of the 1990 levels of 25.8 MtC. Road traffic growth is estimated to grow between 20–25% for the period 2000–2010 (DfT 2003) (see Figure 3).

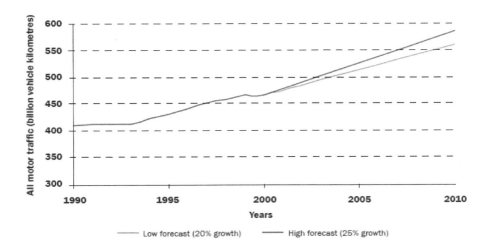

Figure 3   Forecast UK motor traffic

Source: Foley & Fergusson 2003

If not addressed, the increasing road transport CO_2 emissions could endanger the prospect of achieving the Government's 2010 target (Foley & Fergusson 2003). Further measures would therefore be necessary if the transport sector is to deliver CO_2 emission reductions consistent with the Government's obligations under the Kyoto Protocol.

The conclusions for this research provide quantification of the change in CO_2 emissions from the introduction of this tax reform and highlight matters associated with taxation reform to achieve environmental objectives. Moreover, the conclusions inform the development of fiscal and economic instruments to provide incentives and disincentives consistent with obligations addressed through targets for environmental objectives.

Company Car Taxation up to 2002

The system for company car taxation up to 2002 may be illustrated by Figure 4:

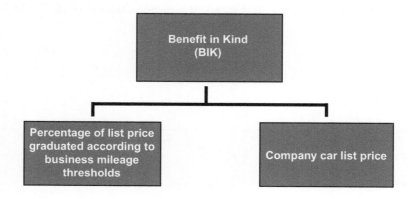

Figure 4   Company car taxation up to 2002

The system of taxation for company cars is based on the principle of BIK whereby a notional income is included as part of an individual's taxable gross salary based on the purported benefit of the company car to the individual. BIK was previously determined by the manufacturers' purchase price (subject to £80,000 maximum) when the car is new including accessories, delivery charges and Value Added Tax (VAT) (list price) and the number of business miles driven by the individual. The higher the purchase price for the car when new, arguably, the greater the benefit. Conversely, the more business miles driven by the individual, arguably, the less benefit the car provides and the greater its requirement for carrying out a particular trade or profession. The BIK up to and including the tax year 2001/2002 was calculated as shown in Figure 5:

Figure 5   **Table of business mileage and tax charges**

Business Mileage	Percentage of list price (subject to a maximum of £80,000)
0–2,499	35%
2,500–17,999	25%
In excess of 18,000	15%

For example, the BIK for an individual driving 16,000 miles per annum in a Ford Focus 1.6LX company car would have been determined as follows (Figure 6):

Figure 6   **Determination of Benefit in Kind (BIK)**

Ford Focus 1.6LX list price:	**£13,210**
Percentage of list price (based upon 16, 000 miles):	**25%**
$\therefore$ Benefit in Kind: (25% x £13, 210) =	**£3,302.50**

The BIK was then aggregated with the individual's gross salary as part of the gross income calculation, which after reliefs and allowances is taxed (Finance Act 2000) at the following rates (Figure 7):

Figure 7   **Income Tax rates (Finance Act 2000)**

Rate (%)	Band of Income (£)	Cumulative Tax (£)
10	1–1,520	152
22	1,521–28,400	5,914
40	28,401–	6,066

Company Car Taxation after 2002

The system for company car taxation after 2002 may be illustrated by the following diagram (Figure 8):

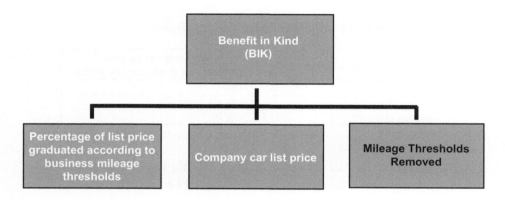

Figure 8   Company car taxation after 2002

The revised system of company car taxation continued to be based upon the principle of BIK and still determined by a proportion of the manufacturers' list price (subject to £80,000 maximum) when the car is new, but took into account the level of CO_2 emission produced by the car to determine the BIK, rather than the number of business miles travelled. The highest charge (35% of list price) and the lowest charge (15% of list price) remained. For the tax year 2002/2003, the BIK charge commenced at 15% of the car's list price for cars emitting less than 165 grams of CO_2 per kilometre (g/km) and increased at a rate of 1% for each five grams of CO_2 per kilometre up to a ceiling of 35%. The new system did not take into account business mileage in the determination of tax charge and removed any incentive for company car drivers to maximise business mileage beyond the thresholds (2,500 miles & 18,000 miles) to minimise tax burden.

Diesel cars were initially subjected to a further 3% supplement, up to the maximum 35% threshold, to reflect the higher emissions of nitrogen oxides as pollutants and particulates that damage air quality and may have an impact on health and in particular certain respiratory diseases. This 3% supplement did not apply for engines meeting strict European emission requirements for nitrogen oxides and particulates until 2005/06. Such engines are referred to as Euro IV compliant.

The qualifying level of CO_2 emissions have been gradually reduced for the first three years as shown in Figure 9:

Figure 9   Table of qualifying levels of CO_2 emissions

Tax Year	Emission
2002/03	165g/km CO_2
2003/04	155g/km CO_2
2004/05	145g/km CO_2

This reduction in the qualifying level of CO_2 emissions was designed to reflect the anticipated improvements in the fuel efficiency of new cars. The arguments for such emission reductions included the voluntary agreements reached with manufacturers to reduce CO_2 emissions by 2008. The increasing rates of tax from 15% to 35%, based on an increase of 1% per 5 grams per kilometre increase of CO_2 and a reducing baseline of 165g/km, 155g/km and 145g/km CO_2 emission for the years 2002/03–2004/05, confirms that company car taxation as a BIK will increase in the first three years of this tax reform (see Figure 11).

For example, the BIK for an individual driving a Ford Focus 1.6LX company car would now be determined as follows (Figure 10):

Figure 10   Determination of Benefit in Kind (BIK)

2002/03
Ford Focus 1.6LX list price: **£13,210**
Percentage of list price (based upon 165 g/Km CO_2): **15%**
∴ Benefit in Kind: (15% x £13,210) = **£1,981.50**

2003/04
Ford Focus 1.6LX list price: **£13,210**
Percentage of list price (based upon 165 g/Km CO_2): **17%**
∴ Benefit in Kind: (17% x £13,210) = **£2,245.70**

2004/05
Ford Focus 1.6LX list price: **£13,210**
Percentage of list price (based upon 165g/Km CO_2): **19%**
∴ Benefit in Kind: (19% x £13,210) = **£2,509.90**

Figure 11   **Rates of taxation for the first three years of reform**

Percentage of List Price (Petrol)	CO$_2$ Emissions (g/Km)			Percentage of List Price (Diesel)
	2002/03	2003/04	2004/05	
15	165	155	145	18
16	170	160	150	19
17	175	165	155	20
18	180	170	160	21
19	185	175	165	22
20	190	180	170	23
21	195	185	175	24
22	200	190	180	25
23	205	195	185	26
24	210	200	190	27
25	215	205	195	28
26	220	210	200	29
27	225	215	205	30
28	230	220	210	31
29	235	225	215	32
30	240	230	220	33
31	245	235	225	34
32	250	240	230	35
33	255	245	235	35
34	260	250	240	35
35	265	255	245	35

Dual-fuel powered cars, designed to run on either petrol or Liquid Petroleum Gas (LPG) or Compressed Natural Gas (CNG) received special treatment in that the CO$_2$ emission figure for gas were used to determine the car benefit. A discount of 1% of the car's list price was given with a further 1% for each full 20g/km of CO$_2$ below the qualifying level for the minimum charge for the year.

Both hybrid (petrol/electric) and electric cars also benefited from a reduced taxation burden in recognition of the fact that such vehicles have the potential for very low emissions including CO$_2$ and that such vehicles had a higher purchase price than conventional cars. An appropriate discount expressed as a percentage of the car's list price was made available. For cars that run solely on electricity a discount of 6% was given, reducing the rate of tax from 15% to 9% of the car's list price. For hybrid electric cars that run on a combination of petrol and electric, the discount was 2%, reducing the rate of tax to 13% of the car's list price with a further 1% for each full 20g/km of CO_2 below the qualifying level for the minimum charge for the year (165g/km CO_2 for 2002/03).

Conceptual Framework

The conceptual framework for this study lies in the connection between the necessity to preserve natural capital and the efficacy of an ecological taxation (through the recognition of price elasticity) to contribute towards preservation of natural capital, either by discouraging its consumption and damage due to pollution and/or the possibility of repair or clean-up of natural capital, through the hypothecation of additional tax revenue raised directly from the polluters via such a taxation reform.

Accordingly, the environment is recognised as a boundary, with CO_2 emissions flowing into the environment and clean-up activity alleviating the damage caused by such emissions. The significant factors pertinent to the study will be identified from the literature in Chapter 2 and developed in Chapter 3, research methodology. These factors are represented in the diagram in Figure 12 and are as follows:

- *company car driver*: the taxpayer for emissions;

- *taxation rate*: to include some internalisation of externalities to impact on resource pricing for a more efficient allocation of resources;

- *price elasticity introduced*: graduated charge based upon g/Km CO_2;

- *price elasticity removed*: now inelastic; there is no longer an incentive to travel further;

- *company car procurement decision/intention*: influenced by the sliding scale of taxation based upon g/km emissions;

- *distance travelled*: impacts on total CO_2 emission produced;

- *on-going technical developments*: resulting in lower-emission cars;

- *quantification of the effects of CO_2 emissions*: internalisation of these costs;

- *tax revenue generated*: the hypothecation of tax revenue towards clean-up costs;

- *clean-up costs*: environmental damage repair costs;

- *prevention costs*: abatement costs caused by raising taxation to curb polluting behaviour; and

- CO_2 *emissions*: arising from car procurement choice and distance travelled.

The interrelationships for these factors may be illustrated by Figure 12:

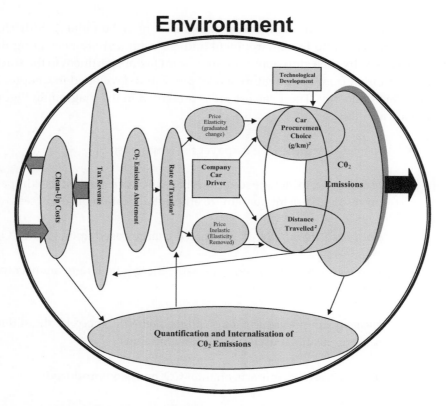

1 Rate of taxation will impact on resource pricing/costing (for a more efficient allocation of resources via internalisation of some externalities into the rate of taxation).

2 Car procurement choice (g/km) and distance travelled are not optional in that they have to be undertaken.

Figure 12   Illustration of the interrelationships of the factors identified for the study

The efficacy of company car taxation reform relies to a certain extent on price sensitivity for a group of mandatory consumers (and polluters), namely company car drivers. The vehicle choice of company car drivers determines the g/km of CO_2 and the amount of tax due, whereas the distance travelled (taking into account the g/km of $CO_{2)}$ will determine the total CO_2 produced. The effects on CO_2 emissions and tax revenue available for environmental repair/clean-up may be hypothesised in the matrix shown in Figure 13.

Figure 13 **Effect of tax rate and distance travelled on CO_2 emissions, clean-up costs and tax revenue**

	←Low Distance	Travelled High→
↑**Low (g/Km)**	Lowest CO_2 emissions Lowest clean-up costs Low tax revenue available	High CO_2 emissions High clean-up costs Low tax revenue available
CO₂ **Emissions** ↓**High (g/Km)**	Low CO_2 emissions Low clean-up costs High tax revenue available	Highest CO_2 emissions Highest cleanup costs High tax revenue available

Research Aim

The aim of this research is to contribute to a more comprehensive understanding of the possible 'mechanisms through which the current structures of an economy might come to reflect – to a significantly greater degree than at present ... [the] ... environmental aspects of economic activity' (Bebbington et al. 2001:22) and in so doing whether environmentally adverse activities may be discouraged or repaired. Moreover, the research emphasises and specifically considers the mechanism of taxation and the price sensitivity of individuals to environmental taxation relating to CO_2 emissions, in so far as these reforms to the UK taxation regime, which may be generalisable, could contribute to a target for lowering CO_2 emissions.

In so doing, this research considers a revenue-neutral taxation reform specifically implemented to discourage CO_2 emissions from a particular category of car user. A positivist paradigm was adopted, utilising the research instrument of a survey for a random sample of company car drivers in order to determine whether the sample were price sensitive to environmental taxation in so far as they were able or prepared to moderate the distance travelled by car and their choice of car. By providing empirical evidence through examining the effect of the change to company car taxation arrangements on business mileage and intended company car selection, together with an analysis of the results of a survey on the implementation of this tax, conclusions were drawn, based upon the evidence, as to whether such an environmental tax at the level imposed would internalise sufficient costs associated with environmental impact and provide adequate incentive to encourage these car drivers to emit less CO_2.

The positivist paradigm adopted for this research arises from the applied research aim to measure CO_2 emissions pre- and post-UK company car taxation reform and to use this CO_2 emission data to test hypothesis objectively and reliably. 'Hypothesis must be testable. Their content must be measurable in some way even if they are not directly observable' (Smith 2003:52).

To consider how the reforms to the taxation arrangements for company cars to reflect the level of CO_2 production and to no longer take into account business miles travelled may have impacted on individuals, and how this may have affected the company car chosen and the business miles driven, this research used empirical results from a questionnaire survey for company car drivers to determine levels of CO_2 production pre- and post-taxation reform. A statistical investigation of this data was carried out, using a difference between means test and a paired t-test to test two specific hypotheses arising from the change in company car taxation. The results indicate whether the revised company car taxation regime could have an influence on the levels of CO_2 production arising from intended business mileage driven by individuals and the levels of CO_2 production from the company car chosen.

The change to the taxation system removed the incentive for drivers of company cars to maximise business mileage beyond certain thresholds and reduce the overall distance travelled by company car drivers. Whether this change resulted in a reduction in CO_2 emissions (compared to the CO_2 emission levels under the previous system of taxation) is fundamental to this study in examining whether, as a consequence of this tax reform, company car drivers are able to or prepared to moderate the distance travelled by car.

The hypothesis: H_o: *There is no significant difference between the current mean level of CO_2 emission and anticipated mean CO_2 emission,* *based upon estimated mileage for the forthcoming year*, was derived and tested for this purpose.

The change to the taxation system also incorporated progressive scale charges to determine the BIK for the individual tax payer. Whether this encouraged company car drivers to choose lower-emission cars, where a choice is permissible, resulting in a reduction in a reduction of CO_2 (compared to the CO_2 emission levels under the previous system of taxation) was also paramount to this research. Studying this change provided an understanding of whether, as a consequence of this taxation reform, company car drivers were prepared to allow the graduated taxation charge to influence their choice of next company car where a choice was permissible, possibly resulting in a reduction in CO_2 emission.

> The hypothesis: H_0: *There is no significant difference between the anticipated mean level of CO_2 emission and anticipated mean CO_2 emission, based upon a proposed replacement company car*, was derived and tested for this purpose.

The hypothesis considered the effect of independent variables on the dependant variables, as opposed to establishing the significance of correlations, in an attempt to demonstrate causality in the possible relationships amongst the variables.

Outline of this Book

To address the research problem this book is divided into six chapters as follows:

This chapter introduced the research, by explaining the problem domain with a sustainability context and emphasising the significance of carbon emissions in particular together with the repercussions of not undertaking some form of corrective or remedial action. Scientific matters relating to carbon were also discussed to appreciate the difficulties for management of carbon in society.

In so doing, this chapter also introduced the theories underpinning the study in an attempt to explain the current situation and to provide an opportunity for further conceptualising of theory later in the study. Moreover, further details were provided of the operationalisation of the specific tax reform that is scrutinised for the purpose of this research and provided some justification as to why the study is significant in the context of the problem referred to earlier.

Chapter 2 provides a discussion and, where appropriate, a critique of the relevant literature pertinent to this problem domain. This chapter emphasises the deficiencies of conventional economic theory in disregarding environmental matters which are fundamental to sustaining the current eco-balance of the planet, by minimising environmental impact which is necessary for long-term sustainability.

The significance of carbon in the sustainability debate and measures to reduce the same are examined through literature, with a taxation emphasis and linkage back to an economic perspective to underpin the latter. It is intended that the reader should appreciate the complexity of taxation relating to carbon matters in this context and because of this, particular emphasis is given to carbon taxation from the literature. In addition it is anticipated that the literature reviewed in this chapter will inform the research findings, or where they cannot, divergence can be explained or reconciled in a defensible manner, based upon theory introduced in this and the subsequent chapters.

Chapter 3 introduces further details of the research study to be carried out and the operationalisation of the same. The research paradigm, conceptual development, research aim and objectives are discussed, prior to the development of the research model, problem definition and hypothesis development. The selection and justification of the research approach is discussed and justified and the development of the survey instrument and data sources is introduced.

Literature is interspersed throughout the chapter to provide some assurance that the methods and approaches are consistent with those generally suggested. The survey and measures taken to ensure the robustness of the same are discussed. The methods employed to analyse the data are explained and possible sources of error are mentioned, prior to a discussion of matters of validity.

Chapter 4 provides details of the analysis of results obtained from the research study carried out. The reliability and validity of the data obtained and the statistical techniques employed for the purpose of hypothesis testing used are discussed. The quantitative analysis for the data obtained from the survey instrument, in the form of a difference between means test and a paired t-test is presented, discussed and conclusions drawn. Descriptive statistics arising from the questions from the survey instrument are graphically presented and discussed individually and collectively and contribute to the conclusions reached for the hypothesis tests.

Chapter 5 reviews the results of the research study discussed in the previous chapter and attempts to concentrate on those findings which may be pertinent to the research questions for the study and to reconcile the outcomes with the literature to provide an opportunity to inform the theory in this area. In so doing the usefulness of the research approach will be reflected upon and a review of the findings and the implications for the same will be addressed.

In particular, Chapter 5 comments upon the significance of the findings and attempts to utilise this, along with the richness of the data obtained, to develop a conceptual framework for ecological taxation. This may be pertinent for the UK taxation regime and may also potentially be applicable generally, possibly providing the basis for reductions of CO_2 consistent with obligations under the Kyoto Agreement. In so doing the implications for CO_2 reductions and ecological taxation are addressed in an attempt to generalise the findings within a framework of valid underlying theory.

Chapter 6 concludes the book from an environmental, scientific, and economic and public policy perspective and takes the opportunity to make general and specific recommendations based upon the literature reviewed throughout the study and the results obtained from the survey. The efficacy of the taxation change under scrutiny is reviewed and the implications arising from such changes will be discussed in so far as it affects Government, company car drivers, fleet managers and manufacturers and individuals. It is envisaged that the recommendations made within this chapter will inform the development of theory in general and emissions-related motor taxation regimes in particular.

In acknowledging the possible limitations of the study carried out, areas for further research are identified, which are consistent with the aims and objectives of this study.

Conclusion

Hasselmann et al. (2003:1923) discussed that 'Climate policy needs to address the multidecadal to centennial time scale of climate change'. The authors acknowledged the value of short-term targets as an important first step. However, for climate change policies, including those relating to carbon emissions, to be effective, they should be developed as long-term programs (Hasselmann et al. 2003). Such an objective would necessitate a broad spectrum of policy measures in addition to market-based instruments best suited to mitigation policies for the short term (Hasselmann et al. 2003).

This book provides some insight into the possibility of achieving short-term CO_2 emissions targets/policy, through fiscal means. The conclusions also contribute to the identification of the characteristics of a framework required for successful implementation of reforms which may be consistent with achieving environmental objectives in the long term.

The findings of this study have implications for, and would be of interest to, academics, policy makers, Government, company car drivers, fleet managers, manufacturers and individuals affected or potentially affected by this or similar taxation reforms.

Our Economic System and Environmental Damage

This chapter will offer a critique of the deficiencies of the existing economic system with respect to the environment and sustainability in the context of economic activity, primarily through the contemplation of literature. Moreover, the recognition of externalities and the consideration of appropriate treatments are discussed. Possible solutions, including internalisation of the externalities, are considered in a sustainability context in general and an emissions perspective in particular.

The environment provides the boundary within which all other systems must operate. The interrelationship between the economic system, economic activity (which is a subset of the economic system) and externalities that arise as a consequence of both and impact on the environment, may be illustrated with the diagram in Figure 14 and are further discussed in the course of this chapter.

Matters relating to internalising costs to reflect the 'Full Cost' of the product were examined as a precursor to a discussion on the role accounting information may play in reporting the Full Costs of an activity, including the consumption of the environment as part of economic activity. The difficulties of such an approach are discussed not only to appreciate the difficulties in themselves in this context, but to deliberate how such difficulties may be pertinent to other approaches to accountability for consumption and/or destruction of the natural environment.

The significance of regulation as a mechanism to curb economic activity and to act as a catalyst to the internalisation of environmental costs in pursuit of Full Costs to lead to optimal environmental policy is examined. A balance may be required between higher costs to curtail polluting activities and the

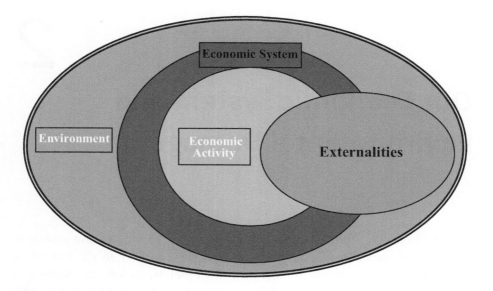

Figure 14   **The interrelationship between the environment, economic activity, the economic system and externalities**

additional revenues generated from imputing such higher costs, which may then be earmarked for environmental repair, or clean-up. Accordingly, the concepts and theories underpinning taxation reform in general and carbon taxes in particular, which are pertinent to the research study carried out, are reviewed. The latter is further contemplated in the context of road transport for the purpose of this study in an attempt to explain the current situation and to provide an opportunity for further conceptualising of theory relating to the specific reforms introduced and discussed in Chapter 1.

Moreover, it is anticipated that the literature reviewed in this chapter, combined with the study itself, may identify characteristics to contribute to an underpinning for a framework for viable strategies for ecological taxation.

Is Economic Theory Deficient?

Bebbington et al. (2001) argued that conventional economics and accounting on a macro and a micro level is deficient as a result of the inability to measure the consequences of economic activity where anything is included which does not have a price attributed to it. This inability to recognise the value of something that exists without the transfer of private property rights (for example, fresh air) may result in economic and business decisions being made with little or no bona fide concern for the environment. In the case of externalities arising from fossil fuels, Boyd et al. (1995) argued that once environmental damage costs are taken into account, then energy is underpriced; using conservative assumptions, the price of oil should be 10% higher, gas 15% higher and coal should be 20% higher (than baseline price levels).

The result of this inability to properly price such resources is that the costs of the same are excluded in evaluating economic benefits for individuals and organisations and are left for society as a whole to bear. A consequence of Carbon Dioxide (CO_2) and other Greenhouse Gas (GHG) emission is climate change, imposing costs on future generations. Stern (2007) notes that such costs are not addressed via markets, or in other ways, allowing the full consequences of the cost of these actions to remain unaccounted for.

Many of the economic indicators for the developed world continue to show improvement, the 'external' costs of these so-called improvements have not been quantified or measured in an agreed way with any degree of accuracy. One may observe the greatest periods of economic growth do coincide with the greatest episodes of pollution, ozone layer depletion, climate change and other types of environmental damage; the consequences of which are far reaching. Goudie (2005) noted that the concentration of CO_2 in the atmosphere has increased by approximately one-third since the year 1750 and that such a CO_2 concentration has not been greater over the past 420,000 years and probably during the past 20 million years.

The recognition that such environmental problems are global issues came in the *Brundtland Report* (1987), published by the United Nations Commission of Envirement and Development (UNCED). The report referred to sustainable development as 'Development that meets the needs of the present without compromising the ability of future generations to meet their own needs' (UNCED 1987:8). This led to the introduction of the term *'sustainable development'*. Yanarella & Levine (1992) and Zimmerman (1994) suggested this heightened awareness amongst international policy makers acted as a catalyst for further debate as to the implications of such a definition. Wilson et al. (2001) observed of the *Brundtland Report* that it offered a political context for ecological issues by emphasising the consequences of excessive consumption whilst contrasting the same with poverty.

Bebbington & Gray (2001) attempted to develop a framework for sustainability and accounting. In attempting this they identified two significant matters. Firstly, the result of attempting to link sustainability to accounting provided an account of the enterprise's unsustainability. Secondly, an acknowledgement that such a link was likely to preclude a business as usual situation.

For an economic organisation to operate in an environmentally sustainable manner there must be some understanding and agreement as to the causes of current unsustainability and the extent of the same (Bebbington et al. 2001). It is only then that the extent of sustainability achieved may be assessed. Bebbington & Thomson (1996) discussed the concept of a spectrum of sustainability from 'strong' to 'weak'. Western entities including governments lean towards a 'weak' sustainability perspective (Bebbington & Thomson 1996). Neumayer (1999) also discussed these differing perspectives, which were introduced in Chapter 1; the divergence arising largely from contrasting views on substitutability of natural capital. This gives rise to uncertainty about the consequences of continuing depletion of natural capital and the extent to which such losses are irreversible.

As the greatest beneficiaries from the current economic model, there is little short-term incentive for Western economies to pursue a radical 'strong' sustainability agenda possibly requiring fundamental changes to our economic system. Instead, the opportunity to achieve some 'weak' degree of sustainability through incremental market-based adjustments of the current system appears most probable.

The current economic status quo is unlikely to change to facilitate a strong sustainability agenda. If the concept of sustainable development is to be embraced, a fundamental reappraisal of the value of things that exist without the transfer of private property rights must take place. Prices and costs need to be realigned to take into account as far as is possible the environmental implications of economic and business decisions.

Attempting to internalise these so called 'externalities' is a significant step in recognising the Full Cost of activities in order that economic and business decisions are taken on a rational and sustainable basis.

From an environmental sustainability viewpoint, current prices may not encompass all environmental matters, resulting in a situation where private decisions taken do not reflect the full or total public cost of the actions. Therefore, some of these costs are borne elsewhere by parties not responsible for causing the cost in the first place. Costs tolerated by others external to the decision or actions are referred to as externalities.

Meade (1973) considered an externality from an economic perspective as an external economy that provides an appreciable benefit (or conversely inflicts an appreciable damage) to an individual or individuals who did not fully approve of the decision or decisions that led to the event in question.

Externalities arise when the global costs of a private decision are not entirely borne by the decision maker, but are borne by society as a whole. Such costs, it is argued, should be monetised and internalised in order that the costs are borne by the person making the decision or taking the action and not society as a whole. The accumulation of CO_2 resulting in climate-related problems is a cost. Climate change caused by human activity is an externality, as explained by Pigou (1912) it remains uncorrected by the market or any institution. Schneider & Goulder (1997) argued that government intervention is required to incorporate such matters into the price of fossil fuels in particular.

Internalising externalities presents a theoretical challenge. If pollution costs, which are imposed on other members of society, are to be included in the decision maker's costs, the costs of the particular pollution must first be identified and monetised. To include the implications of pollution in economic, costing and pricing systems is not an easy task. Stern (2007) notes that the approach to addressing such externalities is further complicated because the impact of pollution is independent to its emission. In addition, the effect of pollution is dependent on geography and other factors such as reliance on agriculture. There is no widely accepted conceptual framework to accommodate this.

Newbery (1980) argued that non-pecuniary externalities arise when the existence of a competitive market is prohibited by set up costs: 'One can think of externalities as synonymous with non-existence of markets, and define an externality to occur whenever the private economy does not have sufficient incentives to create a potential market' (Newbery 1980:139).

Smith (1993) asserted that from an economic standpoint, environmental policy should require that external costs of pollution are fully addressed by those responsible for the pollution. Environmental policy also requires equilibrium to be reached between the costs of controlling pollution and the costs of the pollution itself (Smith 1993).

Ekins (2000a) argued that externalities materialise in circumstances where resource consumption, irrespective of price, is insufficient to address all of the impacts of its use, or in circumstances where there is no price assigned to its use, for example fresh air. It follows that external costs arising from resource use are those costs that have not been internalised and would naturally include pollution costs.

Newbery (1980) asserted that externalities arise in some cases because of property rights not being assigned to individuals. If property rights were defined and assigned, they could be exchanged at a price. However Weitzman (1974) noted that users, who have previously experienced free access to resources, would suffer a fall in income if such property rights were defined and assigned.

Gray & Bebbington (2001) argued that externalities represent part of the price by which the economic gains have been secured and should, therefore, be included in financial reporting, providing an opportunity for comparability. However, the authors add a caveat to acknowledge the debate surrounding expressing all environmental (and social) exchanges in financial terms.

Externalities may also arise as opportunity costs; that is the benefit forgone by not having the particular resource available for future consumption. Such opportunity costs are likely to be subjectively determined and with imprecision. It would be difficult to determine the opportunity cost in perpetuity for the use of scarce resources now.

The recognition of externalities in this context is not insignificant. This may provide the basis for the development of theory and models in pursuit of the valuation and monetisation of the same and in turn could provide business and government an opportunity to account for their actions by providing an opportunity for financial mechanisms to have an influence on organisations' responses to sustainability issues. Bebbington & Thomson (1996) suggested that accounting may influence an organisation in two different ways; firstly in influencing decision making processes within the organisation and secondly by being incorporated into how an organisation communicates to interested third parties.

Recognition of Environmental Impact

The recognition of environmental impact provides an opportunity for association with the activity that caused the impact, to highlight the externality. Ecological footprints provide an opportunity for association with a particular activity and also provide precious linkage back to the *Brundtland Report.*

Ecological footprints provide an opportunity for relative measurement of consumption between countries on a per capita population basis and serve to highlight the excessive consumption and pollution of some nations compared with others, although this may be applied on an organisation or individual basis.

Ekins (2000a) commented that ecological footprints may provide an insight into the effectiveness of conversion of energy and land to provide an understanding of how much resource is appropriated from one area to another. The rationale behind this type of analysis was to highlight countries that do not share resources in a just and equitable basis.

An eco-balance requires the definition or identification of a boundary within an entity. Once defined, energy and material that flow across the boundary may be monitored and outflows compared with inflows. The desired position is that inflows and outflows of energy and material are equal. Where equality is not achieved eco-balance serves to highlight areas that may warrant further scrutiny.

Similarly, Life Cycle Analysis attempts to associate material and energy with activity, but on a more micro level. Fava (1991) defined Life Cycle Analysis as 'an objective process used to evaluate the environmental burdens associated with a product, process or activity…accomplished by identifying and quantifying energy and material usage and environmental releases' (Fava 1991:19). It was suggested that this quantification may then be the basis for impact assessment of the same on the environment for the complete lifecycle of the matter. This may include raw material extraction, process, manufacture, transport, distribution and disposal (or recycle). According to Elliott (2003), Life Cycle Analysis became increasingly relevant as part of any environmental appraisal.

Costing Externalities

The relationship between economic and climatic factors is a complex one. The quantification of the same may also prove problematic and uncertain and inconclusive. Tol (2005) surveyed 28 studies of marginal damage costs of CO_2 and reported estimates of marginal damage caused by a tonne of CO_2 between US$5–$125. This diversity in cost is at least in part affected by the discount rate used in the particular study. Research into climate change and the economic implications of such changes is still at an early stage (Tol 2005). Mahlman (1997) asserted that variability of such estimates were because of a deficiency in our understanding of climate change.

Notwithstanding the likely difficulties alluded to, particularly with respect to the accuracy and hence credibility of the data, the costing of externalities is likely to be informative not least because it permits an overdue debate (Gray et al. 1993). The costing of externalities resulting in the quantification of the same is also attractive, as it may reduce ambiguity and offer a scientific and rational approach for an agreed basis for translation of externalities into financial data.

Implicit in any Cost Accounting approach to the costing of ecological matters, is the requirement to monetise externalities relating to pollution, to take into account that part of the cost that has not been reflected in the market price. Bebbington et al. (2001), in making the case for Full Cost Accounting (FCA), noted that financial measures of performance play a significant role in the management of organisations. Monetisation of externalities, through a process of translation, may facilitate a more complete financial position to be determined.

To mitigate environmental impact, the method chosen to do this must be both conceptually feasible and practically viable. Ekins (2000a) and Antheaume (1997) concurred that the basis for costing externalities arises from either resource consumption or the impact of pollution. In the case of the former, avoidance or abatement costs could be determined based upon the costs associated with the achievement of environmental performance targets. Whereas, with the latter, the cost of the damage arising from the activity may be determined.

It is important to stress that for externality pricing to be credible, the externalities must be attributed to a particular set of activities. The determinant of activities is in itself fraught with difficulty and will of course have implications for what is included and, possibly more importantly, excluded from such costing. This ambiguity for externality pricing for carbon creates uncertainty for incentives to innovate (Stern 2007) with respect to technology to limit or prevent carbon emissions (Taylor et al. 2006).

Internalising Costs

Smith (1998) emphasised the necessity to control emissions via public intervention and suggested that in the absence of government intervention, the polluter may have no motivation to take such external costs on board.

If the market prices of products reflect the 'Full Cost' of the product rather than underestimate environmental damage, consumers may choose not to consume the product, because the cost is prohibitive, may consume less of the product because of the financial penalty or there may be sufficient financial incentive for consumers to substitute their consumption with less environmentally damaging products. Bebbington et al. (2001) recognised this possibility for competitive advantage through change in consumer choices for lower environmental impact of products.

It may be hypothesised that externalities should be imputed via internal costing and pricing systems alongside the costs traditionally incurred by the organisation. In this way, the implications of emissions from (say) CO_2 are costed and incorporated with the costs incurred by the organisation. As a consequence, the decision to permit harmful emissions results in an increase in cost that is neither beneficial to the organisation nor in the interests of global sustainability either.

Higher cost for polluters may discourage pollution by organisations and reduce the take up of products/services; however, the level of cost to reduce demand may not be consistent with the cost of reparation for the environmental damage. The point on the spectrum adopted for sustainability may be significant here in ensuring that a level of cost to discourage polluting behaviour is also sufficient to make good environmental damage.

Smith (1993) provided an economic perspective for an efficient level for pollution abatement in diagrammatical form and suggested that for environmental policy to be optimal, a balance is required between the costs of pollution and the costs of control of the same. Pollution should be curbed to the point where the benefits as a whole for society, from further reductions in pollution, are lower than the costs of pollution control, or the curtailment of activities causing pollution. This is expressed as the 'marginal damage of pollution' being equal to the 'marginal benefit of polluting activities' (Smith 1993:223) and is illustrated in Figure 15.

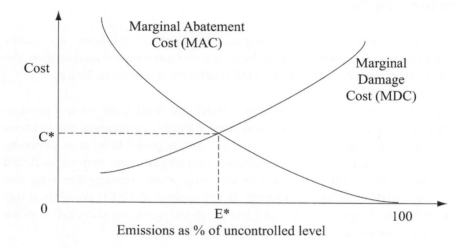

Figure 15   An economic view of the efficient level of pollution abatement
Source: Smith 1993

Barker (2004) expressed Marginal Abatement Cost (MAC) as a discrete incremental cost that will rise as pollution controls are introduced. MAC assumes that least-cost methods of pollution control would be implemented first with more expensive measures introduced later. Nordhaus (1991) suggested 'About 10% of GHG emissions can be reduced at extremely low cost; above that level, the marginal cost of abatement rises sharply' (Nordhaus 1991: 936).

Marginal Damage Cost (MDC) will also rise as emissions rise, acknowledging the possibility that the environment may have some capacity for assimilation, in that larger amounts of pollution would cause appreciably more damage to the environment than smaller amounts of pollution, as smaller amounts of pollution may be accommodated without repercussions. MDCs may be affected by a number of local factors. The costs may be determined with reference to a variety of indicators, such as the number of people affected, plant growth and the number of systems experiencing change (Tol 2005) making estimation of the same problematic.

From the diagram in Figure 15, E* denotes the emission-level point where MAC and MDC are equal (at a cost level of C*) and signifies [the start of] an efficient stage of pollution control.

Notwithstanding the difficulties alluded to earlier; the costs of eliminating all pollution emissions would be greater than the benefits. Within the context of economic environmental policy, it may be argued that whilst pollution reduction is desirable, this may only be embarked upon in so far as the costs of lowering the emissions may be vindicated in terms of the benefits. Smith (2001) emphasised the potential high cost of emission reduction and argued that the avoided costs of climate change should be in line with abatement costs.

It would therefore be necessary to undertake some valuation of the damage caused by pollution in order to ascertain the optimum level of pollution abatement. The efficacy of such valuation is paramount and remains contentious and problematic, not least because of the diversity of possibilities associated with valuation. Johansson (1990) discussed a variety of valuation models for this purpose.

Bebbington et al. (2001) drew attention to the deficiencies in our economic systems and argued that in the context of Western political and business motives, proposals that might be predicated on any reappraisal of the underlying fundamental structure of Western capitalism are unlikely to be considered. Centrally planned economies, with different political motives, are also unlikely to wish to address such deficiencies through such a reappraisal; the costs being more easily overlooked.

Smith (1993) acknowledged that in practice most pollution policies originate from targets and objectives set by political intervention and are not the product of economic modelling predicated upon existing market mechanisms.

Market mechanisms could internalise costs in a number of ways. The United Nations Conference on Trade and Development (UNCTAD) (1996) highlighted the following possible approaches to cost internalisation.

- A regulatory system that assigns costs for previously free goods.

- A system for damages for disregarding the environment.

- An accounting system that encompasses environmental costs as part of the internal decision-making process.

- An eco-labelling system to highlight a product's environmental impact.

- A national tax system predicated upon the consumption of natural resources as opposed to income flows.

- A requirement for manufacturers to have responsibility for the lifecycle uses of the products made.

- A cessation of government programmes that encourage over-use or misuse of natural resources.

Bebbington et al. (2001) referred to four ways of cost internalisation: the democratic/accountability approach; the full privatisation approach; the law, market instruments and structural change approach; and the shadow price approach. Each of these approaches is discussed in turn.

THE DEMOCRATIC/ACCOUNTABILITY APPROACH

If society were better informed about sustainability and environmental issues, they would be likely to make fewer unethical choices. The democratic/ accountability approach is predicated upon the belief that mandatory comprehensive social and environmental reporting by organisations would lead to more informed ethical consumers making more sustainable choices at the expense of the unsustainable decisions. As a consequence, less ethical products would become more expensive as economies of scale would decline, reducing their popularity further.

For an accountability approach to be effective it relies upon appropriate and understandable information being accessible in a form suitable for consumption. This requires unbiased unambiguous disclosure without the use of marketing and advertising to distort the message. There should be an appreciation of democracy for accountability to be important. The consumer should also have an interest in such information, so as not to be intimidated by or feel apathetic toward the vast amount of information that would be available.

Such an approach may already be observed with ethical investment; where fund managers act as agents for investors and undertake to obtain and decipher appropriate information to reduce the unethical investment selections.

THE FULL PRIVATISATION APPROACH

Pearce et al. (1989) advocated the development of economic analysis, to embed costs for all environmental elements in the price. The rationale for this is that many aspects of economic activity are environmental, the latter being free, rather than privately owned. As a consequence, no price is generated for the consumption of (say) fresh air, the use of water or the replacement of natural sound by noise. Pearce et al. (1989) argued that under the full privatisation approach such costs should be incorporated into the price of products by extending private ownership to environmental facets.

Extending private ownership requires modification to the current economic rules to include valuation of environmental resources, thereby facilitating the inclusion of a price for these resources and embedding the same in the price for goods and services.

Those organisations that consume natural resources would see the price of their goods rise, resulting in reduced demand and/or the substitution of goods for less environmentally damaging products where the price would rise disproportionately. Companies may also simultaneously pursue more environmentally sensitive strategies, as these would be cheaper.

Some form of legislative intervention would be necessary for this approach to be effective, along with a feasible methodology for pricing the environmental aspects of economic activity. The quantification of compensation for the consumption or destruction of natural resources is problematic. The economic effect of such measures may also be difficult to model with precision.

THE LAW, MARKET INSTRUMENTS AND STRUCTURAL CHANGE APPROACH

To discourage unsustainable action and to encourage sustainable activity, the structure of the economic environment could be modified by government adjusting the constraints or rules within which organisations function. Government may employ a variety of methods, which are not mutually exclusive, to achieve this. Examples discussed by Bebbington et al. (2001) included:

- Environmental taxes – for example, the carbon content of fuel.

- Environmental grants – to encourage the consumption of the preferred option.

- Environmental regulation – specifying standards of performance and accountability.

- Environmental quotas – placing restrictions on the quantity of a scarce resource that may be consumed.

- Removal of assets from economic activity.

- Environmental fines and penalties.

Such methods may promote practices that minimise damage to the environment and dissuade practices that are least sustainable.

THE SHADOW PRICE APPROACH

Shadow prices, or opportunity costs, provide a quantification of the level of cost incurred if the organisation had acted in a sustainable manner. Bebbington et al. (2001:21) suggest that in this way it is possible through either 'rearrangement, redefinition and reporting of actual costs [or] the use of economic valuation systems [or] the use of existing market prices to calculate the cost that an organisation would have to bear if it had acted in a sustainable manner during the accounting period'. The latter was referred to by Rubenstein (1994) as the *'sustainable cost approach'*. Ekins (2000b) uses a similar basis to conduct *'sustainability gap analysis'* in pursuit of the quantification of costs to a nation of meeting sustainable economic policy.

Such methods would facilitate the production of financial statements that would report on the shadow prices of activities with an environmental impact. Such information could form the basis for a mechanism for redress, via charging or taxation.

The Influence of Accounting

According to Bebbington & Thomson (1996) accounting has the potential to be a principal influence on organisations as they attempt to address sustainability issues. They considered the role accounting had within an organisation and whether this may be redefined in an attempt to address environmental and sustainability issues in two ways: firstly, in leading decision making within the organisation and secondly, in how an organisation communicates to stakeholders.

Berry & Rondinelli (1998) suggested that for accounting to embrace sustainability issues, it may be necessary to remodel accounting to incorporate costs that have previously not impacted on a company's 'bottom line'. The European Union (EU), in the Fifth Action Programme suggested the 'redefinition of accounting concepts, rules, conventions and methodology so as to ensure that the consumption and use of environmental resources are accounted for as part of the Full Costs of production and reflected in market prices' (EU 1992:67).

FCA refers to where methods are implemented to include an economic value for the consumption of the environment as part of the economic activity of an organisation. The Full Costs of an activity must be determined, recorded and reported, including the effects of environmental deterioration. This assumes that such Full Costs would necessitate prices to encompass environmental costs, which Bebbington & Thomson (1996) argue would emphasise more sustainable practices and behaviour throughout the whole production and consumption chain within an organisation.

The International Federation of Accountants (IFAC) defined FCA as 'the commonly accepted term applied to the identification evaluation and allocation of a combined and potentially complex set of conventional costs, environmental costs and social costs' (IFAC 1998:11). IFAC (1998) differentiate (tangible) environmental costs under the two headings of: external environmental costs and internal environmental costs.

Gray (1992) observed that FCA approximation was possible, provided a parallel accounting system was devised which provided details of additional costs that must be borne by the organisation to return the environment and biosphere to the state it was at the commencement of the accounting period.

The recognition of the possibility of FCA also acknowledges the feasibility of a theoretical and regulatory framework of accounting for internalising externalities.

The importance and difficulty of internalising externalities as part of a sustainability agenda should not be underestimated. However, there is growing recognition that the determination of Full Cost may be helpful in so far as it is valuable in determining and offering some quantification to the difference between existing operations and sustainable practices. This may serve to highlight the need to focus on strategies to close the gap between the two, but is unlikely to result in a 'strong' sustainability outcome for organisations, primarily because of commercial pressures.

The United States Environmental Protection Agency (USEPA)/Tellus Institute (1996) categorised FCA under the following headings:

- Usual costs – direct and indirect costs, capital and revenue associated with an activity.

- Hidden costs – additional costs including regulatory and environmental management costs.

- Liability costs – contingent liability costs that are not presently recognised in a conventional accounting context. Such costs may be dependent upon other circumstances (for example, a change in the law). Examples of these costs include fines, clean-up costs and regulatory costs.

- Less tangible costs – costs and benefits that are quantifiable that may arise from enhanced environmental management.

The USEPA/Tellus Institute approach to FCA omitted externalities quantified and imputed via internal costing and pricing systems.

It is apparent that the term 'Full Cost Accounting' (or FCA) is not used in a consistent manner by all commentators. This probably arises because of the inability to determine the *true Full Cost* of any activity.

However, any recognition of the term Full Cost and the application of the same, however partial as in the case of the USEPA/Tellus Institute, is not insignificant and indicated a move, however slow, towards the recognition of internalisation of externalities into economic activities and accordingly the subsequent reduction in polluting activities that may follow as a consequence of the increase in prices for certain goods and services.

The Advisory Committee on Business and the Environment (1996) acknowledged the partial internalisation of externalities through environmental regulation but recognised the significance of economic instruments in achieving internalisation; with an acknowledgement that consideration would need to be given to the effects on business competitiveness. Bebbington & Thomson (1996) suggested that such a caveat demonstrates that sustainable cost determination is also likely to highlight how unsustainable our current activity is. Notwithstanding the authors reservations, in their survey of *Business Conceptions of Sustainability and the Implications for Accountancy,* (Bebbington & Thomson 1996) there was positive commentary by companies with regard to the recognition of the significance of internalising externalities by businesses, although the contrast between accounting measurement activity and a more subjective environmental valuation was acknowledged by respondents, highlighting the need for the development of a conceptual framework.

The EU (1992) recognised the difficulties associated with the implementation of FCA via a conceptual framework and acknowledged there were diverse views on a fundamental redefinition of accounting concepts, rules, and conventions. Bebbington et al. (2001) contributed to the conceptual framework debate with a four-stage approach to FCA (see Figure 16), with each stage building on the former, offering a further level of adaptation to realise Full Cost.

Figure 16   A four-stage approach to Full Cost Accounting

1. DEFINE THE COST OBJECTIVE

FCA permits the valuation of consumption of the environment as part of the economic activity. To define the cost objective, consideration must be given to the purpose of determining the Full Cost. The objective for which the Full Costs are to be calculated is paramount and will inform the scope or limits of analysis.

2. SPECIFY THE SCOPE OR LIMITS OF ANALYSIS

Systems theory provides an insight into the complex interrelationships that can exist in the environment. Bebbington et al. (2001) argued the scope of a FCA exercise must be defined in an attempt to facilitate the measurement of externalities from resource consumption. The supply chain for a particular resource is likely to reveal layers of externalities. The complexity arises as to what level (layer) externalities are quantified to. A framework is required or some rationale must be determined to assist in ascertaining the materiality of the level, either in economic or ecological terms.

3. IDENTIFY AND MEASURE EXTERNAL IMPACT

To identify and measure external impact requires an association to be agreed for a cost objective and the externalities arising from the same. Obtaining data on the cost objective for the purpose of externality quantification is likely to prove problematic. Bebbington et al. (2001) suggested that accounting systems may prove useful here to translate financial data to data relating to activity. Alongside an accounting transaction or posting into a ledger may be the consumption of resources or a movement of materials. It is recognised that consumption may occur directly by the entity, or indirectly via third parties who in turn provide a service to the entity. Such activity data would require further translation into 'impacts data' (Bebbington et al. 2001) to assess the impact of a finite resource within the constraints of the definition of the cost objective.

Notwithstanding the difficulties of translating activity data to impacts data, the former translation of financial data to 'activity data' is likely to prove complex and problematic.

4. COST EXTERNAL IMPACT

Costing the external impact provides an opportunity to monetise the externalities previously ignored. Once impacts data is determined this may be able to be monetised using external costs. This is not without difficulty and requires the identification of which costs to include for this purpose. Tol (2005) identified 103 estimates of MDCs from CO_2 emissions from published studies, highlighting the diversity of cost estimates arising from the variety of applications of a range of discount rates for ecological impacts.

The Scope of Accounting

The identification and recognition of externalities and the quantification of the same are fundamental in any FCA model. The definition of cost objectives, scope or limit of analysis, identification of external impact and finally monetisation of the same may provide an opportunity for an association between externalities and costs and, as a consequence, contribute to the development of a conceptual framework.

Monetisation provides an opportunity via accounting for both reporting and accountability. However, this is likely to have a significant impact upon the financial data that is produced and the value and acknowledgment of the conclusions that may be drawn from the information.

Notwithstanding the adverse impact that the valuation of externalities and inclusion of the same is likely to have on financial statements, FCA does not appear to contradict the fundamentals of existing global economic principles and structure and offers an opportunity for legitimisation of a less than perfect economic model. Accordingly, the likelihood of its acceptance may be increased, but resistance may still be encountered from those with the most unsustainable practices.

FCA, by incorporating many potential costs and benefits, is arguably of greatest value if it is able to extend its influence to the prices for goods and services rather than be merely used as a pure accountability exercise, with little opportunity for reconciliation of the financial statements with the current economic/political paradigm (that is, the status quo). Macve (1997) suggested that FCA would provide the means to improve analysis and scrutiny, but does not in itself provide the solutions.

FCA may also provide significant benefits in influencing policy making or as part of a capital investment appraisal exercise. Popoff & Buzzelli (1993:5) noted that 'plants built by the chemical industry will still be operating 20–25 years from now … and could it tolerate the increased Full Cost of those resources?'

Bebbington et al. (2001:116) concluded that the reservations for developing FCA are 'of both a technical and political nature'. From a technical perspective, FCA will inevitably require organisations to capture and analyse more data. Despite information-gathering costs falling by an order of magnitude Kaplan & Johnson (1991), the costs of a FCA exercise are likely to be material.

The costing of externalities could take a variety of forms, with clean-up costs versus avoidance costs, illustrating the dilemma facing those involved in the preparation of such data. Bebbington et al. (2001) highlighted comparability and interpreting problems that may ensue from the potential lack of uniformity and consistency in approach.

From a political perspective, the outcome of a FCA exercise, notwithstanding the observations made earlier, are likely to be the reporting of higher costs. Tuppen (1996) acknowledged that for the majority of companies the net effect will be an increase in cost. To include environmental costs into product prices is likely to have significant impacts on economies and may as a consequence generate a debate on the unsustainability of corporate agendas.

The effects on costs and prices if a form of FCA were implemented are likely to be so significant that it is not possible, as a part of this book, to offer any meaningful conclusions as to the consequences, but to note that it would have far reaching effects on policy making and resource consumption. However, it is worthy of note that any full FCA exercise, which results in a stable framework for robust carbon pricing for the long term, is likely to encourage investment in low-carbon technologies (Stern 2007) as these become more viable sooner.

The consequence for some industry sectors may be more severe and may raise questions regarding viability and the possibility of a going concern qualification in an audit report. Popoff & Buzzelli (1993) pointed to the destruction of much of the agriculture industry in California if the Full Cost of water were charged. In such circumstances, FCA could still be implemented and the industry subsidised to overcome viability issues. In this way, the Full Cost of the industry is reported and the real level of subsidy may also be visible. Such an approach would be consistent with the fundamental principles of FCA in that externalities are identified as arising and are subsequently measured and reported. However, such an approach was discounted by Baumol & Oates (1975).

Popoff & Buzzelli (1993) emphasised that FCA, as a vital step towards sustainability, could improve environmental performance more than any other measure and that opposition to FCA is effectively concurring with the assertion that environmental costs should not be included in product prices.

The recognition of the necessity of externality valuations for accounting purposes is in itself very significant. Macve (1997) observed the need to increase the traceability of environmental factors for this purpose and to construct accountability based upon incentives.

However, internalisation of externalities would require redefining the boundary of accounting. In the absence of comprehensive legislation, this is likely to place a significant demand on the accounting profession for the derivation of appropriate International Accounting Standards (IAS) to accommodate this and is likely to be a test of the independence of the profession also.

Regulatory Perspective

Regulation provides a mechanism for the state to regulate economic activity and in so doing also provides an opportunity for the state to internalise environmental costs to move towards the achievement of the objective of prices representing Full Costs. Macve (1997) noted that initial organisational lethargy may be overcome with external regulatory stimulus.

Command and control regimes and economic instruments each offer regulatory opportunity to encourage sustainability as shown in Figure 17.

COMMAND AND CONTROL REGIMES

Such regimes stipulate which activities cannot be engaged in and those that can be carried out. In an environmental context, outright bans are used where there is likely to be unacceptable damage arising directly or via an externality. Standard setting provides an opportunity to regulate environmental damage to within acceptable levels. This may be accompanied by a system of permits to place limits on pollution. Similarly, licensing provides an opportunity of control

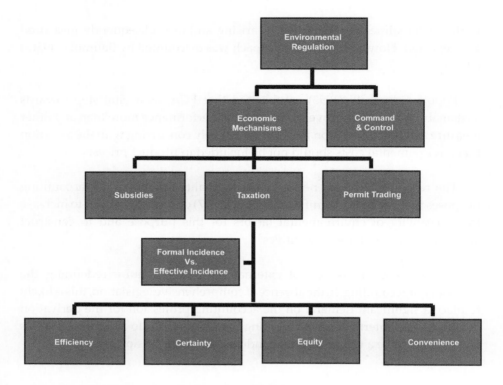

Figure 17   Regulatory perspective for environmental regulation

via restricted opportunity for permission to undertake polluting activities. In addition, compliance costs to obtain licences, together with the imposition of fines for breach of licence conditions provide opportunities to internalise costs. Criminal law may be applied where command and control regimes have been breached to serve as a deterrent to such breaches and to act as a mechanism for enforcement of such regimes.

Voluntary agreements (set by regulatory bodies) can also have a role to play and are mentioned here as a precursor to legislation, the inevitable consequence of not adhering to such agreements.

ECONOMIC MECHANISMS

Economic mechanisms and specific economic instruments may be utilised to encourage the opportunity of avoiding the undesirable activity, but allow the pursuance of the activity, provided additional costs are met. In this way a choice may be made between continuing and avoidance, with the cost implications understood at the outset. As a consequence, the externality may be reduced and the costs of the same may be borne, at least in part by the polluter.

SUBSIDIES

Subsidies are an example of an instrument that may be used to encourage activity for environmental good. The investment in 'green' technology, for example, CFC-free refrigeration may be encouraged by the use of subsidies, which would lower polluting activity and provide a commercially viable alternative for purchasers to choose.

Newbery (1980) discussed subsidising reductions in pollution in place of taxation of the production of the same and concluded that the subsidy for certain organisations would yield a level of emission higher than that which would be generated under taxation and greater than that which would have occurred in the absence of either tax or subsidy. Newbery (1980) suggested that an efficient level of pollution could be reached by providing subsidies to existing firms only and taxing existing customers for the benefits of pollution reductions.

Schneider & Goulder (1997) suggested that following the economic principle of applying the policy instrument closest to a particular market failure should apply and acknowledge that subsidy alone would not directly modify the prices of carbon-based fuels.

However, a subsidy may have a role to play in research and development in lowering an organisation's costs to allow the expansion or acceleration of research and development with respect to CO_2 emissions.

The reduction and eventual elimination of subsidies, sometimes administered in the form of tax concessions, are likely to have a two-fold effect of lowering consumption of those resources and provide an additional incentive for technological development to facilitate minimal use of those scarce resources.

Subsidies that are, for example, taken away from private motorists and given to public transport systems would improve the economic competitiveness of the latter and reduce the same for the former, providing better alignment between ecological and economic goals. This is preferable, rather than placing reliance on less efficient measures as a means of allocating scarce resources such as congestion charging and car parking restrictions.

PERMIT TRADING SCHEMES

Weizsacker & Jesinghaus (1992) suggested if there is a consensus as to the ecological goals to be achieved (for example, CO_2 reduction) then it should be possible, as part of the development of a framework for economic activity, to establish levels of consumption and emission and provide permits for this. Meade (1973) argued that controlling the quantity of pollution does prevent an upper threshold of pollution being breached, where excessive damage may cause disproportionate and irreversible damage to the environment. Beggs (2002) concurred that permits are a type of rationing, whilst ensuring that targets are achieved.

A market could exist for such permits, (Dales 1968) the supply and demand mechanism leading to a price for permits to emit a given amount of pollution, (Pearce et al. 1989) with the emitter of pollution and ultimately the consumer having to pay over and above the costs of the material procured (Weizsacker & Jesinghaus 1992). McKibbin et al. (1999) argued that, from a theoretical perspective, the appeal of permit trading is that it is efficient and guarantees that emissions reductions will be achieved at minimum cost.

Permit trading schemes provide an opportunity for those who under-utilise their allocation of scarce permits, to trade them with those who require permission to pollute further. Permit trading schemes (where there is a scarcity of permits) may encourage good environmental practices and provide financial rewards to those who are able to operate under certain pollution constraints.

Bebbington et al. (2001) suggested that the overall outcome of permit trading schemes may not prevent or even reduce externalities, but would place a limit on the volume of pollution and to allocate that limited volume equitably amongst interested parties.

Large-scale (say) CO_2 reduction target setting would lead to scarcity of CO_2 permits, driving prices up. Peaks and troughs in supply and demand would also affect prices for permits. It is also conceivable that permits may become an attractive speculative investment for some, with the development of a futures market for the same. Those with vested interests (for example, environmental groups) may purchase such permits with no intention of trading them, but purely to prevent the emissions.

Bebbington et al. (2001) also noted that the costs of administration associated with the transaction of permits for these schemes are borne by the participants only, not the regulatory body, thereby not incurring the administrative costs for government.

Grubb et al. (1999) suggested there was considerable opposition to the principle of emissions trading at the time of the negotiation of the Kyoto Protocol, based largely on the premise that it could allow the United States to avoid significant domestic action. There was also some antipathy concerning the possibility of a retrospective windfall for Russia.

The Kyoto Agreement includes a provision for controlling global climate change based upon a system of tradable permits for CO_2 emissions (Article 17). However, this consists of a compromise statement that refers to the necessity to negotiate principles for emissions trading (Grubb et al. 1999). This demonstrates the difficulty in establishing the levels of entitlement for respective parties. Emission entitlements, through the use of permits, places a considerable emphasis on the basis for allocation. There was considerable debate on this matter in the making of the Protocol, with a per capita basis gaining much support at the time.

Notwithstanding the difficulty alluded to, tradable permits for CO_2 emissions become relevant provided that participants have varying marginal costs for carbon emission abatement (McKibbin et al. 1999). In such circumstances the largest gains from trade are possible. Those organisations or countries that have polluted excessively, with little regard for the environment, have arguably the most to gain from a system of tradable permits, as they are likely to be able to achieve a reduction in carbon emissions at relatively low costs (Tulpule et al. 1998).

The UK emissions trading system allows participants in such schemes to either qualify for incentive payments if CO_2 reduction targets are achieved, or financial penalties if they are not. Participants may engage in emissions trading to meet their targets, but decisions on trading will inevitably involve complex calculations and predictions as to the likelihood of a company meeting its targets and the financial consequences of either incentives and/or penalties (Hill et al. 2005).

Tradable permits may provide an opportunity for wealth creation, as permits are assets, tradable by a variety of organisations. The UK emissions trading system commenced in April 2002 and was the world's first emission trading system for GHGs. Initially, the UK emissions trading system operated on a voluntary basis. Participating companies took on voluntary targets for a period of five years with a commitment to make absolute reductions in emissions below their 1998–2000 levels. Gosling (2002) noted that the British Government, by initiating the market in the UK, was attempting to establish London as the location for a world exchange. The EU emissions trading system – trading at company level – commenced in 2005 and is similar except that there is no incentive for meeting the CO_2 targets, but there are penalties for not achieving the same.

The value of such permits is, however, likely to fluctuate over time, with the price per tonne of CO_2 remaining relatively depressed until global emissions trading systems exists, including participation from the US, which refused to ratify the Kyoto Treaty. However, such political resistance may not be of such significance if multinational companies recognise the benefits of participation.

In practice, tradable permits are likely to be limited to emissions for the foreseeable future. Tradable permits based upon emissions are predicated upon the accuracy and reliability of emission measurement data. Such credible data may not be available internationally and thus may restrict the application of such permits to technologically developed countries, unless inputs may be used as emission equivalents.

The European Commission Green Paper (2000) suggested that a comprehensive trading scheme could reduce compliance costs of meeting Kyoto by up to one-third. More recently (2005) the EU emissions trading scheme commenced, with a second phase in 2008–12 and further phases beyond 2012. The scheme is mandatory for energy generators, metal production, cement, brick, and pulp and paper and requires annual audited emissions reports.

Employing tradable permits to ultimately limit emissions remains a viable option, particularly internationally. An arguably important politically desirable quality of such a permit system is that it does not involve the reform of taxation.

TAXATION REFORM

Musgrave (1959) discussed economic reasoning for intervention in a market economy, including resource allocation. He argued that markets left to their own devices would not behave optimally, particularly with respect to 'external effects' for example, pollution.

Bird & Oldman (1990:132) observed: 'The best approach to reforming taxes [is that] one takes into account taxation theory, empirical evidence and political and administrative realities and blends them with a good dose of local knowledge and a sound appraisal of the current macroeconomic and international situation to produce a feasible set of proposals sufficiently attractive to be implemented and sufficiently robust to withstand changing times, within reason, and still produce beneficial results.'

Taxation is 'a compulsory levy made by public authorities for which nothing is received directly in return' (James & Nobes 2000:10). The authors suggest that this levy is used at least in part to endow society with public goods and services in exchange.

In considering taxation reform for the purpose of internalising externalities, it is worth considering existing classifications for taxation. The Organisation for Economic Cooperation and Development (OECD 1976) provides a classification for taxes as shown in Figure 18.

i)   Taxes on goods and services

    a)   Taxes in respect of ownership and use of or permission to use, goods or to perform activities

    b)   Taxes on the production, sale, transfer, leasing and delivery of goods and rendering of services

ii)   Taxes on income profits and capital gains

    a)   Paid by households and institutions

    b)   Paid by corporate enterprises

iii)   Social security contributions

    a)   Paid by employees

    b)   Paid by employers

    c)   Paid by self-employed or non-employed persons

iv)   Taxes on employers based upon payroll or manpower

v)   Taxes on net wealth and immovable property

    a)   Recurrent taxes on net wealth

    b)   Recurrent taxes on immovable property

    c)   Non-recurrent taxes on net wealth and immovable property

vi)   Taxes and stamp duties on gifts, inheritances and on capital and financial transactions

    a)   On gifts and inheritances

    b)   On capital and financial transactions

Figure 18   Adapted from OECD 1976 classification

In any attempt to reform the taxation system, for environmental aims or otherwise, it is worth considering the four 'canons' of taxation proposed by Smith (1776) in an attempt to distinguish potentially beneficial reforms from those which could well be deemed to be unsuitable.

1.   Equity – the fairness of the tax, taking into account the relative contributions of different individuals.

2.   Certainty – the certainty (not arbitrariness) of tax liabilities.

3.   Convenience – the consideration of the way the tax can be paid and the timing of this.

4.   Efficiency – the cost of collection of the tax should be a small proportion of revenue raised. Distortionary effects on the taxpayer should also be avoided.

James & Nobes (2000) contemplated a more economic perspective for appraising tax systems with a view to differentiating prospectively worthwhile reforms from inappropriate ones. The authors devised four criteria, which are not inconsistent with Smith (1776) and provide a framework for possible scrutiny of tax reforms as follows:

•   Efficiency – How could a particular tax proposal impact on the efficiency of the economy? For example, would a particular tax amplify distortions in the price mechanism affecting consumers and producers behaviour? The use of taxation to curb polluting behaviour (offsetting an existing distortion) would be considered here. Administrative and compliance costs and arrangements would also be considered in so far as how expensive the tax proposal would be to administer and to comply with, but also how complex the administrative and compliance arrangements would be.

•   Incentives – To what extent would the tax impact on the behavioural influences of an individual's desire to:

a)   work or undertake certain types of work;
b)   save and take advantage of investment opportunities;
c)   tolerate economic risks associated with business enterprise.

- Macroeconomic considerations – Are there any implications for the levels of employment in the economy?

- Equity – The principle of horizontal equity suggests 'that similar people in similar circumstances should be treated similarly' (James & Nobes 2000:17). Whether a tax is fair, requires a certain amount of subjective judgement. Who is actually affected by a tax, either directly or indirectly is referred to as tax *incidence* and is discussed in more detail later in this chapter.

The incidence of taxation is concerned with the matter of who pays the tax. Kay & King (1991) distinguished between 'formal incidence' and 'effective incidence' of taxation. Formal incidence of a tax refers to those who have the actual legal responsibility for payment; whereas effective incidence is concerned with those who will ultimately bear the tax burden, perhaps as a consequence of a tax levied on a manufacturer being included in the selling price of finished goods, which are ultimately purchased by consumers.

The incidence of taxation may be significant in understanding the role that taxation reform may have for ecological taxation in that the incidence of the majority of taxes are shared with several parties. This is likely to have implications for the ability of a tax to impact on an individual's behaviour and actions and may reduce a tax's effectiveness in achieving specific environmental aims.

Kay & King (1991) argued that the effectiveness of a tax could be improved 'if the tax were more discriminatory … if [for example] it were imposed on a single manufacturer' (Kay & King 1991:8). This could also be the case for a single activity. In such circumstances an attempt could subsequently be made to look for less adversely affected business (or activity) (Kay & King 1991). This highlights the opportunity for taxation reform to modify behaviour and actions, where alternatives exist to the rising costs of continuing with the actions.

Dasgupta et al. (1980) noted that reform of the UK tax system had emphasised that the effects of taxation on patterns of resource allocation are frequently complex, difficult to identify and that this was particularly the case for ecological taxation.

Notwithstanding the above, the taxation system provides an opportunity for fiscal changes to concur with environmental aims of pollution control

(Smith 1997). Direct taxes could be utilised to provide incentives to engage in certain desirable acts (Smith 1993), with a caveat that the use of such taxes may require additional administrative systems and procedures, particularly with respect to enforcement of the same and confirmation of rights to any inducements available.

Smith (1993) suggested that adjustments to the indirect tax system, which could utilise existing administrative mechanisms may prove to be a more efficient approach to the introduction of market-based encouragement for the purpose of pollution control. Kay & King (1991) emphasised that legal liability should be imposed at the point at which the tax can be collected most economically and conveniently; they point to administrative feasibility as an important limitation on tax policy.

Smith (1993) proposed that as an alternative to taxing the pollution emissions from cars, additional tax could be levied on fuel purchases, on the basis that the fuel will be burned and the amount of pollution is proportional to this. However, such a measure is likely to prove regressive and may have far reaching distributional consequences also.

Kaufmann (1991:139) described the use of a carbon tax as a 'least-cost policy'. Gaskins & Stram (1991) suggested that policies which lessen costs are advantageous, because they are economically more efficient than command and control regimes.

Taxation reform, implemented via taxation on fossil fuels, to work towards environmental objectives is consistent with the polluter pays principle, in that polluters are made to bear the costs of polluting via the taxation system. 'The harder it is for someone to substitute other things for the taxed activity, the greater the proportion of the incidence of the tax which he will bear' (Kay & King 1991:8).

Pearson & Smith (1990) argued that 'a tax (if set at the right level – an important proviso!) will often be more economically efficient than directly stopping polluting behaviour through legal curbs. Taxes are better than regulation in controlling some sorts of pollution because they allow individuals to weigh up the costs and benefits of their behaviour on a case-by-case basis' (Pearson & Smith 1990:2).

The desirable characteristics of environmental taxes are two-fold: Firstly, environmental taxes permit the manifestation of the true economic costs of goods and provide important revenue. Secondly, there is an unremitting incentive for innovation to develop lower polluting products or processes (Pearson & Smith 1990).

However, the significance of price elasticity is acknowledged in that the level of taxation to curb polluting behaviour may not be consistent with the clean-up costs for the same, creating a potential dilemma as to the level of taxation levied and the desired effects. Notwithstanding this, the 'true economic cost of goods' may be paramount in introducing an environmental tax and provides an explanation for the emphasis given to this by Pearce et al. (1989) to finding economic worth for the environment. Pearson & Smith (1990) concluded that it was improbable that a generally accepted measurement of worth for the environment would emerge in the short term.

However, Weizsacker & Jesinghaus (1992:18) suggested that such an obstacle may not need to be overcome prior to the introduction of ecological taxation reform. They make mention that such reform has the advantage that 'a government's exchequer never has to prove that any of the elements which are taxed in our society cause damage [they] are generally accepted on account of the undisputed need for public spending'.

Ecological taxes provide an opportunity for those responsible for the pollution, to modify their polluting behaviour, to reduce or avoid the taxation burden that would ensue or to continue with the polluting activities, unabated, and bear the costs of the same in the form of taxation.

Ecological taxation could take many forms, including taxation on the profits of the organisation's polluting activity, or taxation on the level of pollution caused (possibly through emission data) provided the accuracy and reliability of measurement data is sufficient that the data remains credible. Or alternatively, a tax on the raw materials used to cause the pollution could be relied upon where inputs may be used as emission equivalents. For example, the carbon content (per heat unit) of oil is approximately 40% higher than natural gas (Manne & Richels 1990).

Tietenberg (1985) concluded, as a consequence of a simulation approach, that with the use of environmental taxes, compliance costs could be reduced by 50%. Pearce (1991) also suggested that compliance costs could be reduced with environmental taxes. This arises from a tax mutual to all polluters giving rise to varying rates of pollution abatement as each individual's costs of pollution abatement may be different.

Pearson & Smith (1990) considered where economic behaviour may be influenced by environmental taxes in an attempt to reduce the true costs of economic activity and identified three areas:

- carbon taxes;

- road transport taxes; and

- fertiliser taxes and trade effluent discharge charges (soil and water pollutants).

Recent taxes introduced into the UK for this purpose include the Landfill Tax and Climate Change Levy, Vehicle Excise Duty (VED) for motorcars and changes to company car taxation as outlined in Chapter 1. Road tolls and congestion charging also fall into this category.

Agnolucci & Ekins (2004) identified an 'announcement effect', where measures are taken to reduce environmental impact from the time of the environmental tax announcement to implementation of the same. The existence of an announcement effect implies that organisations will recognise that current environmental practices will not be optimal post-environmental tax reform and, in taking steps to reform these, identify that abatement measures would be more viable than they were previously.

James & Nobes (2000) acknowledged the complexity of successful tax reform. Bird & Oldman (1990) acknowledged the balance required between theory and realism when reforming taxes. The European Environment Agency (EEA 1996) suggested that piecemeal reform in the form of a shift in taxes from labour to pollution as part of a package of tax reforms, whilst simultaneously addressing market failures, is likely to be the most successful approach. Ekins (1999) noted that governments will continue to introduce environmental taxation piecemeal, with the two-fold attraction that this taxation appears to offer, firstly, cost-effective environmental policy and, secondly, a source of revenue. James & Nobes (2000) concluded that piecemeal reform is more likely to be carried through, but express some caution as to whether reform implemented in this way would achieve its original aims.

It is partially in acknowledgement of this concession to piecemeal reform that carbon taxes on their own are given particular prominence and emphasis in this literature review. There is also a close association of carbon taxes to the particular tax reform of company car taxation taking into account the level of CO_2 emission, studied as a part of this book. In addition, the piecemeal implementation or carbon taxes of the type alluded to above in various forms for environmental ends is highly probable.

Carbon Taxes

'The taxation of energy or of carbon emissions as a policy option to mitigate climate change is increasingly being considered by industrialised countries' (Brack 1998:7). Carbon taxes have received considerable attention as an example of how an application of the price mechanism may provide environmental benefits (Pearson & Smith 1990). Stern (2007) observes that taxation may be used to create an explicit price for carbon. Carbon taxes may be levied on fossil fuel users according to the levels of carbon emissions when the fuel is combusted.

For example, the levels of carbon emitted from coal is considerably higher than oil, to produce the same value of heat. Similarly the levels of carbon emission are higher for oil than natural gas.

Pearce (1991) concluded that a carbon tax is most likely to manifest as a specific excise tax on the carbon content of fuels. Such a tax would vary for each fossil fuel (oil, coal and gas) because of the differences in the carbon content. Moreover, Smith (1993) suggested that the close association between CO_2 emissions and the carbon content of fossil fuels burnt provides further justification why the use of carbon taxes is an appropriate application of such a fiscal instrument.

Pearce (1991) suggested that a carbon tax could be consumption or production-based, the latter would effectively be an extraction tax and is likely to provide benefit to those carbon-exporting countries with oil, coal and gas resources and would disadvantage net carbon importers.

Much of the discussion of carbon taxes in the literature relates to consumption as this is likely to have the greatest effectiveness in curtailing carbon production via fossil fuel consumption and it is on this basis that carbon taxes are discussed further.

Pearce (1991:940) discussed the role of carbon taxes and suggested 'while most taxes distort incentives an environmental [carbon] tax corrects a distortion, namely the externalities arising from the excessive use of environmental services'. Pearson & Smith (1990) argued that the environmental costs of CO_2 emissions remain the same irrespective of their source. As a consequence all CO_2 generating activity should tolerate a charge in proportion to the amount of CO_2 produced. Carbon taxes may prove to be a valuable instrument for reducing CO_2 emissions, not least because carbon taxes are an on-going incentive to derive ever cleaner technology and adopt energy conservation measures (Pearce 1991).

Ekins (1994:578) emphasised the social benefit of carbon taxes, suggesting that such advantage 'derives from the carbon tax's "double dividend" characteristic' in that carbon taxes not only attempt to redress the environmental externality of fossil fuels by internalising the same, to a degree, but also have the potential to replace existing taxes, which may be distortionary, providing increased efficiency (Ekins 1994). Ekins (1997) attempted to model a shift from labour taxes to environmental taxes, but the results proved inconclusive. The Third Assessment Report of the Intergovernmental Panel on Climate Change (IPCC) (2002) concurred with the 'double dividend' view, whilst attempting to differentiate between a 'weak' and a 'strong' form of double dividend.

However, Weyant (1998) had reservations concerning the possibility of a double dividend and suggested that carbon taxes were inclined to be a less efficient source of revenue than income taxes. Bovenberg & Goulder (1996) emphasised that the levels of other taxes were significant in predicting the consequences of environmental taxes such as carbon taxes.

Pearce (1991:942) argued that carbon taxes may be easily modified as additional information becomes available. Carbon taxes are 'a policy instrument capable of responding to successive revision of [scientific] data'.

Of the EU member states, Sweden, Norway, The Netherlands, Denmark, Finland, Austria, Germany and Italy have already implemented some form of carbon tax, based upon the carbon or energy content of the fuel (Carter 2001) with varying degrees of success. Most countries taxed mineral oil (except marine and aviation fuel) in the economy in any case (Brack 1998). So far the effectiveness of such taxes has been relatively low, partially due to low tax rates and for dispensations given to energy intensive industries (OECD 1999). Carter (2001) suggested that carbon and energy taxation in Europe has had minimal success in reducing emissions and argued that this is partially as a consequence of the tax being levied at a level which is too low in order that the tax is politically acceptable.

The Regional Environmental Center for Central and Eastern Europe (REC) (2004) asserted that there are only a limited number of studies that have attempted to evaluate the environmental effectiveness of the implementation of carbon taxes so far and pointed to methodological difficulties and complexities in carrying out such evaluation studies for the lack of proper studies. Notwithstanding these observations, there appear to be some significant studies that provide the basis for a contribution to the development of theory in this area. One such study is the Swedish Environmental Protection Agency (SEPA). They concluded that a CO_2 tax has contributed to a reduction in CO_2 emissions consistent with Swedish environmental policy (SEPA 1997).

However, Hanisch (1998) claimed that in Finland, where CO_2 taxes have been implemented since 1990, CO_2 emissions had continued to rise, because of strong economic growth.

Kaufmann (1991) asserted that with the introduction of a carbon tax, fuel specific charges would arise, which will result in higher taxes on coal than oil and higher taxes on oil than natural gas. This may result in a reduction in consumption of certain fuels and lower CO_2 emissions by acting as a catalyst to technological improvements and through fuel substitution.

Pearson & Smith (1990:6) noted 'the primary effects of a carbon tax would be to raise the price of energy, so reducing the amount of energy demanded by the economy, and also encouraging a reduction in the amount of carbon used per unit of energy generated'. If it were the intention to reduce CO_2 emissions in the short term, the rates of tax introduced would have to be very high, whereas if the intention were to reduce CO_2 emissions in the longer term, taxation increases could be more modest (Pearson & Smith 1990). These conclusions from a discussion of elasticity of demand were based upon the experience of significant increases in energy prices during the 1970s.

This view was reaffirmed by Manne & Richels (1993) who made mention of an increase in prices for fossil fuels dampening energy consumption and asserted that an increase in fossil fuel prices resulted in fossil fuels being less attractive compared to other supply-side possibilities. 'We need only look back to the oil price shocks of the 1970s to see how well the price mechanism works' (Manne & Richels 1993:5).

However, an important observation to make is that whilst both Pearson & Smith (1990) and Manne & Richels (1993) claimed that carbon taxes would lower the consumption of carbon-intensive fuels and hence reduce CO_2 emissions, such taxes may not dampen total energy consumption; the possibility of fuel substitution exists. In their discussion of price elasticity, Manne & Richels (1993:5) concluded that 'carbon taxes create incentives for fuel switching away from carbon-intensive fuels'.

Indeed, high levels of carbon tax may encourage fuel switching unless the prices of carbon-free fuel substitutes, for example, nuclear energy, are raised also. The possibility exists for levies to be placed on carbon-free fuels also, possibly through taxation, according to the level of environmental damage incurred (for example, environmental decommissioning costs for nuclear energy) alongside carbon taxes for fossil fuels.

The outcome may be improved energy consumption, because of the increase of prices of all fuels. However, there may be no significant change in the levels of CO_2 production as the price differential between carbon and non-carbon fuels may not be significant enough to encourage consumers to switch fuels. Indeed, one could speculate that with the high environmental costs arising from nuclear energy, any levy could be material to influence consumers to not switch from fossil fuels.

Manne & Richels (1993) concluded that a selective combination of carbon and energy taxes may be counterproductive. They contended that the primary motive of carbon taxes should be to lower CO_2 emissions and not energy conservation. Kaufmann (1991) observed that that it is the end-user price that determines the degree of substitution (between fossil fuels) and conservation. Kaufmann suggested one criterion for the determination of the efficacy of a carbon tax may be the degree of substitution from higher carbon-producing fossil fuels per heat unit to lower carbon-producing fossil fuels per heat unit.

The rate of increase of the price of a particular fossil fuel, as a consequence of the introduction of a carbon tax, based on the carbon content of the fuel concerned will be dependent upon the variation in the price between fuels. This rate of increase may be significant in determining the extent of fuel substitution. Kaufmann (1991:144) highlighted that coal is significantly cheaper per unit of heat than other fossil fuels. The rate of increase that a carbon tax would therefore need to bring to bear on coal would be 'a ratio much greater than the emission rate of coal relative to oil or natural gas'.

In addition, the problem is further complicated by the fact that fossil fuel prices vary between nations and even sectors. Hoeller et al. (1990) suggested that it may be necessary to determine end-user prices that are specific for particular nations and sectors.

Kaufmann (1991) raised the question as to whether the primary motive of a carbon tax is to internalise the costs connected with the emission of CO_2, which could ignore any motive for conservation and sustainability. This may determine a different total price for particular fossil fuels that may not reduce carbon emissions, either through fuel substitution or efficiency. Accordingly, a carbon tax may be more effective if levied as a rate with a base rate assigned to the lowest carbon content fossil fuel (natural gas) with rates proportionate to their carbon content for oil and coal (Kaufmann 1991). However, a careful modelling of end-user prices to gauge precisely the outcome of a carbon tax on CO_2 emissions would be necessary.

The introduction of a carbon tax in the UK would change relative prices and this would have an effect on the international competitiveness for products (Ekins 1994). Tulpule et al. (1998) also observed that (notwithstanding the opportunity for fuel substitutability) carbon emission penalties (possibly in the form of taxes) would increase production costs for emission intensive industries. This would lead to higher prices for consumers.

Ekins (1999) suggested that the use of economic instruments, such as carbon taxes, should not increase the overall burden of taxation for businesses which would adversely affect business competitiveness. He adds a caveat that such impact on environmentally intensive sectors is part of the essential purpose of environmental taxation, in order to persuade these sectors to make more efficient use of scarce resources and to simultaneously pursue new, less environmentally demanding products and processes.

A carbon tax may affect the relative competitive trade position, particularly for those parts of the economy that are heavily dependent on fossil fuels, for example manufacturing, by increasing the price of industrial inputs and, as a consequence, increased prices of consumer goods (Pearson & Smith 1990). The higher prices for consumers would in turn encourage consumers to substitute products from these sectors for less environmentally damaging products.

However, the size of increase cannot easily be quantified but will be influenced by the carbon intensity of the product and the size of the carbon tax as well as the extent to which such a tax is offset by other fiscal measures. Pearson & Smith (1990) attempted to evaluate how broad groups of industries could be affected if a carbon tax were introduced using a categorisation of industry type and the introduction of a measure of 'output per unit of energy used' using industry categorisations (Pearson & Smith 1990:15). The higher the value of output, the less susceptible an industry would be to fossil fuel price increases.

This reveals that a carbon tax is more likely to have an effect on coal than other fossil fuels because of the relatively higher carbon intensity of the fuel and also suggests that, as a consequence of coal being used for 'non-premium' applications, it would be more difficult to pass on this higher cost to the consumer (Ferriter 1997).

The possibility of macroeconomic gains in the area of employment arising from the introduction of a carbon tax exists (Ekins 1994). Competitiveness of labour would increase as it became relatively cheaper. This may be particularly significant for those countries with high unemployment, which could, as a consequence of the introduction of a carbon tax, benefit from an increase in employment.

McKinney & Schoch (2003) asserted that carbon taxes (like other indirect taxes) are regressive. Poorer people would suffer the tax as a higher proportion of total income compared to relatively wealthy people. This view was shared by Harris & Goodwin (2003). Pearson & Smith (1990) acknowledge the possibility of macroeconomic effects of a carbon tax but add a caveat that such macroeconomic effects could be dependent on what the proceeds of such a tax were used for.

Pearson & Smith (1990) recognised the possibility of a change in industrial competitiveness and balance of payments, but placed reliance on a floating exchange rate to adjust accordingly to maintain competitiveness. Smith (1993) conceded that the consequences for industry (and households) are that such taxes would result in significant increases in tax payments, but that the additional revenue collected from such taxes would be available to mitigate some of the adverse effects of this through reductions in indirect taxes elsewhere. Ekins (1994) maintained that there does not have to be a long-term adverse effect on the international competitiveness of a nation arising from the introduction of a carbon tax, provided that revenues from the tax are recycled back to avert this in the carbon-intensive sectors of industry.

Baranzini et a.l (2000) also concurred that that carbon taxes may be a viable policy option and that their main negative impacts may be recognised and mitigated through the design of the tax and the use of the generated fiscal revenues.

Pearson & Smith (1990) concluded that (post-carbon tax implementation in the UK) the preference would be for the UK to focus on production with low-energy content, with other non-carbon taxing countries focusing on production with a high-energy content. The authors concluded that a single country introducing carbon taxes is unlikely to lower global CO_2 emissions but rather redistribute these emissions. For carbon taxes to be effective in lowering global CO_2 emissions they should be introduced on a global basis.

Braithwaite & Drahos (2000) concurred with the proposal of a global carbon tax and recommended that an international agreement be reached to introduce carbon taxes at a relatively low level to begin with increasing gradually over time. Uzawa (2003) discussed proportional tax schemes, where the emission tax is levied proportional to a measure of national income. However, an international (coordinated) approach to taxation could prove problematic. The difficulty in creating an international body that would be both sufficiently independent and prominent to levy and spend the tax appropriately was highlighted by Victor (2001).

Ekins (1994) discussed modelling the effects of a carbon tax and appraised the many detailed reviews of studies for a variety of CO_2 abatement economic modelling and concluded that distinctive taxes have different distortionary effects on the economy. Boero et al. (1991) attempted to classify such models into two broad categories of firstly, long-term comparative prices and equilibrium distribution of resource models and secondly, short-term alterations and disequilibria models. This was in an attempt to assess the Gross Domestic Product (GDP) implications of achieving various CO_2 emission reductions.

A reduction of GDP was noted as a result of the introduction of a carbon tax modelled at different levels according to the desired CO_2 emission reduction and the time period considered. Stern (2007) also concurred that increasing fossil fuel costs would have a negative impact on GDP. Variations in GDP reductions from different commentators may be explained by differences in the extent of emissions abatement, the extent of use of low-emission technologies, the approach to modelling and also the extent to which revenue from carbon taxes would be used to offset or reduce other taxes and which taxes were reduced.

Smith (1993) conceded that pollution issues such as global warming and acid rain which taxation could possibly address were not constrained by national boundaries and, as a consequence, acknowledged the significance of the international perspective for environmental tax policy making and that, because of the possible ramifications of environmental taxes on trade and the competitive position of a nation, countries are unlikely to introduce environmental taxes at an optimal level prior to international agreement on the objectives of policy.

However, Ekins (1994) placed great emphasis on the conclusion that a unilateral introduction of a carbon tax would not impair international competitiveness, but added a caveat that revenues from the tax are recycled as discussed earlier.

The European Commission (EC) favours the introduction of an EC-wide (harmonised) carbon tax. The rationale for this is that GHGs, including CO_2 are homogeneously mixed pollutants resulting in uniform damage across all EC nations and indeed the whole world. Such a harmonised European carbon tax regime would also go some way towards addressing the concerns of EC member states over their relative competitiveness. Mohr (1990) concurred that carbon tax harmonisation could provide benefits. However, Pearce (1991) was less conclusive concerning this matter, suggesting that the degree of harmonisation is open to debate.

The situation may be further complicated by some EU member states, such as Sweden, Norway, The Netherlands, Denmark, Finland, Austria, Germany and Italy. These countries have already implemented some form of carbon tax, based upon the carbon or energy content of the fuel, albeit with significant variations between countries. This has resulted in the average price of a tonne of carbon being inconsistent between countries.

The table in Figure 19 demonstrates the inconsistency for taxes on energy products of selected European countries.

Figure 19   Energy products for European countries

Source: Baranzini et al. 2000

Tax rates for European countries are for 1998 in national currencies and then converted with 1997 purchasing power parities (PPP 1997). (PPP source: OECD Main Economic Indicators July 1998, Paris).

Taxes on Energy Products in Some Selected Countries, in Purchasing Power Parity										
Country	Petrol (gasoline) unleaded		Diesel		Diesel/Gas Oil *(industrial use)*		Coal *(industrial use)*		Natural Gas *(industrial use)*	
	$PPP / 1000 litre	$PPP / ton CO_2	$PPP / 1000 litre	$PPP / ton CO_2	$PPP / 1000 litre	$PPP / ton CO_2	$PPP / 1000 kg	$PPP / ton CO_2	$PPP / 1000 m³	$PPP / ton CO_2
Denmark	395	164	272	95	206	72	163	67	28	15
Finland	558	232	324	113	55	19	33	14	28	15
France	590	245	370	129	78	27	0	0	1	1
Germany	495	205	313	109	40	14	0	0	33	17
Netherlands	583	242	336	117	102	36	11	5	55	29
Norway	520	216	403	140	46	16	46	19	93	49
Spain	490	203	356	124	104	36	0	0	8	4
Sweden	456	189	295	103	183	64	126	52	105	56
Switzerland	356	148	372	129	1	1	0	0	0	0

Pearson & Smith (1990) discussed the distributional consequences of a carbon tax on domestic fuel with reference to consumer behaviour as a consequence of the introduction of Value Added Tax (VAT) on electricity and gas. They placed reliance on data from Baker et al. (1990) and a methodology described in Blundell et al. (1989) to conclude that the introduction of a tax on domestic fuel would reduce consumption of energy significantly. However, they observed that the distributional effects of this change were undesirable with the poorest households reducing energy consumption, but no significant reduction for the richest decile.

It could, therefore, be necessary to allow for some increase in the income for certain low-income groups, for example pensioners, with the aim of redistributing the tax burden arising from a carbon tax, to mitigate the tax increase for these income groups. Or alternatively, as a subsidy to (say) offset possible health-related problems to avoid incurring certain public health costs. In this way low-income groups may not be more vulnerable as a consequence of rising energy prices, but would still have an incentive to consume less energy.

Taxes introduce an opportunity to attribute a monetary value to an externality. The taxation system provides a mechanism for internalisation of previously disregarded externalities into economic entities. In so doing, taxation provides a reporting, and hence accountability, opportunity for economic entities along the lines of FCA. It follows that carbon taxes could have a significant role to play in valuing and limiting carbon emissions. 'Environmental taxes can be powerful policy instruments in steering the market towards lower-carbon options and bringing forward investments in near commercial options' (Foley 2003:21). The effectiveness of carbon taxes as a means to carbon pricing must be supported by credible policy, in so far as it may convince a range of interest groups (Stern 2007) and facilitate long-term planning and investment.

The potential for the use of taxation for environmental aims has not gone unnoticed by policy makers. Ekins (1999) noted that the use of various forms of environmental taxation in OECD countries has increased by more than 50% between the periods 1987–1994.

A carbon tax could promote economic efficiency and has the potential to substitute distortionary taxes (Ekins 1994). Where such taxes are contemplated they should be introduced with a view to achieving a neutral macroeconomic outcome and be 'imposed gradually and with long-term prior anticipation' (Ekins 1994:577). Other taxes should be modified accordingly 'so that the total fiscal package is broadly inflation and revenue neutral' (Ekins 1994).

It is also paramount to emphasise that in estimating the impact of carbon taxes, 'the underlying energy elasticities are crucial' (Pearce 1991:947).

Meade (1973) argued that setting a tax rate to control the quantity of pollution does not prevent an upper threshold of pollution being breached, where excessive damage may cause disproportionate and irreversible damage to the environment, whereas the introduction of licences or permits does. Notwithstanding that, the introduction of taxation based upon CO_2 emissions could be seen to be advantageous irrespective of whether global warming is proven to arise from CO_2 emissions, or indeed whether or not global warming is likely to have significant future cost implications.

Car Taxation

Pearson & Smith (1990) suggested three reasons why motorcars may be singled out for special attention for ecological taxation. Firstly, significant taxes already exist for cars (and other forms of road transport). This provides the opportunity for modification of taxation in this area rather than introducing a completely new taxation regime as the latter may prove politically very unpopular and administratively complex and possibly inefficient. Secondly, cars make a significant contribution to externalities, via pollution noise and congestion. Thirdly, car transport is very energy intensive. Finally, it is anticipated that road traffic will continue to rise for the foreseeable future, which will intensify environmental matters associated with this form of transport.

EXISTING CAR TAXES

Existing UK car taxes comprise taxes on fuel (petrol and diesel), with differing rates of taxation for leaded and unleaded petrol, diesel and low-sulphur fuels. They also include VED, which is now graduated according to CO_2 emissions, and VAT, which is charged on the purchase of a vehicle and also on the fuels and the repair and maintenance costs for the vehicle. Besides these, the individuals benefiting from the use of a company car are also subject to further taxation in the form of a Benefit in Kind (BIK) as explained in Chapter 1, which provides the main context for this study.

EXTERNALITIES

Smith (1993) categorised environmental externalities associated with road transport as noise, pollution of the atmosphere, and the impact on the natural landscape due to new road-building. As the volume of road traffic continues to increase, so do the significance of these externalities.

Car emissions comprise: lead, CO_2, nitrogen oxides, carbon monoxide and hydrocarbons. Although the latter two pollutants have been reduced from cars in recent years with the introduction of catalytic converters, such equipment does require an increase in the concentration of the petrol to air ratio for the platinum and rhodium within the catalytic converter to absorb these pollutants effectively. The outcome is a reduction in fuel consumption of approximately 5% coupled with a corresponding increase in CO_2 emissions. Such pollution is not subject to the price mechanism as outlined earlier in this chapter.

MEASURES

To reduce the current level of CO_2 emissions from cars would require the introduction of measures to encourage a considerable reduction in the CO_2 generated per kilometre travelled. Pearson & Smith (1990) suggested two uses of taxation to reduce fuel consumption and hence emissions:

Firstly, increase the marginal cost of car transport. According to Pearson & Smith (1990) an increase in the marginal cost of travelling by road would reduce the aggregate distance travelled. Fuel price increases would result in consumers purchasing less fuel and as a consequence travelling fewer miles. This is an example of price elasticity of demand. However, it is worth contemplating a caveat that fuel price increases may not necessarily result in a reduction in the aggregate distance travelled if the fuel is directly substitutable by another. In the UK, the increase in tax on leaded petrol improved the market share of unleaded petrol from 4% in April 1989 to 30% in March 1990 (Kirby et al. 1995).

The revised system of company car taxation introduced in 2002 and outlined in Chapter 1 removes the incentive for drivers of company cars to maximise business mileage beyond certain thresholds (2,500 miles and 18,000 miles).

Whether such a change will reduce the overall distance travelled by company car drivers is evaluated as part of this book to gain some insight into price sensitivity to environmental taxation by company car drivers; in so far as they are able or prepared to moderate the distance travelled by car. Such empirical evidence provided through examining the effect of the change to company car taxation arrangements on possible business mileage may ascertain whether the results of the study concur with the literature in this chapter, which advocates that fiscal incentives, or the discontinuance of unsuitable incentives, can reduce carbon emissions.

Secondly, increase the number of kilometres per litre. Incentives such as graduated VED for cars (now introduced) discriminate in favour of lower-emission engines (Pearson & Smith 1990) and encourage the acquisition and use of smaller, more fuel efficient cars that emit lower pollutants. Such measures have the added advantage over increasing fuel prices that it can be distributively more appealing (Pearson & Smith 1990). Those living in areas with poor public transport systems are not punished by the high cost of fuel, but are encouraged to pollute less by switching to smaller less polluting cars.

Pearson & Smith (1990) also observed that the existing (now previous) system for taxing company cars promoted larger cars. They emphasised that, as a consequence of this (now previous) system of taxation, the largest tax inducement is achieved by providing a car with a large engine capacity. They concluded to avoid this inducement to acquire larger engine cars, it would be necessary to formulate scale charges in a more progressive manner.

The revised system of company car taxation, introduced in 2002 and outlined in Chapter 1, does incorporate progressive scale charges by taking into account the level of CO_2 emission produced by the car together with a proportion of the manufacturers' list price (subject to £80,000 maximum) when the car is new, to determine the BIK for the individual tax payer.

In so doing there is a recognition that whilst a 1000cc car should more fuel efficient than (say) a 1500cc car, for some models the converse is the case (possibly arising from technological advances in engine management technology, vehicle gross weight or aerodynamics) and, because of this, a tax based purely upon engine size may not be as effective an environmental tax as one based upon emissions.

A change with the potential to reduce CO_2 emission may be more attractive than raising petrol prices (Pearson & Smith 1990). Whether such a change will curtail this incentive to buy larger cars is evaluated as part of this research to determine price sensitivity to environmental (emissions) taxation by company car drivers in so far as they are able or prepared to moderate their choice of car.

As discussed in Chapter 1, empirical evidence provided by examining the effect of the change to company car taxation arrangements on intended company car selection may ascertain whether the results of the study concur with the literature in this chapter, which suggests that fiscal incentives (or deterrents) can reduce emissions.

In examining the choices made by individuals in the selection of company cars and the distance travelled under the revised tax regime, and comparing this to choices made under the previous system, conclusions may be drawn as to the intentions of company car drivers as a consequence of this taxation reform. It is worth noting that company car ownership for many is not voluntary and choice may be restricted to a certain extent by the size of vehicles to undertake certain work (for example, estate cars for transporting samples).

Conclusion

Notwithstanding the difficulties alluded to in externality valuation, the *Brundtland Report* provides valuable linkage between the concept of sustainability and the recognition of environmental impact arising from economic activities. The report has acted as a catalyst for debate for costing externalities and the possibilities for internalising such costs, along with the implications of the same for individuals and organisations. This debate is informed by the regulatory perspective and has evolved post-Kyoto.

The literature in this chapter offers a critique of some of the deficiencies of our economic system, relating to environmental damage in general and pollution and carbon emissions in particular. There is also recognition that emissions abatement policies, when applied independently to individual countries as opposed to consistently to all countries, may raise production costs, leading to higher prices, which may have an impact on competitiveness.

As part of the discussion in this chapter, an attempt was made to identify a way forward to mitigate the environmental impact arising from economic activities within the existing economic framework, where acceptance of the same is likely to be high. Taxation may provide such an occasion.

Taxation provides an opportunity for the inclusion of externalities without wholesale review/change in economic theory or political perspective (for example, Marxism). Carbon taxes provide the potential for a 'double dividend' (Pearce 1991:940) in that they raise revenues for government and curb polluting behaviour. Such gradual (incremental) piecemeal changes in taxation could benefit society in moving towards a more sustainable position with minimal resistance coupled with the opportunity of earmarking revenue for specific environmental rectification purposes.

However, it should be reiterated that the externalities arising from carbon emissions arise globally. Batabyal & Beladi (2001) noted of their research into carbon taxes that it is predicated on the supposition that unilateral carbon reduction in one country does not bring about significant changes of carbon emissions elsewhere. In the same way, as consumers may substitute but not lower overall consumption of fuels because of measures to encourage lower consumption and emissions, companies may also substitute geographical locations in the form of countries to reduce their exposure to financial disincentives for carbon emissions.

Much of the literature in the latter part of this chapter proposes reforms linked to carbon emissions. The significance given to the regulatory perspective in this chapter ,together with an emphasis on taxation and carbon emissions, is due to their significance in the research study carried out.

Implicit in the earlier discussion is the concept of externality valuation for the purpose of determining the level of taxation, albeit this may be incremental to provide sufficient opportunities for modification of polluting behaviour. However, such a strict application of the polluter pays principle (which OECD countries embraced in 1972) via a system of taxation reforms may be problematic.

Weizsacker & Jesinghaus (1992:23) observed that 'in a host of cases, the polluter pays principle cannot be applied in any strict sense because either repair is impossible (e.g. in the case of species extinction), or the damage is nearly impossible to quantify (e.g. damage as a result of an enhanced greenhouse effect) or it is impossible to apportion legal responsibility for pollution'.

Moreover, the rate of taxation required to curb or preclude polluting requires data for elasticity of demand. Pearce (1991) emphasised that accurate estimates for energy elasticity are paramount. However, the rate of taxation necessary to achieve this is unlikely to be the same as the repair cost. This raises the question as to what should underpin the setting of the rate of such a tax.

The use of tax-based environmental policies creates improvement opportunities for both the environment and the fiscal system. However, potential environmental gains may not be realised if there is bias towards revenue considerations in establishing tax rates. 'Environmental spending may be determined simply by the availability of earmarked revenue' (Smith 1993:235). Nordhaus (1975) observed that UK tax policy has in the past been influenced by electoral factors, rather than demand management motivations.

However, Smith (1993) noted that there has been a tendency for countries to earmark the proceeds from environmental taxes for environmental matters in practice. Tax earmarking or tax hypothecation 'involves assigning the revenue from a particular tax to a specific part of public expenditure' (James & Nobes 2000:136). An example of hypothecation in the UK is National Insurance (NI) contributions that are used for specific health and welfare benefits. There are opposing views as to the efficacy of earmarked taxes. It is plausible that earmarked taxes could inflict a constraint on budgetary decisions, reducing the efficiency of government.

Alternatively, Buchanan (1963) suggested the converse that such a constraint may actually improve budgetary decisions. Teja & Bracewell-Milnes (1991) also concur that tax earmarking could offer greater public sector efficiency than expenditure from a single fund and suggested that it would be beneficial to have a closer link between the specific benefits received from a public service and the contribution that is required for this purpose. This, the authors argue, coupled with a greater willingness on the part of individuals to pay their taxes if they understood how the money was being earmarked, could prove beneficial also.

A tax system does require the cooperation of the vast majority of taxpayers if it is to function effectively, so matters pertaining to tax compliance are worthy of mention here. Tax compliance refers to the extent to which taxpayers comply with tax law. The gap between compliance and non-compliance may be measured (actual revenue received compared with complete fulfilment of tax obligations) (James & Nobes 2000) and is referred to as the 'tax gap'. Wallschutzky (1993) considered tax compliance issues and noted that much of the research in this area appeared to be directed towards why some taxpayers do not comply. James & Nobes (2000) concluded that the motives of the tax payer are paramount. The authors gave emphasis to the possibility of detection, non-compliance penalties and activities designed to promote voluntary compliance. The latter also encompasses stance towards the nation state and revenue authorities as central factors.

Tax revenue should arguably be utilised for the benefit of society. The benefits of the process, at least from a compliance point of view, are likely to be greater if any compliance policy takes account of the wide range of motivations of taxpayers to avoid a rigid and confrontational system (Schmolders 1970), which can result in a high degree of disaffection and opposition amongst taxpayers. Internal Revenue Service (1991) suggest that education, along with simplification, may have a role to play in convincing individuals of the value of a responsible approach towards taxation in pursuit of this.

Pearce (1991) concluded of carbon taxes that countries would first look to politically 'soft' measures before implementing carbon taxation and suggested energy saving campaigns as an example. However, if these so-called 'soft' measures do not prove effective in reducing CO_2 emissions, precious time would have been lost in arresting environmental damage, the consequence of which is that any tax increases later would have to be higher (Pearce 1991).

The revised system of company car taxation, introduced in 2002 and outlined in Chapter 1, provides an opportunity for CO_2 emission reduction, via lower consumption and also fuel substitution. The extent to which the reforms are consistent with the four 'canons' of taxation proposed by Smith (1776) should become perceptible later in this book from the research study and the findings from the same in the latter chapters.

3

Measuring Attitudes and Behaviour amongst Company Car Drivers

The aim of this research is to contribute to a more comprehensive understanding of the possible 'mechanisms through which the current structures of an economy might come to reflect – to a significantly greater degree than at present … [the] … environmental aspects of economic activity' (Bebbington et al. 2001:22). We will specifically consider the mechanism of taxation and the price sensitivity of individuals to environmental taxation relating to Carbon Dioxide (CO_2) emissions, in so far as changes to a principle and method in the UK taxation regime, which is potentially applicable generally, may contribute to the Kyoto Target for lowering CO_2 emissions.

The research acknowledges (from the literature) the significance of carbon taxes to potentially reduce CO_2 emissions and contemplates the matter of implementation of the same. The objectives of this research are to (based upon the literature) recognise the significance of economic activity in permitting externalities to arise that have an impact on the environment via carbon emissions and to consider the efficacy of a change in a principle and method in the UK taxation regime to reduce such emissions.

In so doing, the intention of the research is to consider a revenue-neutral taxation reform specifically implemented to discourage CO_2 emissions from a particular category of car driver. The study attempted to analyse the results of a survey on the implementation of this tax, to draw conclusions, based upon the evidence, as to whether such an environmental tax at the level imposed would internalise costs associated with environmental impact and provide adequate incentive to encourage these motor car drivers to emit less CO_2 by:

- • encouraging company car drivers to choose lower-emission vehicles than they would have otherwise chosen (reducing CO_2 emissions per kilometre); and

- • no longer encouraging some company car drivers to drive more miles than perhaps necessary (reducing total kilometres).

The research will ascertain whether the results of the study carried out concur with the literature in Chapter 2, which advocates that fiscal incentives or the discontinuance of unsuitable incentives can reduce carbon emissions.

Burke (1997) acknowledged that the evaluation of ecological or 'green' taxes is problematic and cited complexity and counteracting effects of regulations together with problems of data collection and suggested that 'adequate evaluation of practical experience with such taxes [of the type undertaken in this study] is still comparatively rare' Burke (1997:88).

This data, collected from the research method employed, will also permit a deliberation of the paradox arising from environmental taxation, in so far as the level (rate) of taxation required to internalise sufficient costs to cover reinstatement of the environment (clean-up costs) may not be consistent with the level (rate) of taxation to discourage emissions in the first place. This paradox is addressed in an attempt to draw conclusions as to the efficacy and appropriateness of this environmental tax relating to carbon emissions, to contribute to the Kyoto Target for lowering CO_2 emissions.

Moreover, the study provides an opportunity to observe the implementation of a 'green tax' and in the course of the latter chapters of the book, to draw conclusions based upon the evidence and the literature reviewed, for the tenants of carbon taxes to comment on and make recommendations for the efficacy of emissions-related motor taxation regimes.

This chapter provides details of the research methodology adopted for the study carried out later in the book. In so doing, the chapter will outline the method applied to address the research objectives and the questions arising from the same, outlined in Chapter 1 and in pursuance of this, to contribute to the body of accumulated knowledge (Remenyi et al. 1998) by testing hypothesis using quantitative evidence obtained through a survey.

This chapter also provides details of the survey instrument, the research approach adopted and the justification for this. Sample selection, size and data collection are also discussed. Matters relating to the robustness of testing and, as a consequence, the reliance that may be placed on the findings are also addressed. The difficulties of the approach adopted are also referred to not only to appreciate the difficulties in themselves in this context, but to deliberate as to how such potential shortcomings could impact on the research study.

This research is exploratory in that the subject matter, a single revenue-neutral reform of the company car taxation system and the impact of this on individuals' attitudes to company car acquisition and overall levels of CO_2 production from the same, has not been studied before. However, the theory underpinning this study and the use of taxation (carbon taxes) as an instrument for reducing CO_2 emissions has been considered in prior research. Such research has taken the form of a simulation analysis 'and the corresponding effect of this [carbon] tax on the purchasing power and the economic behaviour of households' (Symons et al. 1994:19).

A diagrammatic representation for the relationship between the research problem, hypothesis development, information used to analyse the problem and the research methodology is illustrated in Figure 20.

The positivist paradigm adopted for this book arises from the applied research aim to measure CO_2 emissions pre- and post-UK company car taxation reform and to use this data to test hypothesis objectively and reliably. 'Hypothesis must be testable. Their content must be measurable in some way even if they are not directly observable' (Smith 2003:52).

Notwithstanding the recognition of some of the possible subjective behavioural matters involved in the choice of company car, where a choice exists, (for example, performance, family considerations, brand loyalty, perceived brand image, specific accessories, safety, reliability), a deductive approach would appear more appropriate for carrying out this research study, providing an opportunity for greater reliability in measurement (Smith 2003). Such an approach is preferred for a highly structured environment, where the empirical testing of theoretical models would be undertaken. The credibility of such testing is reliant on the appropriateness of quantitative and statistical methods (Smith 2003). A deductive approach should provide an opportunity to test the hypothesis outlined and discard the theoretical suppositions which

**Figure 20   The relationship between the research problem, hypothesis
development and information used to measure an expectation
of the post-taxation reform**

cannot be confirmed. Those hypothesis which remain (that is, not discarded)
may be used to inform the development of the theory in this area and possibly
offer some predictive capability also.

An illustration of the deductive approach (Smith 2003) is shown in Figure 21.

'A valuable part of the initial planning process is the development of a
conceptual representation of the research project. This can help to clarify the
important relationships…the explanatory and intervening variables, as well as
the demonstration of causation' (Smith 2003:24). The conceptual matter of this
research requires an examination of the relationship and any casual link between
the following key variables; choice of company car, the form of company car
taxation, amount of taxation for the company car, CO_2 emissions (g/km),

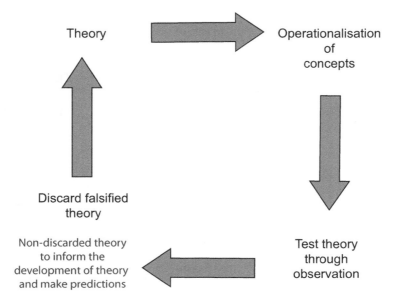

Figure 21   The deductive approach taken to the research
Source: Smith 2003:26

business mileage travelled and the total emissions arising as a consequence of the expressed procurement intentions.

The combination of the aforementioned factors when subsequently compared with the CO_2 emissions arising under the conditions existing for the pre-2002 taxation regime, enable a comparison to be made as to the efficacy of the taxation reform for lowering CO_2 emissions from company cars, be it based upon an intended reduction in business mileage, a choice of a lower-emission car or a combination of both factors.

This may be illustrated in a conceptual schema diagram shown in Figure 22.

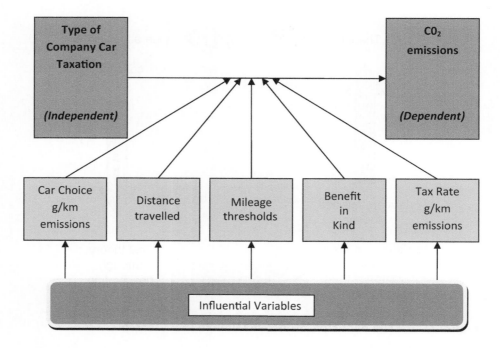

Figure 22   Conceptual schema diagram for the key variables

Research Hypotheses

The hypotheses for this research are concerned with proving the significance of environmental carbon taxes in reducing pollution, by reducing CO_2 emissions through the evaluation of a specific taxation regime. The hypotheses considered the effect of independent variables (the taxation) on the dependent variables (CO_2 emissions), as opposed to establishing the significance of correlations, in an attempt to demonstrate causality in the possible relationships amongst the variables.

DEVELOPMENT OF THE PROPOSED RESEARCH MODEL

The proposed research model, which provides the basis for the investigation carried out, drew from existing literature where environmental taxes 'might have a role in adapting economic behaviour to reflect the true costs of economic activity' (Pearson & Smith 1990:4) and also considered simulation models on consumer behaviour and the distributive outcome of adding Value Added Tax (VAT) to electricity and gas costs (Pearson & Smith 1990). In addition, the observations of Baker et al. (1990) concerning the effects of adding a tax on domestic fuel and power were considered. These studies, whilst considering the consequences of introducing a tax, have concentrated on the distributional impacts of the same and have emphasised the regressive nature of such taxes as opposed to the reduction of emissions as a consequence of an alternative choice being made by the consumer.

As discussed earlier, the research places considerable emphasis on a deductive approach and the use of quantitative data in pursuance of the same. The model, which leads to the hypotheses development, reflects this. The investigated constructs are illustrated in Figure 23.

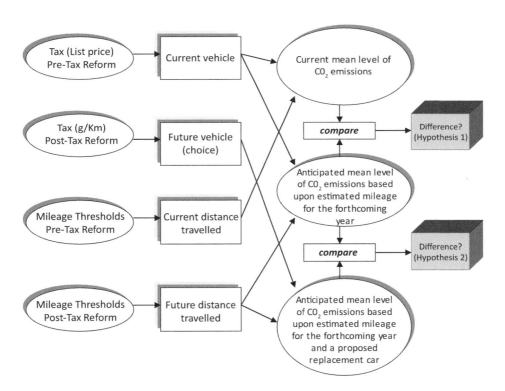

Figure 23   Proposed research model

PROBLEM DEFINITION AND HYPOTHESES DEVELOPMENT

The study examines whether company car drivers are price sensitive to environmental taxation in so far as they are able or prepared to moderate the distance travelled by car and their choice of car to reduce their taxation burden. It also examines whether the reductions of CO_2 emissions were of a sufficient order of magnitude to conclude that the revised taxation regime could have an influence on the behaviour of this group of motorists and lower their levels of CO_2 emissions from cars.

This research uses empirical data to determine levels of CO_2 emissions pre- and post-taxation reform. This data is utilised to test two hypotheses. The outcome reveals whether the revised company car taxation regime could have an influence on the levels of CO_2 production because of firstly, business mileage travelled by individuals being reduced and secondly, as a consequence of the company car chosen producing less CO_2 g/km.

In addition, the use of the empirical data and descriptive statistics obtained from the data is used to corroborate the outcome of hypothesis testing and to draw further conclusions in general, based upon the richness of the data, as to the efficacy of the taxation reforms for environmental aims and for individuals affected.

The hypotheses have been stated in the null forms, declaring no relationship between CO_2 emission levels for pre- and post-taxation reform. In testing these hypotheses, there was the possibility that the following errors may occur: a Type 1 error, the rejection of a null hypothesis, which is true; or Type 2 error, the acceptance of a null hypothesis, which is false. Smith (2003:53) provided a legal analogy for a Type 1 and Type 2 error. 'In a legal scenario, the conviction of an innocent man would constitute a Type 1 error, while the freeing of a guilty man would provide a Type 2 error.' It is usually considered more desirable to reduce the probability of Type 1 errors, as the outcome of such errors could prove more acute or expensive.

The two hypotheses formulated arise from the single revenue-neutral taxation change introduced in the UK and are stated in the null forms, declaring no relationship between CO_2 emission levels for pre- and post-taxation reform. If either or both of these hypothesis is not supported, consideration must be given as to the explanation for this, together with findings from both data collected, which can be credibly measured, and the literature to support the

MEASURING ATTITUDES AND BEHAVIOUR AMONGST COMPANY CAR DRIVERS

study. Should the outcome prove inconclusive, or where inconsistencies in the outcome cannot be explained, the possibility of repeating the study with a larger sample size exists.

Sub-problem 1 and Hypothesis 1

The revised system of company car taxation introduced in 2002 and outlined in Chapter 1 no longer takes into account business mileage in the determination of tax charge. This removed the incentive for drivers of company cars to maximise business mileage beyond certain thresholds (2,500 miles and 18,000 miles) to minimise their individual tax burden.

Does such a change to the taxation system reduce the overall distance travelled by company car drivers, resulting in a reduction in CO_2 compared to the CO_2 emission levels under the previous system of taxation? (As a consequence of this tax reform are company car drivers now able to or prepared to moderate the distance travelled by car?)

> H_o: *There is no significant difference between the current mean level of CO_2 emission and anticipated mean CO_2 emission, based upon estimated mileage for the forthcoming year.*

Sub-problem 2 and Hypothesis 2

The revised system of company car taxation introduced in 2002 and outlined in Chapter 1 now incorporates progressive scale charges by taking into account the level of CO_2 emission produced by the car together with a proportion of the manufacturers' list price (subject to £80,000 maximum) when the car is new. This is used to determine the Benefit in Kind (BIK) for the individual tax payer.

Does such a change to the taxation system prompt company car drivers to choose lower-emission cars, where a choice is permissible, resulting in a reduction in CO_2 compared to the CO_2 emission levels under the previous system of taxation? (As a consequence of this tax reform are company car drivers now able to or prepared to choose lower-emission cars?)

> H_o: *There is no significant difference between the anticipated mean level of CO_2 emission and anticipated mean CO_2 emission, based upon a proposed replacement company car.*

Research Methodology

Remenyi et al. (1998), in describing research methodology, gave emphasis to the mechanistic structure within which research can take place. Leady (1989) emphasised the operational aspect of the framework, within which the research is conducted. Galliers (1992) provided a taxonomy of methods or approaches, which are not mutually exclusive, for undertaking research as follows:

- action research;

- case studies;

- enthnographic;

- field experiments;

- focus groups;

- forecasting;

- futures research;

- game or role playing;

- in-depth surveys;

- laboratory experiments;

- large-scale surveys;

- participant-observer;

- scenario discussions; and

- simulation.

Smith (2003:54) categorised research methods into five categories:

1.   model building involving scientific reasoning;

2.   historical research using archival data and/or secondary sources;

3.   case studies requiring considerable exploration in the field;

4.   surveys, involving large-scale sampling; and

5.   experiments either in the field or laboratory type conditions.

The methodology itself is significant in achieving the research aim, but Quinn (1998) advocated caution in allowing the methodology to dominate the research.

For the purpose of this research, it was considered appropriate to adopt an empirical methodology based upon a survey to confirm theoretical conjecture concerning the environment and price sensitivity to tax reforms (elasticity of demand). The choice of methodology arises primarily from the focus of the book and the research question in particular, which is based upon company car drivers stated intentions and the need to measure and quantify CO_2 emissions pre- and post-UK company car taxation reform. This quantified CO_2 emission data was used to test the hypothesis objectively and reliably. An empirical methodology would also permit some quantification of possible overall CO_2 emission reductions for the sample, which may be extrapolated for the population as a whole, to draw further conclusions relating to total CO_2 emissions.

The research approach offers the opportunity for two distinct categories of research to be pursued; each offers acceptable methods to add to the body of knowledge.

Empiricism, which according to Remenyi et al. (1998) began with the work of Locke (1690), observes matters via passive observation or through experiment. Such observations are collected and assembled into evidence in order that conclusions can be drawn which are claimed to add to the body of existing knowledge.

A logical positivist or quantitative paradigm 'implies that the researcher is working with observable social reality' (Remenyi et al. 1998:32). This allows for an objective analysis and interpretation of matters based upon quantifiable observations that facilitate statistical analysis. Such research relies on a scientific approach with a demonstrable robust method, clearly defined criteria, known procedures and reliable statistical results that can be interpreted. The difficulties in pursuing empirical investigation should not be underestimated. Remenyi et al. (1998) discussed the difficulties in obtaining credible evidence which can be used for this purpose.

In contrast, the phenomenological, or non-positivist is considered as a research theorist who studies the matter without any direct involvement with the subject, nor the collection of evidence. Instead, reliance would be placed upon the work of others to contemplate a new or revised theory. In this way it may also be claimed that the researcher has contributed to the body of knowledge. Cohen & Manion (1987) asserted that phenomenology is a theoretical assertion that promotes the study of direct experience taken at face value; and that behaviour is not determined by reality in an objective or physical sense, but rather by phenomena of experience.

Such qualitative research has become a more accepted research paradigm for social science research in the area of business and management (Rosenthal & Rosnow 1991) possibly because of its ability to cope with both complex matters (Wheatley 1992) and unique occurrence of events (Saunders et al. 2003).

There appears to be little congruence between these apparently conflicting approaches to research. The former appears to be placing emphasis on evidence, the latter more reliant on theory. The relationship between the two may appear to be irreconcilable, which may present some difficulty for researchers looking to credibly advance the body of knowledge. Remenyi et al. (1998) noted that 'there are always theoretical assumptions associated with the collection of evidence and there is always evidence that underpins theory ... [however] ... empirical research is the dominant paradigm in business and management research' (Remenyi et al. 1998:32).

Research approach intends to contribute relevance to research by utilising an intentionally premeditated development of conditions for the collection of data and subsequent analysis of the same in a manner that permits this with minimum procedure (Selltiz et al. 1981).

It is recognised that appropriate design of any research approach is paramount in order to usefully contribute to the body of existing knowledge (Remenyi et al. 1998).

In developing the research approach to be adopted, consideration has been given to earlier studies carried out with a similar theoretical underpinning to this study. Such studies relied upon empirical testing via simulation and were carried out in a largely structured environment.

The data-gathering arrangements for this study facilitated the gathering of evidence, which is consistent with the objectives of the research study and provided an opportunity for the establishment of causality (that is, beyond description) to offer an explanation of the underlying causes for what is observed. The evidence obtained was also capable of being generalised to similar circumstances (Bennett 1986).

The environment for this study was highly structured and appeared capable of empirical testing. This, together with an obligation to demonstrate rigour in the scientific enquiry undertaken and a further proviso for the generalisability of the findings, to address the title of this book and moreover, the research question articulated, requires multiple observations to be credible, suggesting it was appropriate to pursue a quantitative approach. It is acknowledged that empirical testing of theoretical models requires robustness of quantitative and statistical methods (Smith 2003).

An issue arising from the decision to study a revenue-neutral tax reform, which is allied to research approach, is whether to undertake a longitudinal study, which would require a period of time sufficiently long enough for the taxation changes to be implemented and observed, or alternatively a cross-sectional research study, requiring an examination of the matter at the time of the research study. Given that the taxation reform had been introduced with little prior anticipation, together with the requirement to obtain quantitative data from a survey instrument for this single reform only, a cross-sectional study was undertaken.

In this way, subsequent tax changes and counteracting effects of regulations (Burke 1997) that may confuse the conclusions would not affect the study. As a consequence, the research concentrates on how matters are decided at the time of the research study (Remenyi et al. 1998).

Surveys provide an opportunity to conveniently obtain large quantities of data (Oppenheim 1966) for cross-sectional research. However, survey methods have been criticised primarily because of their lack of ability to allocate subjects randomly to actions and also an inability to discount rival hypotheses (Smith 2003). Brownell (1995) suggested that studies involving surveys could be designed to minimise validity concerns and proposed the use of good theoretical underpinning in the construction of relationships.

Jung (1995) raised an important objection to the use of averaging possibly arising from the use of questionnaires and suggested that averages are far too non-specific to illustrate the possible subjective variety of an individual. Marsh (1989) also questioned the validity of aggregate simple averages arising from a series of differing points of view.

Notwithstanding these remarks, mail survey and face-to-face interview remain the most popular survey methods for accounting research (Smith 2003), although Young (1996) pointed to a decline in the popularity of mail surveys. Remenyi et al. (1998) confirm that questionnaires are commonly used in business and management research.

A survey approach was preferred for this study in order to access a sufficiently large number of respondents without incurring undue cost, which could be analysed quantitatively, but also offer some qualitative evidence to support the findings of the research.

The theory underpinning this research is capable of empirical testing and there exists a generalisable public opinion that may be tested via questions (Remenyi et al. 1998). For the purpose of this research, the use of a survey fulfils Popper's (1959) defining attributes of scientific theory in terms of:

- hypothesis formulation and quantitative and statistical testing of the same;

- attempts at falsifying the theory, through the two hypothesis formulated stated in the null forms, declaring no relationship between CO_2 emission levels for pre- and post- taxation reform; and

- conclusions drawn will result in false propositions being left behind.

Survey Instrument

The survey instrument is designed to fulfil the requirements of this research in the following ways:

Firstly, to provide descriptive statistics to confirm the validity of the responses elsewhere in the questionnaire, to provide summarised statistical data for use with the data referred to later in this chapter and to provide additional evidence to support the outcome of the hypothesis tests carried out and assist in drawing conclusions for the study.

Secondly, to obtain data on current mileage and intended future mileage, current make, model and engine cubic capacity of car, intended choice of future make, model and engine cubic capacity of car. This data provided the basis for calculation of CO_2 emission data and was used in determining quantitative CO_2 emission data for current mean level of CO_2 emission, anticipated mean CO_2 emission, based upon estimated mileage for the forthcoming year and anticipated mean CO_2 emission, based upon estimated mileage for the forthcoming year and a proposed replacement company car.

This repeated measures design was used to test the two hypotheses developed by examining the differences between the variables to determine whether they are statistically different, rather than the difference occurring purely by chance.

Thirdly, to provide a basis for discussion of the richness of the data obtained. This is particularly pertinent when drawing conclusions as to the efficacy of the taxation reform and provided an opportunity to link the research data to the findings of the hypothesis tests and also back to the earlier literature.

The survey instrument was used to obtain from company car drivers specific information as to their choice of next company car, post-tax reform, to provide quantitative data. This data was analysed using quantitative methods to establish whether lower CO_2 emission cars would be chosen and whether overall distance travelled by company car drivers would also reduce, resulting in a reduction in CO_2 compared to the CO_2 emission levels under the previous system of taxation. The philosophy underpinning the use of a questionnaire as a survey instrument is that there must exist a generalisable opinion from the sample, representative of the population as a whole, that may be examined and tested via the use of predetermined questions. In the case of this research, the survey instrument must also be capable of providing the source for quantitative data on CO_2 emission levels in order that the hypotheses established earlier could be tested.

Denscombe (1998) suggested that questionnaires can yield greatest benefit when:

- used with large numbers of respondents geographically dispersed;

- the responses are brief, uncomplicated and uncontroversial;

- the social climate permits honest answers;

- there is a requirement for uniformity in response to standard questions;

- time permits lead-time for piloting, production and response time delays;

- resources are sufficient to cover dissemination costs; and

- respondents are able to understand the questions.

Questionnaires as a research tool or as part of a procedure are embedded in commitments to particular visions of the world (Hughes 1997). Such an approach must be employed within assumptions about the nature of society, the respondents and the relationship between the two. It is acknowledged that questionnaires provide some limitations in terms of the data that respondents would be willing to provide (Selltiz et al. 1981). In addition, questionnaires do not provide the researcher with the opportunity to investigate issues in great depth and there is unlikely to be an opportunity to supplement questions, given the responses received. These limitations may be minimised with well-formulated questions which are relatively narrow in scope (Smith 2003).

The survey instrument developed addresses a number of fundamental design and planning matters at the outset.

Type of survey to be carried out: A mail survey was decided upon on, primarily on the basis of cost. A survey approach was preferred for this study in order to access a sufficiently large number of respondents without incurring undue cost. The results of the survey could be analysed quantitatively, but also offer some qualitative evidence to support the findings of the research.

Respondent population identification: The respondents targeted for the survey were company car drivers who were affected by the change in taxation and may have been able to mitigate the effect of their individual tax burden by exercising some choice in the selection of their next company car.

Responses required: Respondents were required to provide specific details of their existing company vehicle, the approximate number of miles driven for the current (2001) year, the anticipated annual mileage for the forthcoming year (2002) and the preferred company car, where a choice exists, when the current vehicle was due for replacement.

From this information CO_2 emission data may be determined and used to statistically test the hypotheses established earlier. Questions were included to validate the responses to the specific details mentioned above. Respondents were also asked to provide brief details on individual attitudes to environmental taxation. Finally, respondents were asked to rank features of company cars in order of preference in the hope that anonymised data may also be of interest to motor car manufacturers who in turn may be prepared to sponsor the research.

Response categories: The majority of questions are closed, requiring a tick box response, with the exception of factual details required concerning make, model and cubic capacity of engine (to determine g/km emissions) and mileage details (actual and estimated).

Sequencing of questions: Questions were sequenced in an order which could provide some insight into the taxation change for the reader and to guide respondents through the survey. Questions at the beginning of the survey were shorter and possibly easier to respond to, with questions requiring more thought in the middle of the survey. Finally, questions relating to personal details were positioned towards the end of the survey allowing the early part of the survey to focus on the research matter (Bryman 2001).

Layout of the survey instrument: The questionnaire was five pages in length with a separate colour sheet at the start and end of the questionnaire to explain the purpose of the survey instrument and to obtain personal data should the respondents wish to disclose this. The survey was designed to be completed in less than 20 minutes (Smith 2003).

Sample selection and size: Determination of the appropriate sample size is complex. The following matters were taken into account:

- type of sample;

- variability in the population;

- time;

- costs;

- accuracy of estimates; and

- confidence in making generalisations to the population

(Remenyi et al. 1998).

For the purpose of this study, a probability sample was required for the positivist research in order that statistical techniques may be applied to the sample. In probability sampling each individual has a known, but not necessarily equal likelihood of selection (Remenyi et al. 1998). In selecting a sample, it was paramount that, if the findings are to be considered credible, the sample avoided bias and remained representative of the population as a whole.

Smith (2003) noted that random selection of samples is usually deemed preferable, however this may not yield a sample that is either representative or of use in so far as a random sample may not provide any representatives for a group within the population as a whole. To overcome this situation, systematic sampling (selecting every nth item from a sampling frame) or directed sampling (obtaining items from specified groups) may be considered, but caution must be exercised not to infringe the assumptions of statistical techniques (Smith 2003) and invalidate the experiment as a consequence.

Information on company car drivers is held by the Inland Revenue, obtained via P11D returns made for company directors and employees. Regrettably, the Inland Revenue were unable to release such personal information, for confidentiality and data protection reasons. This was problematic when attempting to determine the size of the total population. Accordingly, scientific means of sample selection may be inappropriate. Remenyi et al. (1998) suggested that sample sizes in practice may not be exactly adhered to. On occasion the chosen sample sizes are to fit with company policy or are chosen because they would be deemed as credible. Lehmann (1989) concurred that such an approach to sampling is permissible.

The sampling frame for this study has been based upon the premise that company cars are provided by companies and as a consequence a sampling frame may be drawn from an appropriate register or year book for companies (Smith 2003). Sample selection was made on this basis by means of systematic sampling of companies to participate in the survey, by disseminating copies of the questionnaire to employees with company cars.

Pilot Testing: The survey instrument was pre-tested using a sample of 30 company car drivers, as discussed earlier, selected as likely to be representative of the population as a whole on dimensions of age, sex and seniority of position. Following the pilot test, revisions were made to the questionnaire to include an explanation of the taxation change and to lengthen the explanation associated with some tick box answers, in order that the choice between alternatives was more obvious to the reader. Questions relating to income were also removed as the pilot study revealed some difficulty in obtaining accurate and reliable answers.

Survey Questions

A discussion of the questions used in the survey instrument, together with a rationale for the inclusion of the same is presented in this chapter, with an analysis of the data from the survey in the following chapter. Each question is reproduced from the questionnaire for ease of reference.

Question 1: Do you currently drive a company car?

Do you currently drive a company car?

☐ Yes.

☐ No (Please go to question 15).

A prerequisite to participation in the survey was to be a company car driver.

The respondents targeted for the survey should all be company car drivers who were affected by the change in taxation. Question 1 was included to confirm that all respondents were company car drivers. Questionnaires where the respondents answered no to this question were discarded and not included in the subsequent analysis.

Question 2: Current car make, model and engine cc?

Please state:

Car Make: _____ Model: _____ Engine cc: _____

The responses for this question was firstly used to confirm the validity of the response provided, by comparing the data provided by respondents with manufacturers published data for UK and European sourced vehicles. This served to confirm that the make and model variant with a particular size engine was a valid combination. Vehicles that were not produced in the UK or mainland Europe may on occasion still be sourced from Europe as a consequence of, in some cases, considerable differences in the new car price. This may result in some variation between UK and mainland European model specification that could impact on the size of the engine and CO_2 emission data. After considering this possibility, if such a combination remained invalid, the response was discarded.

The make and model variant with a particular size engine was used to obtain manufacturer's CO_2 emission data (g/km) in each case for use with question 3 for the hypothesis testing discussed later in this chapter.

Question 3: Current annual mileage?

Approximately, how many miles do you currently drive on company business?

_____ miles per annum.

The responses to this question were used in conjunction with the response from question 2 to determine the total CO_2 emission from the respondents' company car for the current year. This data is used later in Chapter 4 for the hypothesis testing of Hypothesis 1.

Question 4: Are you aware of the changes to company car taxation affecting individuals that will be implemented in April 2002?

Are you aware of the changes to company car taxation affecting individuals that will be implemented in April 2002?

☐ Yes.

☐ No (Please go to question 6).

The responses for this question were firstly used to determine whether the respondent was aware of the changes to company car taxation and to direct respondents to a text paragraph to explain the changes concerning CO_2 emissions and business mileage. Respondents were in a position to reply to the remaining questions with similar knowledge of the changes. Despite a paragraph of text being included in the questionnaire summarising the changes, it was considered that the intention of this paragraph was to add context to the questionnaire by reiterating the major parts of the changes rather than to provide sufficient detail for an individual, who had no prior knowledge of the changes to make an informed response to the survey. As a consequence, responses from such individuals were deleted from the sample as they may have been misleading and could have subsequently altered when the detail of the changes to company car taxation was more fully understood.

Question 5: How did you find out about the changes to company car taxation affecting individuals?

How did you find out about the changes to company car taxation affecting individuals?

☐ Employer.

☐ Media.

☐ Motor car manufacturer.

☐ Other.

It is recognised that carbon taxes 'imposed gradually and with long term prior anticipation' (Ekins 1994:577) are likely to be implemented more successfully. Data was gathered on the contribution that the employer, media, motorcar manufacturer and others made in informing individuals of the taxation changes in order to identify the most valuable sources for communicating information to company car drivers.

Question 6: Estimated annual mileage for the following year (after reiteration that 'company car taxation will no longer take into account the number of business miles driven').

From April 2002, company car taxation for individuals will no longer be based solely upon the list price of the car. Instead it will be based upon the percentage of a car's list price graduated according to its CO_2 emissions. Therefore drivers of cars that produce more grammes of CO_2 per km will pay more company car taxation. Company car taxation will no longer take into account the number of business miles driven.

From April 2002, company car taxation will no longer take into account the number of business miles driven. With this knowledge, please estimate your annual business mileage for next year: _____ miles per annum.

The responses to this question were used in conjunction with the response from question 2 and question 12 to determine the total CO_2 emission for the respondent's company car for the current year and the forthcoming year. A mean and standard deviation was obtained from this data for the statistical hypothesis (significance) testing Hypothesis 1.

Question 7: Comparison of business mileage for the next year (question 6) with the estimate of current business mileage (question 3).

Comparing your estimate of business mileage for next year (question 6) with your estimate of current business mileage (question 3).

☐ My annual business mileage will reduce because there is no longer a tax incentive in driving more miles than necessary.

☐ My annual business mileage will reduce because of other factors affecting my job.

☐ My annual business mileage will increase because of other factors affecting my job.

☐ My annual business mileage will remain approximately the same.

The responses to this question were used to confirm the appropriateness of answers from question 3 and question 6 and to obtain data on the reasons why an individual's business mileage may vary (including taxation change).

Question 8: Extent of choice of vehicle, when the company car is due for replacement?

To what extent do you have a choice of vehicle, when your current car is due for replacement?

☐ Extensive choice (wide variety of makes/models and engine sizes to choose).

☐ Good choice (variety of make/models, but engine size choice limited).

☐ Some choice (choice of up to 3 make/models, engine size choice limited).

☐ No choice (make and model specified by employer – go to question 12).

The responses to this question provided data on whether respondents were able to moderate CO_2 emissions as a consequence of vehicle choice, by obtaining information on the extent of choice available to individuals. The responses provided to this question were also used to validate the responses provided to question 2 on current make, model and engine cc, and question 12 on proposed make, model and engine cc, in so far as if a respondent indicates little or no choice is available when the current car is due for replacement, the response to question 12 should not be dissimilar to question 2.

Question 9: Will the taxation change have an influence on your choice of next company car? (3 categories.)

> From April 2002, company car taxation will take into account the amounts of grammes of CO_2 emitted per km. Will this taxation change have an influence on your choice of your next company car?
>
> ☐ Yes – I will try to choose a car with a low g/km of CO_2 emission, to reduce my tax burden.
>
> ☐ No – I will choose a car based upon other features.
>
> ☐ Don't know – I do not fully understand how this change is likely to affect me personally.

Responses to this question provided data on the reasons behind an expressed preference for the selection of next company car and whether such a preference was on the basis of taxation arrangements or features of the vehicle. The responses to this question also provided an opportunity to validate the response to question 12, concerning the preference for the respondents' next company car make, model and engine cc.

Question 10: If the amount of company car taxation were doubled, would such a taxation increase have an influence on your choice of your next company car? (3 categories.)

> If the amount of company car taxation were doubled, would such a taxation increase have an influence on your choice of your next company car?
>
> ☐ Yes – I will try to choose a car with a low g/km of CO_2 emission.
>
> ☐ No – I will choose a car based upon other features.
>
> ☐ Don't know – I do not fully understand how this change is likely to affect me personally.

Responses to this question provided data on the influence of 'punitive' (doubled rate) taxation on individuals' expressed preference of the intended selection of next company car. This was in an attempt to firstly confirm price elasticity concerning this ecological tax reform and to observe the significance of elasticity by considering such a hypothetical change to the amount of taxation.

Question 11: If the amount of company car taxation were halved, would such a taxation decrease have an influence on your choice of your next company car? (4 categories.)

If the amount of company car taxation were halved, would such a taxation decrease have an influence on your choice of your next company car?

☐ Yes – I would consider a car with a higher g/km of CO_2 emission.

☐ Yes – I will try to choose a car with a low g/km of CO_2 emission.

☐ No – I will choose a car based upon other features.

☐ Don't know – I do not fully understand how this change is likely to affect me personally.

In a similar manner to question 10, this question again attempted to provide additional evidence of price elasticity concerning this ecological tax reform and to observe the significance of elasticity by considering such a hypothetical change to the amount of taxation.

Question 12: Next Car Make Model and Engine cc.

If you already have a vehicle in mind for your next company car, please give details (or if you have no choice, give details of the car specified by your employer):

Car Make: _____ Model: _____ Engine cc: _____

Similar to question 3 earlier, the responses for this question were firstly used to confirm the validity of the response provided, by comparing the data provided by respondents with manufacturers published data for UK and European sourced vehicles. This served to confirm that the make and model variant with a particular size engine was a valid combination.

The make and model variant with a particular size engine was used to obtain manufacturers CO_2 emission data (g/km) in each case. This data is used later in this chapter for the quantitative hypothesis testing for Hypothesis 2.

Question 13: Do you think the change in company car taxation is a good idea? (4 categories.)

Do you think the forthcoming change in company car taxation is a good idea, as it may reduce CO_2 emissions, which contribute to global warming?

☐ Yes.

☐ Yes – Provided that low-emission vehicles are available for me to choose, in order that I may pay less company car taxation.

☐ No.

☐ Don't know.

The responses to this question provided information on whether respondents were sympathetic or at least unopposed to environmental taxation, when directly affected by the change, in the form of the reforms to company car taxation.

Question 14: Consideration of hybrid/electric car with very low/zero emissions.

Would you consider a hybrid/electric car with very low/zero CO_2 emissions if such a choice was available to you and the amount of company car taxation payable were lower than you are anticipating paying for the next year: (tick more than one box if appropriate)

☐ Yes – If the taxation burden was lower by 25%.

☐ Yes – If the taxation burden was lower by 50%.

☐ Yes – If the taxation burden was lower by 75%.

☐ No – I would not consider such a car, because the range (distance travelled before recharging/refuelling) of the car is poor compared to conventional vehicles.

☐ No – I would not consider such a car, because the performance of the car is poor compared to conventional vehicles.

☐ No – I would not consider such a car, because (please state) _____.

This question was included to gather some information on respondents' attitudes to alternative powered cars as an incentive for motor manufacturers to consider sponsoring this research.

The responses to this question also provided information on whether respondents were prepared to consider alternative forms of very low-emission company cars and if so whether a reduction in the taxation burden would influence or act as an incentive to switch.

Question 15: Measures to reduce the number of miles driven per annum.

Which of the following measures are likely to reduce the number of miles driven by you per annum? (Tick more than one box if appropriate.)

	Business Mileage	**Private Mileage**
Increase in company car taxation relating to the number of business miles travelled.	☐	☐
Increase in the cost of car fuel.	☐	☐

Introduction of congestion charging in cities for peak traffic times.	☐	☐
Introduction of road pricing, where a charge is made for the number of miles travelled.	☐	☐

The responses to this question provided information on the view of respondents as to other measures that were likely to mitigate the distance travelled by the company car driver. In this case respondents were able to tick more than one box if appropriate.

Question 16: Ranking of features in choosing a car.

Please rank the following features that may be important to you in choosing your next company car. (1= most important, 9 = least important)

☐ Performance.

☐ Image.

☐ Brand (make/model).

☐ Safety.

☐ CO_2 emission.

☐ Accessories.

☐ Colour.

☐ Reliability.

☐ Dealer support.

The responses for this question were used to gauge the perceived importance of CO_2 emission given the changes in company car taxation and also to determine whether the ranking of CO_2 emission as an important feature was consistent with the response to question 9, where respondents were asked to state whether they would try to choose a car with a low level of CO_2 emission.

Question 16 was also included to obtain information on a company car driver's preferences for certain features, in an attempt to provide additional information to car manufacturers to obtain financial assistance to carry out this research.

Question 17: Questions about the respondent.

Respondents provided personal contact details to enter a prize draw as an incentive to respond, together with details on age and gender. Anonymity of responses was assured to encourage participation. This final question was confined to a separate sheet of paper and was separated from the other response data upon receipt.

Questions about you.

Please provide the following information. This will only be used to enter you into the prize draw, send you a summary of the survey responses if requested, or to contact you in the event of a query about your responses and will not be revealed to any third parties.

Name: _____

Address: _____

Tel: _____

Email: _____

Male/Female:

☐ Male

☐ Female

Age group

☐ 25 or under

☐ 26–35

☐ 36–45

☐ 46–55

☐ 56 +

It is hoped to conduct some follow-up interviews. If you would be willing to participate please tick the box. ☐

Thank you for taking the time to complete this survey. Please return it in the pre-paid envelope provided or via email to: companycarsurvey@fccafcma.freeserve.co.uk

The Survey

The primary source of data for this research was obtained from individuals completing and returning identical questionnaires used as the survey instrument to provide a generalisable opinion from the sample. The secondary sources for evidence for the research study was obtained from the literature, professional and industry bodies and government departments, providing an opportunity not only to develop the theoretical underpinning for this study, but also to determine whether the findings of this study concur with other credible reliable and notable studies.

Respondents (company car drivers) provided details of whether they were aware of the changes affecting company car drivers, how they found out about the changes, whether individuals have a choice of car, together with their existing company vehicle, the approximate number of miles driven for the current year and the preferred company car, when the current vehicle was due for replacement. From this information, quantitative data for an individual motor vehicle (based upon make and model) CO_2 emission levels measured in g/km was obtained from motor vehicle manufacturers. This together with information provided by respondents on distance travelled was used to determine the total CO_2 emission levels for the following:

- current total emissions based upon existing vehicle g/km and current mileage (Hypotheses 1 & 2);

- future total emissions based upon existing vehicle g/km and anticipated mileage for the forthcoming year (Hypothesis 1); and

- future total emissions (new) based upon next vehicle choice g/km and anticipated mileage for the forthcoming year (Hypothesis 2).

A problem with survey responses is whether the respondents are representative of the population as a whole, that is, whether respondents and non-respondents differ significantly. Non-response can prove problematic if systematic differences between respondents and non-respondents can be demonstrated and that such differences will have an impact on the outcome.

With this in mind, emphasis was given to Dillman's (1978) Total Design Method (TDM) in an attempt to encourage a response. In particular consideration was given to:

- careful screening of titles and addresses;

- the presentation of the survey to prevent the appearance of spam/ junk mail;

- providing an incentive for completion;

- clear and unambiguous instructions; and

- return address details and envelopes.

A covering letter informed the participants that the research was being conducted to ascertain the views and attitudes of company car drivers to the new tax regime to determine whether these new tax arrangements would have any impact on the levels of CO_2 emissions from company cars. The letter asked respondents to return the questionnaire directly to the author, using an attached reply paid envelope or to a reply email address. The letter provided assurances that individual responses would remain confidential and that only anonymised and aggregated data would be published.

Two follow-up reminders were sent in an attempt to obtain further responses. The first follow-up reminder proved to be considerably more successful than the second. The timing of the survey (November) was designed not to coincide with year-end for most organisations (Smith 2003) and took into account an average lead time associated with the acquisition of a new company car, such that respondents should have received the questionnaire at or around the time that they may be considering procurement. It was hoped that this consideration of timing would encourage responses, but also make it easier for fleet managers to disseminate the survey at a time when other material concerning the acquisition of replacement cars would be sent to individual company car drivers.

Screening of Results

All responses received were given a unique identifier. The responses were initially scrutinised to identify spoilt questionnaires which were discarded, leaving the balance as useable for the subsequent data analysis. The response data referred to in data sources earlier was transferred into an MS-Excel™ spreadsheet for analysis. Partially completed and spoilt questionnaires were discarded.

Given the possibility of risk of errors from the manual data capture process and the importance of the accuracy of g/km CO_2 emissions data for the subsequent hypothesis testing, an attempt has been made to highlight and correct missing data and data irregularities within the spreadsheet dataset with respect to g/km CO_2 emissions. An approach suggested by Smith (2003) of an application of simple descriptive statistics in the form of a calculated mean and standard deviation for each column containing CO_2 emission data was adopted. Monitoring these columns will then establish which data items lay outside a predetermined range. Smith (2003) suggested three standard deviations around the mean value with warning limits at the 95% confidence limit (1.96 standard errors) and action limits at the 99% level (2.58 standard errors).

If the sample mean fell outside the limits for the latter, which could only occur by chance in 1% of the cases, this could indicate a problem with the data

(Lucey 2002). In such circumstances the data should be further scrutinised to establish whether such items are data errors or outliers.

The data set contained no missing values after the removal of the spoilt responses and sufficient data existed for the data analysis.

A test for normality of the data was evaluated through the construction and inspection of a normal distribution curve for the CO_2 emission data for 'Current Total Emission', 'Future Total Emission' and 'Future Total Emission (new)'.

Non-response bias was investigated using a two sample t-test of the difference between means. Early responses (the first 15 from the sample) were compared to the late responses (the last 15 from the sample) for the following nominal variables:

- current mileage;

- current total emission;

- future mileage;

- future total emission; and

- future total emission (new).

A statistically significant difference between the early responses and late responses could indicate a non-response bias.

Standard error of the difference between two means:

$$\sqrt{\frac{s_1^2}{n_1} + \frac{s_2^2}{n_2}} = s\,(\mu_1 - \mu_2)$$

Where:

S_1 = *standard deviation of sample 1, size* n_1

S_2 = *standard deviation of sample 2, size* n_2

The t score is calculated as:

$$t = \frac{\mu_1 - \mu_2}{s\,(\mu_1 - \mu_2)} \quad \text{with } n_1 + n_2 - 2 \text{ degrees of freedom.}$$

In assessing the possibility of non-response bias which could result in either an increase or decrease in the values obtained, the tests have been carried out as a two-tailed test at the 5% level of statistical significance (95% confidence limit).

The data for this analysis is reproduced in Figures 24–28 as a summary table for each of the nominal variables referred to.

Figure 24   **Summary data for t-test: early vs. late responses: current mileage data**

t-Test: Paired :	Current Mileage	
	First 15 Responses	*Last 15 Responses*
Mean	21533.33	21100.00
Variance	30123809.52	51364285.71
Observations	15.00	15.00
Pearson Correlation	0.40	
Hypothesized Mean Difference	0.00	
df	14.00	
t Stat	0.24	
P(T<=t) one-tail	0.41	
t Critical one-tail	1.76	
P(T<=t) two-tail	0.82	
t Critical two-tail	2.14	
	No significant difference	

Figure 25   Summary data for t-test: early vs. late responses: current total emission data

t-Test: Paired:	Current Total Emission	
	First 15 Responses	*Last 15 Responses*
Mean	6304598.33	6208970.10
Variance	2676366192673	6009804887043
Observations	15.00	15.00
Pearson Correlation	0.39	
Hypothesized Mean Difference	0.00	
df	14.00	
t Stat	0.16	
P(T<=t) one-tail	0.44	
t Critical one-tail	1.76	
P(T<=t) two-tail	0.88	
t Critical two-tail	2.14	
	No significant difference	

Figure 26   Summary data for t-test: early vs. late responses: future mileage data

t-Test: Paired:	Future Mileage	
	First 15 Responses	*Last 15 Responses*
Mean	21266.67	21100.00
Variance	32066666.67	51364285.71
Observations	15.00	15.00
Pearson Correlation	0.43	
Hypothesized Mean Difference	0.00	
df	14.00	
t Stat	0.09	
P(T<=t) one-tail	0.46	
t Critical one-tail	1.76	
P(T<=t) two-tail	0.93	
t Critical two-tail	2.14	
	No significant difference	

Figure 27   Summary data for t-test: early vs. late responses: future total emission data

| t-Test: Paired: | Future total emission | |
	First 15 Responses	Last 15 Responses
Mean	6225757.33	6208970.10
Variance	2832870336405	6009804887043
Observations	15.00	15.00
Pearson Correlation	0.42	
Hypothesized Mean Difference	0.00	
df	14.00	
t Stat	0.03	
P(T<=t) one-tail	0.49	
t Critical one-tail	1.76	
P(T<=t) two-tail	0.98	
t Critical two-tail	2.14	
	No significant difference	

Figure 28   Summary data for t-test: early vs. late responses: future total emission (new) data

| t-Test: Paired: | Future total emission (new) | |
	First 15 Responses	Last 15 Responses
Mean	5543112.27	5599534.53
Variance	1909185259648	330013384366
Observations	15.00	15.00
Pearson Correlation	0.45	
Hypothesized Mean Difference	0.00	
df	14.00	
t Stat	-0.13	
P(T<=t) one-tail	0.45	
t Critical one-tail	1.76	
P(T<=t) two-tail	0.90	
t Critical two-tail	2.14	
	No significant difference	

At the 5% level of significance for (15-1) 14 df the value for the t distribution = 2.14.

The calculated t scores were lower than + or -2.14 (5% significance level 14df) for each of the nominal variables. As a consequence there is nothing to suggest evidence of non-response bias. Any variation between the two means under consideration could have occurred purely by chance.

Data Analysis

The response data is analysed in Chapter 4 and further discussed in Chapter 5. The analysis utilised descriptive statistics and statistical tests, the latter specifically to determine whether the difference between an observed and expected value for CO_2 emission is statistically significant so that it may not be attributed to chance. The former to offer a degree of corroboration and assurance for, firstly, the responses obtained, secondly, the statistical tests carried out and, thirdly, to provide a basis for discussion of the richness of the data obtained. This is particularly pertinent when drawing conclusions as to the efficacy of the taxation reform and provided an opportunity to link the research findings back to the literature. The research results presented were obtained from data capture via a flat file Symantec™ database. Quantitative analysis was carried out using Microsoft Excel™ software.

The survey instrument provided information from company car drivers as to their existing company car, choice of next company car post-tax reform together with the number of business miles travelled pre-taxation reform and the anticipated number of business miles travelled post-taxation reform to determine quantitative data for CO_2 emission levels (pre- and post-taxation reform). The philosophy underpinning the use of a questionnaire as a survey instrument and the subsequent data analysis carried out is that there must exist a generalisable opinion from the sample, representative of the population as a whole.

The quantitative data on CO_2 emission levels calculated from the data provided by the respondents has been used to calculate the mean pre- and post-taxation reform, taking into account mileage changes and company car changes, to determine whether there was a significant difference between the two means for the data under consideration.

For this purpose, the test of difference between means was used to test the hypotheses as follows:

$$\mathbf{H_0:} \quad \mu_1 - \mu_2 \; = \; 0$$

$$\mathbf{H_1:} \quad \mu_1 - \mu_2 \; \neq \; 0$$

From the data, the distribution of sample mean differences is normally distributed, enabling parametric tests to be applied. The sample was considered a large sample as $n > 30$. (Where $n < 30$ the t-distribution would apply). Normal area tables were used for the testing of the difference between two means.

The variables used for the standard error and z-score calculation for the difference between two means (Hypothesis 1) were as shown in Figure 29:

Figure 29   **Standard error and z-score (variables) for the difference between two means: Hypothesis 1**

Current CO$_2$ emission$_{(1)}$	Future CO$_2$ emission$_{(2)}$
n_1	n_2
μ_1	μ_2
S_1	S_2

The variables used for the standard error and z-score calculation for the difference between two means (Hypothesis 2) were as shown in Figure 30:

Figure 30   **Standard error and z-score (variables) for the difference between two means: Hypothesis 2**

Future CO$_2$ emission$_{(2)}$	Future CO$_2$ emission (new)$_{(3)}$
n_1	n_2
μ_1	μ_2
S_1	S_2

The standard error of the difference between two means is calculated as:

$$\sqrt{\frac{s_1^2}{n_1} + \frac{s_2^2}{n_2}} = s\,(\mu_1 - \mu_2)$$

Where:

S_1 = *standard deviation of sample 1, size* n_1

S_2 = *standard deviation of sample 2, size* n_2

The Z score is calculated as:

$$Z = \frac{\mu_1 - \mu_2}{s(\mu_1 - \mu_2)}$$

Hypothesis testing of sample data provides for the possibility of the stated hypothesis being rejected, or the sample being unrepresentative of the population as a whole, which applies to all samples to a greater or lesser extent. It was therefore appropriate to establish whether or not any differences identified from the sample data obtained may be attributed to purely random factors. To accommodate this, the hypothesis testing included statistical tests, which were conducted at the 5% level of significance, to conclude that there is a (statistical) 95% confidence that the difference between means was not due to factors occurring by chance.

Consistent with the stated hypothesis, the direction of variation in such tests is not a concern, so as to detect whether there was a significant variation in either direction (increase or decrease in values). The tests have been carried out as a two-tailed test at the 5% level of statistical significance (95% confidence limit). As a consequence, if the calculated Z score from the data for current CO_2 emission and future CO_2 emission means (Hypothesis 1) and current CO_2 emission and future CO_2 emission (new) means (Hypothesis 2) is lower than + or -1.96, for each of the hypothesis tested, there is nothing to suggest that there is any difference between the two means under consideration. (H_0: μ_1-μ_2 = 0). Any variation in the sample data could have occurred purely by chance.

There would be insufficient evidence to reject the null hypothesis (H_1: μ_1-$\mu_2 \neq 0$). H_0 would therefore be accepted.

In addition, in such a repeated measures situation a more robust statistical test is also available. A paired t-test facilitates the difference between each pair to be determined and to observe these differences, where they are not zero, to determine whether these differences were large enough and in the same direction, not to be attributed to chance.

By incorporating the standard deviation of the differences, the t-test controls for individual dissimilarity between subjects in the sample. The observed differences would be wholly attributable to changed conditions.

The data collected and to be analysed meets the criteria for a paired t-test in that:

- the data must be from the same sample;

- the data must be organised in pairs; and

- there is a relationship between each pair of data points.

Again, consistent with the stated hypothesis, the direction of variation is not a concern, so as to detect whether there is a significant variation in either direction (increase or decrease in mileage and CO_2 emission). The tests have been carried out as a two-tailed test at the 5% level of statistical significance (95% confidence limit).

For the sample of size, in this case of 497, if the calculated t-statistic is lower than + or -1.96, for each of the hypothesis tested, there would be nothing to suggest that there is any difference between the pairs of data under consideration, as any variation in the sample data could have occurred purely by chance. There would be insufficient evidence to reject the null hypothesis for each case. H_0 would therefore be accepted.

The Microsoft Excel™ t-Test: Paired Two Sample for Means analysis tool and formula was utilised to perform a paired two-sample student's t-test to determine whether a sample's means are distinct. The resultant data is displayed in Chapter 5.

Matters of Validity

To demonstrate causality (Mill 1874) beyond a casual association requires the experiment to hold all other variables constant (except the independent variable and dependant variable). The greater the degree of control over other variables likely to cause 'extraneous influences in experiments' (Ryan et al. 2002:122) the higher the internal validity. Where internal validity is low, for example with a biased sample, there will be difficulty in drawing valid conclusions.

In designing this research study the likelihood of drawing valid conclusions has been improved by attempts to build in controls into the research design, the application of robust quantitative techniques and the corroboration with descriptive statistics from the data collected as outlined earlier in this chapter. Finally, the consideration and corroboration of the outcomes with the literature and other notable findings from industry and professional bodies and government bodies provides further additional assurance of validity.

Positivist research may be evaluated using the criteria of reliability, objectivity and validity; the latter refers to goodness of fit linking theory and reality (Gummesson 1991). The application of statistical techniques for the difference between means and paired t-tests should lead to reliable and objective testing of the hypotheses outlined earlier in this book. The validity of the findings should provide some linkage back to the earlier theoretical discourse.

The use of a paired t-test, alongside a test of difference between means, attempts to offer some assurance of the reliability and validity of the statistical techniques used via a degree of triangulation for the research, albeit within the same paradigm. It is the expectation that if both the statistical tests applied lead to similar conclusions which may be in turn subsequently corroborated by the literature, that conclusions may be drawn from the sample data, which may be applied to the population of company car drivers as a whole.

However, it is acknowledged that returned questionnaires may have been completed incorrectly or inappropriately. The manual data entry processes was burdensome and the risk of input error existed. Validation checks were introduced to scrutinise returned questionnaires in an attempt to eliminate these sources of error in the data. Measures were taken to ensure that all relevant boxes on returned questionnaires were completed; where a choice had to be made between alternatives, only one choice was made; where ranking was used, that the specified range of values for this purpose was adhered to; and also to ensure that respondents' expressed intentions were consistent with the next vehicle choice. Verification checks were also introduced before and during data entry to minimise the risk of erroneous data and to identify and correct missing or invalid values, the latter is pertinent for incompatible combinations of make, model and engine size.

The possibility of inaccuracy exists from the application of quantitative analysis to relatively small sample sizes. The risk of inaccuracy lessens with larger sample sizes (of the type obtained for this study) together with careful selection of an appropriate sampling technique (of the type discussed earlier in this chapter) and with careful and methodical scrutiny of the data gathered.

Conclusion

The conceptual framework discussed in Chapter 1 provided the basis to explore the connection between the externalities arising from carbon emissions and use of taxation or other fiscal instruments to mitigate the latter taking into account elasticity consumer reaction and behaviour. The proposition of the relationship being that the use of taxation can reduce emissions and pollution. The methodology outlined in this chapter describes an orderly and systematic approach adopted in the collection and screening of data and the application of statistical techniques for the purpose of testing the hypotheses derived in order that conclusions may be drawn from the study.

The following chapter presents the analysis of the data collected and endeavours to interpret the same using descriptive statistics and the quantitative techniques outlined earlier in this chapter.

4

Assessing the Potential Effectiveness of Ecological Taxation

In this chapter we will deal with the analysis of data and findings of the study, in terms of descriptive statistics for survey responses and the use of quantitative data, for the purpose of testing the hypotheses presented in Chapter 1 and discussed in Chapter 3. Further details of the application of the methodology, including detailed consideration of non-response bias, confirmation of normality assumptions, the tests applied to the data and whether the sample data obtained was representative of the population as a whole, are also included in this chapter.

Background

Of the 566 responses received to the questionnaire, 69 responses were deemed spoilt/unusable and were removed leaving 497 as useable. Sufficient data had been captured for data analysis. A summary of the responses, respondents' age profiles and gender are shown in Figures 31, 32 and 33 respectively.

Returned Responses	Spoilt / Unusable Responses	Usable Responses
566	69	497

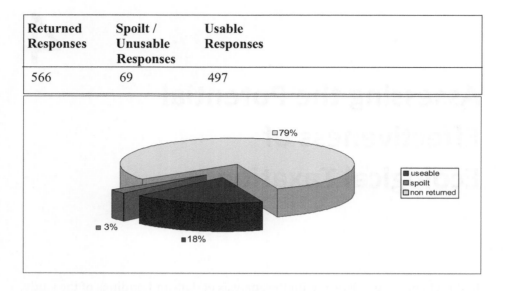

Figure 31   Summary of responses

INFORMATION ON RESPONDENTS

Figure 32   Analysis of respondents' age profiles

Age (years):	<=25	26–35	36–45	46–55	56+
n:	19	194	193	68	23
Percentage:	3.82%	39.03%	38.83%	13.68%	4.63%

Gender

As discussed in Chapter 3, non-response bias was investigated using a two-sample t-test of the difference between means. Early response data for nominal variables for current mileage, current total emission, future mileage, future total emission, future total emission (new) (the first 15 from the sample) were compared to the same nominal variable late response data (the last 15 from the sample).

Statistical difference between the early responses and late responses were not significant and served to confirm that non-response to the survey was not as a consequence of any particular bias and that the responses received were

Sex:	Male	Female
n:	371	126
Percentage:	74.65%	25.35%
n: 497		

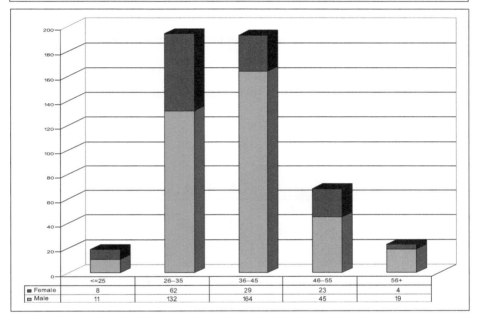

	<=25	26–35	36–45	46–55	56+
Female	8	62	29	23	4
Male	11	132	164	45	19

Figure 33   Analysis of respondents' age and gender profiles

a valid reflection of the views of the population. A summary table for this was included in Chapter 3.

Normality of the data used for Hypothesis 1, outlined in the previous chapter, was confirmed through the construction and inspection of a distribution histogram for the Carbon Dioxide (CO_2) emission data for 'Current Mileage' and 'Future Mileage'. Potential outliers were identified and removed at this stage. Sample sizes exceeded the minimum sample size of n>30, which is preferable for normality assumptions (Curwin & Slater 1996).

Figure 34 shows a distribution (histogram) of 'Current Mileage'.

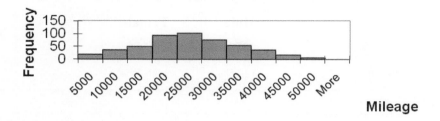

Figure 34   Distribution of respondents' 'Current Mileage'

Figure 35 shows a distribution (histogram) of 'Future Mileage'.

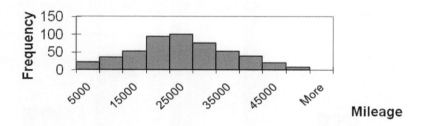

Figure 35   Distribution of respondents' 'Future Mileage'

Normality of the data used for Hypothesis test 2, outlined in the previous chapter, was also confirmed through the construction and inspection of a distribution histogram for the CO_2 emission data for 'Current CO_2 g/km' and 'Future CO_2 g/km'. Potential outliers were identified and removed at this stage. Sample sizes exceeded the minimum sample size of n>30, which is preferable for normality assumptions (Curwin & Slater 1996).

Figure 36 shows a distribution (histogram) of 'Current CO_2 g/km'.

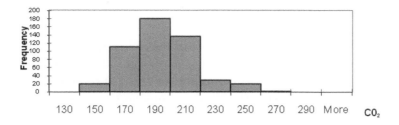

Figure 36   Distribution of respondents' 'Current CO$_2$ g/Km'

Figure 37 shows a distribution (histogram) of 'Future CO$_2$ g/km'.

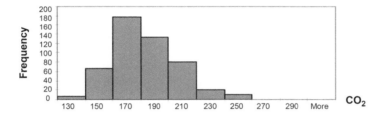

Figure 37   Distribution of respondents' 'Future CO$_2$ g/Km'

The mean CO$_2$ of 185g/km for existing company cars from the survey sample was compared with the mean g/km CO$_2$ emissions for new cars sold in the UK to the quarter ending November 2001 in an attempt to determine whether the sample data obtained and used in this analysis was representative of the population as a whole. The mean CO$_2$ of 185g/km for existing company cars from the survey sample is similar to the mean CO$_2$ of 178g/km for the population of new cars sold in the UK to November 2001 (SMMT 2005). The difference of 7g/km (less than 4%) could be explained by the sample data not including private buyers who would personally benefit from lower Vehicle Excise Duty (VED) and better fuel consumption and as a consequence may be more likely to choose lower-emission vehicles.

Responses to the Survey Questions

Of the 497 respondents who were aware of the changes, 223 respondents had found out about the changes from their employer, 109 respondents via the media, 16 respondents via a car manufacturer and 149 respondents via other sources, highlighting the significance that employers had played in bringing this matter to the attention of employees. Figure 38 shows a pie chart for responses to question 5.

Figure 38   Responses to question 5

Both the employer and the media contribution in informing employees should be recognised, in so far as if further similar taxation reforms in this area are to be introduced then reliance could be placed upon these methods of informing individuals. Given the significance of prior anticipation in successful taxation implementation and that 30% of respondents found out about the changes to company car taxation affecting individuals from other sources, it would be valuable to carry out further investigations to ascertain more information about these sources.

Responses revealed a mean engine size of 1872cc (standard deviation of 298cc) and mean CO_2 emission of 185 g/km (standard deviation of 22 g/km). The 'current' mean mileage of respondents was 23,433 miles with a standard deviation of 10,153 miles.

Initial Findings

A comparison was made of the distribution of respondents total anticipated businessmilesfortheforthcomingyear(2002/03)whichnolongertookintoaccount the number of business miles driven of 11,637,250 miles (mean 23,414 miles) with the distribution of respondents current total (2001/02) business mileage of 11,646,100 miles (mean 23,433 miles). This comparison revealed a total difference of 8,850 miles. This very small difference may suggest that CO_2 emission from the respondents' company car for the current year and the forthcoming year, based upon mileage, may not be significant.

In addition, in an attempt to corroborate these initial findings, the sample data from the 497 respondents was scrutinised to determine whether, as a consequence of the mileage thresholds of 2,500 miles and 18,000 miles being withdrawn, there would be an impact on individuals' estimated mileage levels for the forthcoming year (that is, as a result of the withdrawal of mileage thresholds referred to above, will any individuals' mileage fall below the previous threshold, where it was formerly advantageous from a personal taxation point of view to remain?)

Of the 497 respondents, nine company car drivers, who previously exceeded 18,000 miles would reduce their mileage below this threshold and one company car driver, who previously exceeded 2,500 miles would reduce their mileage below this threshold. This very small number of threshold changes would suggest that the reforms to the taxation arrangements for company car drivers, to no longer take into account business miles travelled, has had no significant impact on individuals and their business miles travelled. This implies that company car drivers were not driving more miles than necessary.

The mean data referred to above of 23,414 miles and 23,433 miles is used later in this chapter, together with their respective standard deviations of 10,242 and 10,153, for the statistical hypothesis (significance) testing for Hypothesis 1 referred to in the previous chapter. The outcome should be consistent with this discussion to offer additional evidence to support the initial conclusions reached here.

Is Business Mileage Likely to Change?

Figure 39 shows the responses given for the reasons why business mileage may change or remain constant. The majority (90%) of respondents indicated that business mileage was unlikely to change after the introduction of the revised tax, with similar responses (4%) and (5%) for annual business mileage increasing and reducing respectively because of other factors. The answers to this question are consistent with the previous question, revealing little change in business miles travelled because of the taxation change. Only six respondents (1%) indicated that annual business mileage would reduce because there is no longer a tax incentive to drive more miles than necessary.

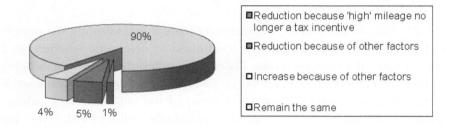

Figure 39   Responses to question 7

The actual number of respondents who previously exceeded either the 18,000 miles threshold or 2,500 miles threshold, but did not intend to in the forthcoming year was ten in total. Of these ten (9+1) respondents that indicated an anticipated change in business mileage for the forthcoming year, to result in a mileage change below previously established thresholds discussed earlier, only three of these respondents identified the business mileage reduction 'because there is no longer a tax incentive in driving more miles than necessary'. The remaining seven respondents cited the reason as 'my annual mileage will decrease because of other factors affecting my job'.

Choice of Car

It is recognised that the extent to which individuals can mitigate the tax charge may be hindered by the degree of the choice of vehicles available to choose from. The primary objective of fleet managers is to provide vehicles that are fit for purpose whilst simultaneously minimising asset lifecycle costs. The vehicles offered for choice would reflect that. This could reduce the potential emission reduction benefits arising from the introduction of this tax as the objectives of the fleet manager may not be consistent with the requirements of the company car driver. This, in addition to constrained choice (that is, very low-emission cars may not be available to choose) could have an impact on the possible levels of CO_2 reduction achieved in reality. However, in the case of this survey, respondents were asked to respond within the context of vehicles available to them in order that an assessment may be made as to the effect of the taxation changes within the constraints within which they had to operate.

Figure 40 shows a pie chart for responses to question 8.

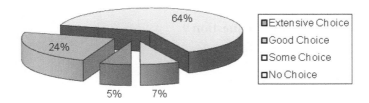

Figure 40   Responses to question 8

Of the 497 respondents, 463 were able to exercise some choice over the next company car when the current vehicle was due for replacement, indicating that the majority of individuals did have an opportunity to mitigate, at least to some extent, the effect of the Benefit in Kind (BIK) taxation affected by CO_2 emissions. Those respondents (34) who have no choice in the selection of their next company car, as the make and model is specified by the employer, were asked to omit questions 9, 10 and 11, as these concerned the effect that the taxation change and hypothetical taxation changes would have on individuals' procurement intentions.

A small majority of the responses (56%) indicated that choice would, to some extent, be influenced by CO_2 emission in that they 'will try to choose a car with a low g/km of CO_2' to reduce their individual tax burden. The responses to this question are not inconsistent with the outcome of the analysis of Hypothesis 2 discussed in the previous chapter and tested later in this chapter.

Figure 41 summarises the responses to question 9.

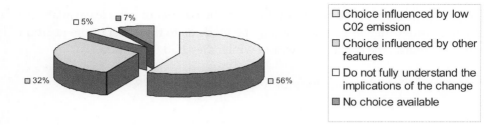

Figure 41   Responses to question 9

Hypothetical Tax Changes

Figure 42 summarises the responses given to question 10 concerning whether a hypothetical doubling of company car taxation would have an influence on the choice of an individual's next company car.

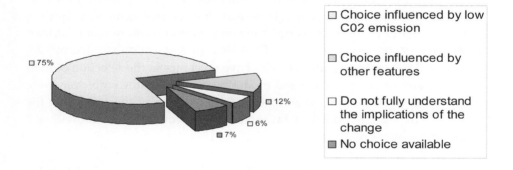

Figure 42   Responses to question 10

Figure 43 compares the responses to this question with those for question 9, to give an indication as to whether a more punitive tax would discourage the selection of higher-emission cars further.

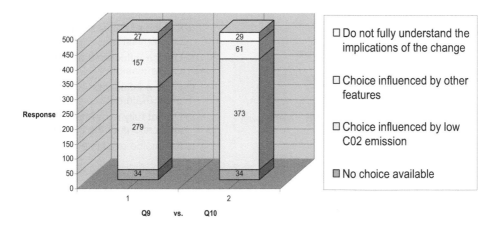

Figure 43   Responses to questions 9 and 10 compared

The hypothetical change in taxation arrangements, if they were more punitive (tax charge doubled) would have an influence on future car choice, with the number of respondents that 'will try to choose a car with a low g/km of CO_2' to reduce their individual tax burden increasing from 56% to 75%.

Whether a hypothetical halving of company car taxation would have an influence on the choice of next company car was examined in question 11. The number of respondents that 'will try to choose a car with a low g/km of CO_2' to reduce their individual tax burden reduced to 29% from 56% (tax charge as proposed) in question 9 and 75% (tax charge hypothetically doubled) in question 10. The response data provided additional evidence that company car drivers' selection of their next company car based on CO_2 emission was elastic.

Figure 44 summarises the responses given.

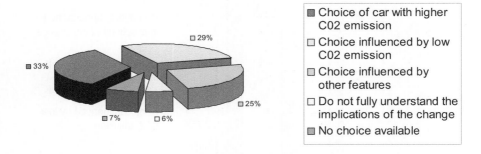

Figure 44   Responses to question 11

Figure 45 compares responses given for questions 9, 10 and 11 and shows whether a more or less punitive tax would have an influence on the selection of higher-emission cars. This provides some evidence that the level of taxation charge has an influence on company car selection with respect to CO_2 emission. It confirms a degree of price sensitivity amongst company car drivers with respect to company car taxation to support the outcome of the testing of Hypothesis 2.

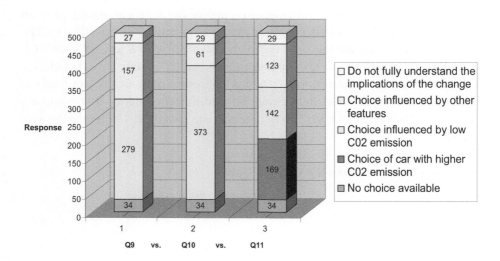

Figure 45   A comparison of the responses given for questions 9, 10 and 11

Next Car

Responses revealed a mean engine size of 1874cc (standard deviation of 278cc) and mean CO_2 emission of 174 g/km (standard deviation of 22 g/km). Whilst the next car mean engine size is similar to the engine size for the existing car (1871cc), the mean CO_2 emission had reduced by 11 g/km (6%). This data is used later for the hypotheses tests discussed in the previous chapter.

At the time of the survey, 88% of the respondents ruled out considering choosing hybrid/electric cars with very low/zero emissions, on the basis of poor range (28%), poor performance (23%) and other reasons (37%). At that time there were only two mass-produced cars that fell into this category (Honda and Toyota). Neither of these cars featured in the survey responses either as an existing vehicle or as an intended choice.

Figure 46 summarises the responses given to question 14.

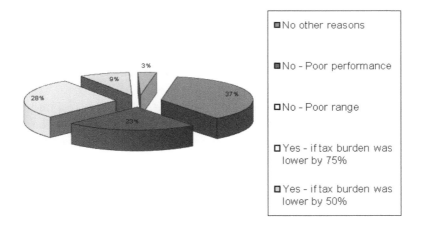

Figure 46   Responses to question 14

However, 77% of respondents thought the change in company car taxation was a good idea (35% of respondents believing that it may reduce CO_2 emissions and a further 42% of respondents believing it to be a good idea, provided low CO_2 emission vehicles were available to choose). It would appear that when respondents were considering low CO_2 emission vehicles for their own choice, or referring to reductions in emissions arising from low CO_2 emission vehicles, it is not anticipated that this would be as a consequence of embracing alternative technology vehicles, such as hybrid/electric cars, but as a result of more fuel efficient and lower-emission conventional cars. This was borne out by the larger number of diesel cars proposed as a replacement vehicle, (question 12) which do provide greater fuel efficiency and lower CO_2 emissions, but do have higher particulate emissions and offer marginally less performance (Brake Horsepower – BHP) and an increase in noise and vibration.

It is acknowledged that individuals' resistance to alternative technology vehicles, such as hybrid/electric is likely to diminish as the technology matures and as a greater variety of models become available.

Only 12% of respondents indicated that they would consider electric/hybrid vehicles if the tax burden was 50% lower (3%) or 75% lower (9%), indicating that at the time of the survey considerable incentive would have to be offered to encourage a minority of company car drivers to migrate to such vehicles. These responses ignore any prejudices that fleet managers may have to procuring emerging technology, particularly with respect to uncertainty about residual values and asset lifecycle costs.

Is the Change in Company Car Taxation a Good Idea?

Figure 47 summarises the responses given and shows that respondents were supportive of environmental taxation in the form of revised company car taxation, with a greater proportion of respondents being supportive provided that low-emission cars are available, to mitigate any increase in company car taxation. Only 16% were opposed to the taxation based on CO_2 emissions rather than the use of vehicle list price only.

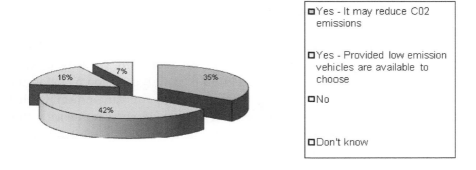

Figure 47   Responses to question 13

Other Measures to Reduce the Distance Travelled

The introduction of road pricing was seen as the most effective measure for reducing the distance travelled by the company car driver, followed by an increase in the cost of fuel. An increase in business miles car tax was the least popular, as this tax burden could be borne by the individual rather than the company.

The responses do indicate that respondents' preference for measures to reduce the number of miles driven per annum may be influenced by whether the individual or the company would bear the increase in taxation charge.

Figure 48 summarises the responses given.

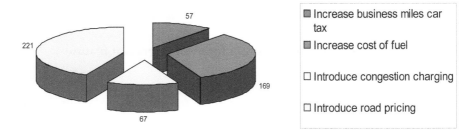

Figure 48   Responses to question 15

Ranking of Features in Choosing a Car

In question 9, 56% of respondents indicated that the level of CO_2 emission would have an influence on their choice of next company car. However, in question 16, only 9% of respondents (45) ranked CO_2 emission as being the most important factor in selecting their next company car, indicating that whilst levels of emissions are of interest and would have some influence on the procurement decision, other factors may also be taken into account and given greater priority and weighting in the decision.

Figure 49 summarises the responses given.

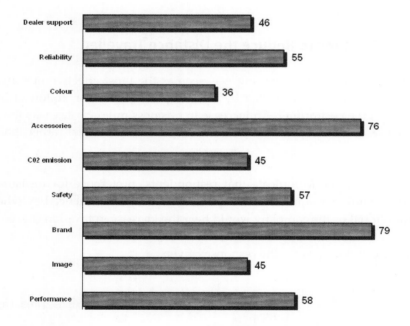

Figure 49   Responses to question 16 for most important feature

Figure 50 summarises the responses given for the ranking of nine features considered to be important for company car drivers.

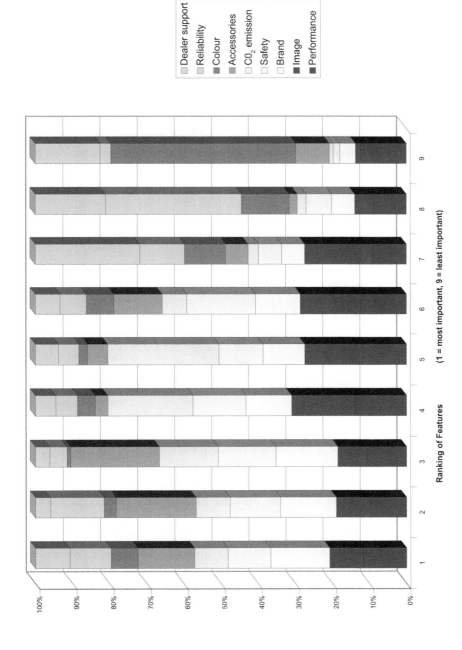

Legend:
- Dealer support
- Reliability
- Colour
- Accessories
- CO_2 emission
- Safety
- Brand
- Image
- Performance

Ranking of Features   (1 = most important, 9 = least important)

Figure 50   Responses to question 16 for ranking of all features

Whilst in question 16, only 9% of respondents ranked CO_2 emission as being the most important factor in selecting their next company car, this percentage is not inconsistent with the percentage of other respondents' ranking of other features as being the most important factor in selecting their next company car.

In addition, where respondents were asked to rank the nine features (1= most important, 9= least important), 87% of the respondents ranked CO_2 emission between 1–5, indicating that CO_2 emission is recognised as important by the majority of company car drivers. This feature has the highest cumulative response for ranking between 1–5 (as illustrated by Figure 51) suggesting that CO_2 emission levels are of interest and are likely to have some influence on the procurement decision, not withstanding other features.

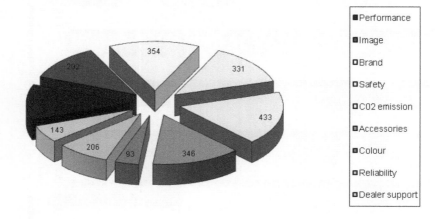

Figure 51   Cumulative response for ranking between 1–5, for question 16

Responses to question 10 (if the amount of company car taxation were doubled, would such a taxation increase have an influence on your choice of your next company car? (3 categories)) showed an increase from 56% to 75% for those respondents who would allow low CO_2 emission to influence their next choice of company car, for this hypothetical more punitive level of taxation. In such circumstances, it may be contemplated that the cumulative response for ranking of features from 1–5, for question 16 illustrated above, may become greater for CO_2 emission at the expense of other features.

Other Notable Matters

From the sample data, a comparison of the current total level of CO_2 emission ('current total emission') of 3,464,871,766g with the anticipated total CO_2 emission, based upon estimated mileage for the forthcoming year ('future total emission') of 3,461,640,412g revealed an overall reduction of 3,231,354g of CO_2.

Whereas a comparison of the anticipated total level of CO_2 emission based upon estimated mileage for the forthcoming year ('future total emission') of 3,461,640,412g with the anticipated total CO_2 emission, based upon estimated mileage for the forthcoming year and a proposed replacement company car ('future total emission new') of 3,245,891,211g revealed a larger reduction of 215,749,201g of CO_2. In this case, the mean grams emission per mile has fallen from 0.599g to 0.561g, a reduction of approximately 6% per mile.

A comparison of CO_2 emissions pre-taxation reform with CO_2 from emissions based upon respondents intentions post-taxation reform, the current total level of CO_2 emission ('current total emission') the anticipated total CO_2 emission, based upon estimated mileage for the forthcoming year and a proposed replacement company car ('future total emission new'), revealed an overall reduction of 218,980,555g.

This data is summarised in Figure 52.

Figure 52   Summary emission data

Current Total Emission	Future Total Emission	Future Total Emission (new)	Change
3,464,871,766g	3,461,640,412g		-3,231,354g
	3,461,640,412g	3,245,891,211g	-215,749,201g
3,464,871,766g		3,245,891,211g	-218,980,555g

The CO_2 emission reductions, identified within the sample data, as a consequence of the changes to a principle and method in the UK taxation regime, provides evidence of statistically significant reductions of CO_2 emissions overall. This finding which is potentially applicable generally and may contribute to the Kyoto Target, will be examined in the hypothesis tests outlined in the previous chapter and carried out later in this chapter.

A comparison of the mean current engine size (engine cc) with the mean engine size of the proposed replacement company car, revealed little difference (1871.96cc compared to 1874.29cc). This suggests that the emission reduction of 215,749,201g of CO_2 from the sample data referred to above has not been obtained by company car drivers selecting cars with a smaller engine capacity (downsizing), but through either switching to diesel cars – which provide lower CO_2 emission levels, partially because of greater fuel economy – or through selecting a similar sized engine car which provides greater efficiency of fuel use, resulting in lower emissions.

The sample data reveals the number of diesel cars had increased from the 'current' level of 11.3% (56 cars) of sample size to 37.6% (187 cars), based upon a proposed replacement company car.

The mean CO_2 of 185g/km for existing company cars from the sample data concurs with the mean of 185g/km for 2000/01. For the Lex Fleet of 178,000 cars (Fleet News 2007) respondents proposed replacement company cars with a mean CO_2 of 174g/km indicating a trend of lower-emissions company cars, which is not inconsistent with the mean CO_2 of 178g/km for new cars sold in the UK for the quarter to November 2001 (SMMT 2005).

The majority of the respondents (76%) were 'currently' 'high-mileage' company car drivers and are, as a consequence, likely to pay more taxation as a result of the abolition of the favourable tax treatment for this category of company car drivers. As one would anticipate from the relatively small decreases in CO_2 emission, arising from the reduction in business miles based upon their intended mileage for the forthcoming year, the majority of respondents who were classified as 'high-mileage' company car drivers, for the forthcoming year, fell slightly to 74% of the sample.

The survey instrument did not provide free format boxes to allow respondents the opportunity for additional narrative comments. Despite this, a number of respondents (23) had added various comments to the returned questionnaire doubting the reasons for the introduction of such a change in taxation and expressing concern that lower CO_2 emission vehicles may not be available to offset the increase in taxation likely to be suffered by individuals. Such expressions as 'stealth tax', 'another Labour tax' and 'what will they think of next to tax', suggested that, at least for some individuals, the change in taxation would have undesirable financial consequences, which may not be mitigated by an alternative choice of car. All respondents who added these additional comments travelled in excess of 18,000 miles per annum and would no longer benefit from a reduction in taxation as a consequence of 'high' business mileage. No questionnaires were returned annotated with positive narrative comments concerning the change in company car taxation. Of the questionnaires deemed spoilt and excluded from further analysis, 21 of these had been excessively annotated with similar and less polite comments concerning the taxation reform, making further use of them as part of the response problematic.

Hypotheses Tests

Survey respondents (company car drivers) provided details to determine the current annual CO_2 emission; based upon the respondents' existing vehicle and estimated mileage for the current year. This data is described as 'Current Total Emission'. Survey responses also provided details to determine the anticipated future annual CO_2 emission, based upon the respondents' existing vehicle and estimated mileage for the forthcoming year. This data is described as 'Future Total Emission'. A mean and standard deviation was calculated for 'Current Total Emission' and 'Future Total Emission' and the differences between the means were measured to test the first hypothesis. Furthermore, survey responses also provided details to determine the anticipated future annual CO_2 emission, based upon the respondents' preferred company car, when the current vehicle was due for replacement and estimated mileage for the forthcoming year. This data is described as 'Future Total Emission (new)'. A mean and standard deviation was calculated for 'Future Total Emission' and 'Future Total Emission (new)'. The differences between the means were measured to test the second hypothesis.

TEST OF HYPOTHESIS 1

Hypothesis 1 restated:

> **H$_0$:** *There is no significant difference between the current mean level of CO_2 emission and anticipated mean CO_2 emission, based upon estimated mileage for the forthcoming year.*

> H_0: $\mu_1 - \mu_2 = 0$

> H_1: $\mu_1 - \mu_2 \neq 0$

The distribution of sample mean differences was normally distributed, enabling parametric tests to be applied. The sample of 497 is considered a large sample as n > 30. (Where n < 30 the t-distribution would apply). Normal area tables are used for the testing of the difference between two means and t-distribution tables for 496 *df* (the value for the t distribution for the more robust statistical test to be applied). The latter facilitates the difference between each pair of variables to be determined and to observe these differences, where they are not zero, to determine whether these differences are large enough and in the same direction, not to be attributed to chance. The tests have been carried out as a two-tailed test at the 5% level of statistical significance, therefore the direction of variation is not a concern, as no expectations about the variation were declared as part of the hypothesis.

Current CO_2 emission$_{(1)}$	Future Total CO_2 emission$_{(2)}$
n_1 = 497	n_2 = 497
μ_1 = 6,971,572.97	μ_2 = 6,965,071.25
S_1 = 3,174,602.45	S_2 = 3,193,164.42

$$\sqrt{\dfrac{s_1^2}{n_1} + \dfrac{s_2^2}{n_2}} = s\,(\mu_1 - \mu_2)$$

Where:

S_1 = *standard deviation of Current CO_2 emission, size n_1*

S_2 = *standard deviation of Future Total CO_2 emission, size n_2*

$$\sqrt{\dfrac{3{,}174{,}602.45^2}{497} + \dfrac{3{,}193{,}164.42^2}{497}} = 201{,}974.1588$$

The Z score is calculated as:

$$Z = \dfrac{\mu_1 - \mu_2}{s(\mu_1 - \mu_2)}$$

Where:

$\mu_{1\_}$= *mean of Current CO_2 Emission.*

μ_2 = *mean of Future Total CO_2 Emission.*

Z = *6,971,572.97 - 6,965,071.25* = **0.03219**
———————————————————
201,974.1588

If the calculated Z score is lower than + or -1.96, for the hypothesis tested, there is nothing to suggest that there is any difference between the two means under consideration. As a consequence, there would be insufficient evidence to reject the null hypothesis. H_0 would therefore be accepted. The calculated Z score of 0.03219 is within the score for a two-tailed test at the 5% significance level of + or -1.96. Therefore, applying this test in this case there is insufficient evidence to reject the null hypothesis (H_o). At the 5% significance level there is nothing to suggest that there is any difference between the two means for mean 'Current Total Emission' and mean 'Future Total Emission'.

By incorporating the standard deviation of the differences, the t-test controls for individual dissimilarity between subjects in the sample. As a consequence, observed differences are wholly attributable to changed conditions. The Microsoft Excel™ t-Test: Paired Two Sample for Means analysis tool and formula were utilised to perform a paired two-sample student's t-test. The resultant data is summarised in the table in Figure 53.

Figure 53   **Summary data for Paired t-test: Current mean level of CO_2 emission and anticipated mean CO_2 emission, based upon estimated mileage for the forthcoming year**

t-Test: Paired: Test for Hypothesis 1	Current Total Emission	Future Total Emission
Mean	6971572.97	6965071.25
Variance	10078100728735	10196299026915
Observations	497.00	497.00
Pearson Correlation	1.00	
Hypothesized Mean Difference	0.00	
df	496.00	
t Stat	0.59	
P(T<=t) one-tail	0.28	
t Critical one-tail	1.65	
P(T<=t) two-tail	0.55	
t Critical two-tail	1.96	

At the 5% level of significance for (497-1) 496 *df* the calculated t scores are lower than + or - 1.96 (5% significance level 496 *df)* for each of the nominal variables. There is nothing to suggest that there is any difference between the two pairs of data under consideration, as any variations between the same could have occurred purely by chance. The inability to reject the null hypothesis using the parametric tests described in the previous chapter and applied to the survey responses in this chapter, would suggest that the change in the taxation regime is unlikely to act as an incentive to reduce business mileage. This finding was consistent with the analysis of responses to question 7 of the questionnaire with 90% of respondents indicating that annual business mileage for the forthcoming year will remain approximately the same.

In addition, as discussed earlier, in an attempt to corroborate these findings, the sample data from the 497 respondents was scrutinised to determine whether, as a consequence of the withdrawal of mileage thresholds of 2,500 miles and 18,000 miles, any individuals' mileage would fall below the previous threshold (where it was formerly advantageous from a personal taxation point of view to remain). It revealed a very small number of threshold changes of (9+1) ten company car drivers. This would suggest that the reforms to the taxation arrangements for company car drivers, to no longer take into account business miles travelled, does not impact on individuals' business miles travelled, which in turn provides additional assurance for the parametric tests inability to reject the null hypothesis. The sample data also indicated that the total mileage travelled post-taxation reform was only 8,850 miles lower than before the revised taxation arrangements were introduced.

Notwithstanding any reductions of business mileage arising from other factors affecting respondents, this small change in business mileage on its own may indicate that the reforms to the taxation arrangements for company car drivers, to no longer take into account business mileage travelled, may have had little or no impact on individuals' annual mileage. This also provided additional assurance for the parametric tests ability to accept the null hypothesis for Hypothesis 1.

TEST OF HYPOTHESIS 2

Hypothesis 2 restated:

> H_0: There is no significant difference between the anticipated mean level of CO_2 emission and anticipated mean CO_2 emission, based upon a proposed replacement company car.

$$H_0: \quad \mu_1 - \mu_2 = 0$$

$$H_1: \quad \mu_1 - \mu_2 \neq 0$$

The distribution of sample mean differences is normally distributed, enabling parametric tests to be applied. Consistent with the analysis of Hypothesis 1, the sample of 497 is considered a large sample as n > 30. Normal area tables are used for the testing of the difference between two means and t-distribution tables for 496 *df* for the value for the t distribution (for the more robust statistical test to be applied). As stated earlier, the latter facilitates the difference between each pair of variables to be determined and to observe these differences, where they are not zero, to determine whether these differences are large enough and in the same direction, not to be attributed to chance. Again, these tests were carried out using the Microsoft Excel™ t-Test: Paired Two Sample for Means analysis tool and formula to perform a paired two-sample student's t-test. The resultant data is summarised in the table in Figure 54.

The direction of variation is not a concern as, again consistent with the hypothesis, this has been carried out as a two-tailed test (at the 5% level of statistical significance).

Future Total CO_2 emission$_{(2)}$	Future Total CO_2 emission (new)$_{(3)}$
$n_1 = 497$	$n_2 = 497$
$\mu_1 = 6,965,071.25$	$\mu_2 = 6,530,968.23$
$S_1 = 3,193,164.42$	$S_2 = 2,955,043.14$

$$\sqrt{\frac{S_1^2}{n_1} + \frac{S_2^2}{n_2}} = s\,(\mu_1 - \mu_2)$$

Where:

S_1 = *standard deviation of Future Total CO_2 Emission, size n_1*

S_2 = *standard deviation of Future Total CO_2 Emission (new), size n_2*

$$\sqrt{\frac{3,193,164.42^2}{497} + \frac{2,955,043.14^2}{497}} = 195,155.5072$$

The Z score is calculated as:

$$Z = \frac{\mu_1 - \mu_2}{s(\mu_1 - \mu_2)}$$

Where:

μ_1 = *mean of Future Total CO_2 Emission.*

μ_2 = *mean of Future Total CO_2 Emission (new).*

$$Z = \frac{6,965,071.25 - 6,530,968.23}{195,155.5072} = \mathbf{2.22439}$$

The tests have been carried out as a two-tailed test at the 5% level of statistical significance, therefore the direction of variation is not a concern, as no expectations about the variation were declared as part of the hypothesis. If the calculated Z score is lower than + or -1.96, for the hypothesis tested, there is nothing to suggest that there is any difference between the two means under consideration. As a consequence, there would be insufficient evidence to reject the null hypothesis. H_0 would therefore be accepted. The calculated Z score of 2.22439 is outside the score for a two-tailed test at the 5% significance level of + or -1.96. Therefore applying this test in this case there is sufficient evidence to reject the null hypothesis (H_0).

The rejection of the null hypothesis was corroborated with the standard deviation of the differences with the paired t-test, which controls for individual dissimilarity between subjects in the sample. As stated earlier, observed differences are wholly attributable to changed conditions.

The data for this analysis is shown in a summary table and is reproduced in Figure 54.

Figure 54   **Summary data for Paired t-test: Anticipated mean level of CO$_2$ emission, based upon estimated mileage for the forthcoming year and anticipated mean CO$_2$ emission, based upon estimated mileage for the forthcoming year and a proposed replacement company car**

t-Test: Paired: Test for Hypothesis 2	Future Total Emission	Future Total Emission (new)
Mean	6965071.25	6530968.23
Variance	10196299026914.70	8732279949141.93
Observations	497.00	497.00
Pearson Correlation	0.95	
Hypothesized Mean Difference	0.00	
df	496.00	
t Stat	9.49	
P(T<=t) one-tail	0.00	
t Critical one-tail	1.65	
P(T<=t) two-tail	0.00	
t Critical two-tail	1.96	

At the 5% level of significance for (497-1) 496 *df* the calculated t scores are higher than + or -1.96 (5% significance level 496 *df*) for each of the nominal variables. As a consequence, there is a difference between the two pairs of data under consideration, as any variations between the same could *not* have occurred purely by chance. The rejection of the null hypothesis and, as a consequence, the acceptance of the alternative hypothesis, H_1 using the parametric tests described in the previous chapter and applied to the survey responses for preferences for the choice of next company car, taking into account the effect of CO_2 emissions on an individual's personal taxation position in this chapter, would suggest that the change in the taxation regime is likely to act as an incentive to choose lower CO_2 emission vehicles than an individual was currently driving.

This finding was consistent with the analysis of responses to question 9 of the questionnaire with 56% of respondents indicating they would try to choose a car with a low g/km of CO_2 emission to reduce the taxation burden. This increased to 75% of respondents (question 10) indicating they would try to choose a car with a low g/km of CO_2 emission to reduce the taxation burden if the taxation burden were to be doubled for CO_2 emissions.

In addition, as discussed earlier, in an attempt to corroborate these findings, the sample data was scrutinised to determine whether this may influence the choice of the company car chosen by individuals, as a result of the reforms to the taxation arrangements for company cars, to reflect the level of CO_2 production. Of the 497 respondents, 215 company car drivers (43% of sample) expressed an intention to select their next company car with a lower level of emission (g/km) than their current car. Whilst 67 company car drivers (13% of sample) selected their next company car with a higher level of emission (g/km) than their current car.

The number of individual company car intended choices resulting in a lower g/km CO_2 emission on their own may indicate that the reforms to the taxation arrangements for company car drivers, to take into account levels of CO_2 emission on a g/km basis, could have had an impact on an individual's vehicle choice and provided additional assurance for the parametric tests ability to reject the null hypothesis for Hypothesis 2.

The sample data reveals that, on average, the g/km CO_2 emission from the next company car chosen would be 10.57g/km lower than before the revised taxation arrangements were introduced. When combined with anticipated business mileage for the forthcoming year, this represents a total reduction of 218,980,556g of CO_2 and, on average, a reduction of 440,604g of CO_2 per company car. Notwithstanding any reductions of CO_2 as a consequence of more efficient engines, lower g/km CO_2 emissions from the sample data on their own may indicate that the reforms to the taxation arrangements for company car drivers, to take into account levels of CO_2 emission on a g/km basis, could have had an impact on individuals' vehicle choice. This provides further assurance for the parametric tests ability to reject the null hypothesis for Hypothesis 2.

Summary

The reform of company car taxation was designed to be revenue-neutral and now takes into account the level of CO_2 emission produced by the car to determine the BIK, rather than the list price along with the number of business miles travelled. The new system does not take into account business mileage in the determination of tax charge and therefore no longer encourages drivers of company cars to maximise business mileage beyond certain thresholds (2,500 miles and 18,000 miles) to minimise their individual tax burden. In this way, the changes could have both an impact on the number of business miles travelled and the choice of next company car.

An analysis of the descriptive statistics revealed that there was widespread understanding of the proposed changes and to the way company car drivers would be taxed in the future and the financial implications arising from the same. The descriptive statistics indicate that the change in the taxation system affecting 'high-mileage' drivers (in excess of 18,000 miles) would do little to reduce the mileage travelled, with the vast majority of business mileage remaining unchanged. This was borne out by the sample data and confirmed by Hypothesis test 1.

The majority of company car drivers were able to exercise some choice over their next company car. Choice of company car by an individual is a complex matter, with many factors (within a given budget) being taken into account in selecting the next vehicle. There is also a qualitative and not entirely rational dimension involved for some in the selection decision. Notwithstanding this, the significance of CO_2 emission linked to a system of company car taxation does appear to have some influence on the procurement decision. However, there are other factors that are prominent in the selection decision, notably brand and accessories. The level of CO_2 emission appears to be more significant to company car drivers if the level of taxation were to be more punitive, indicating price elasticity. The vast majority of respondents (75%) would allow the level of CO_2 emission to influence their choice of next company car when a hypothetical doubling of the tax charge was proposed, compared with 56% under the revenue-neutral proposals to be implemented in the tax year 2002/03, indicating a degree of price elasticity with this ecological tax reform.

The underlying theoretical propositions relating to price elasticity arising from economic theory would suggest that company car drivers are price sensitive to environmental taxation (price elasticity), in so far as they can mitigate their intentions, in order to minimise individual personal taxation. This has been borne out by responses from individuals to hypothetical increases (and reductions) in taxation and also the outcome to the second hypothesis test.

The first hypothesis test revealed, at the 5% level of statistical significance, insufficient evidence to reject the null hypothesis, suggesting that the change in taxation would not have a significant effect on the levels of CO_2 produced from the number of business miles travelled, demonstrating that business mileage was by and large out of the control of the company car driver. This finding was supported by the data with only a very small number of threshold changes from company car drivers, who previously exceeded 18,000 miles and 2,500 miles reducing their mileage below these thresholds.

The second hypothesis test revealed, at the 5% level of statistical significance, sufficient evidence to reject the null hypothesis, suggesting that the change in taxation would have a significant effect on the levels of CO_2 produced from the selection of next company car. This outcome also concurred with the descriptive statistics with 43% of sample expressing an intention to select their next company car with a lower level of CO_2 emission (g/km) than their current car and an overall reduction of 218,980,556g of CO_2 when combined with anticipated business mileage for the forthcoming year.

At the time of the survey, the technology for 'alternative' cars had not reached maturity. Until greater variety of ultra-low emission models become available with more proven technology, CO_2 reductions from company car drivers were unlikely to be achieved by the widespread adoption of such vehicles. At the time of the survey, 88% of the respondents ruled out considering choosing hybrid/electric cars with very low/zero emissions. Instead, it is likely that any reductions would be achieved through downsizing of engine size or by a switch to diesel engines, which offer greater fuel efficiency and lower CO_2 emissions. The survey responses indicated that the latter is an increasingly popular choice to mitigate an increase in company car taxation. Of those 56 respondents who currently had a diesel company car, only four intended to choose a petrol vehicle when the car became due for replacement. In general, larger diesel engines may be chosen compared to their petrol equivalents and still benefit from a fall in CO_2 emissions (although some other pollutants do increase).

The discussion of results in the subsequent chapter will provide context to the overall problem domain for the book, as informed by the literature in Chapter 2. In particular, whether the generalisability of the findings of the research contributes to a more comprehensive understanding of the efficacy of emissions-related motor taxation regimes and whether such changes to a principle and method in the UK taxation regime, which is potentially applicable generally, may provide an opportunity for significant reductions of CO_2 emissions to be achieved.

5

The Inelasticity of
Business Mileage

This chapter provides further scrutiny of the results and a critical review of the findings from the study, with respect to the literature considered in Chapter 2 and the theoretical underpinning discussed in Chapter 1 of this book. The theoretical contribution is discussed and the implications for significant reductions of Carbon Dioxide (CO_2) emissions are also highlighted. In so doing, this chapter will review the results obtained from the research study, in particular the quantitative data from the survey instrument and the outcome of the hypothesis tests carried out in the previous chapter. The descriptive statistics used in the previous chapter will also be referred to in an attempt to review the results, which may be pertinent to the research undertaken.

In assessing the appropriateness of the research approach used in an attempt to gain assurance that the findings 'add something of value to the body of accumulated knowledge' (Remenyi et al. 1998:23) an assessment could be made as to whether the results obtained demonstrated the operationalisation of the research model via testing of the hypothesis outlined in Chapter 1 and further discussed in Chapters 3 and 4. 'Hypothesis must be testable. Their content must be measurable in some way even if they are not directly observable' (Smith 2003:52).

The research approach proved to be successful in capturing sufficient data pre- and post-taxation reform for CO_2 emissions based upon vehicle g/km and mileage to enable the hypothesis testing in the form of a difference between means test and a paired t-test to be carried out. Sufficient data was also obtained to facilitate the production of descriptive statistics to better understand the problem domain examined and to provide a degree of corroboration for the quantitative analysis carried out in pursuit of the hypothesis tests.

Furthermore, to demonstrate rigour in the scientific enquiry undertaken and a further proviso for the generalisability of the findings (requiring multiple observations to be credible), it is appropriate to consider whether survey responses were consistent with responses for other notable prior research and whether such research reached analogous conclusions based upon similar analysis.

Despite the outcomes of the research being consistent with other studies carried out, which are discussed in the course of this chapter and notwithstanding the assurances that the literature may provide as to the usefulness of the research, further replication studies with larger sample sizes would prove beneficial to confirm the outcome of the relationships within the data and the conclusions reached from the hypothesis testing.

The research approach deliberately considered 'intended choice' of next company car, which may transpire to be different to actual choice. It also considered 'estimated mileage for the forthcoming year', which may be different to actual mileage. Intentions were examined rather than actual choices and mileage, as the survey was designed to evaluate the pre- and post-taxation reform position.

Summary of Results

The sample data collected was corroborated with data from the Society of Motor Manufacturers and Traders (SMMT 2005) to confirm that the data obtained was representative of the population as a whole. A summary of the data collected and subsequently used for the purpose of hypothesis testing (and some of the descriptive statistics) is shown in Figure 55.

Figure 55   Summary quantitative data for hypothesis testing

	Current Engine CC (existing)	Current CO$_2$ g/km (existing)	Current mileage	Current Total (1) Emission	Future mileage	Future Total (2) Emission	Future Engine CC (new car)	Future CO$_2$ g/km (new car)	Future Total (3) Emission (new)
Mean	1871.96	184.78	23432.80	6971572.97	23414.99	6965071.25	1874.29	174.22	6530968.23
Standard Error	13.37	0.99	455.43	142400.38	459.44	143233.00	12.46	1.00	132551.80
Median	1895	181	23000	6796416	23000	6757800	1896	170	6371640
Mode	1998	181	20000	6796416	26000	8032128	1998	156	7192230
Standard Deviation	298.04	22.06	10153.10	3174602.45	10242.57	3193164.42	277.85	22.38	2955043.14
Sample Variance	88830.33	486.82	103085464.54	10078100728735.20	104910223.44	10196299026914.70	77198.09	500.80	8732279949141.93
Range	1737	134	47000	18321683	48000	18479365	1928	118	14999098
Minimum	1242	136	3000	825417	2000	667735	998	130	608202
Maximum	2979	270	50000	19147100	50000	19147100	2926	248	15607300
Sum	930363	91838	11646100	3464871766	11637250	3461640412	931522	86586	3245891211
Count	497	497	497	497	497	497	497	497	497
Stats check	OK	OK	OK	OK	OK	OK	OK	OK	OK

Consideration of Findings

The data used for the research problem also provided an opportunity to make use of the richness of the data obtained to make further deductions concerning the study that are related to the hypothesis declared and tested. This permits conclusions for the implications for implementation of 'ecological taxation' to be drawn and the implications for CO_2 reductions arising from this and similar tax changes. Accordingly, the findings contribute to a more comprehensive understanding of the implications of changes to a principal and method in the UK taxation regime, which is potentially applicable generally.

HYPOTHESIS 1

H_o: *There is no significant difference between the current mean level of CO_2 emission and anticipated mean CO_2 emission, based upon estimated mileage for the forthcoming year.*

The outcomes of the difference between means and paired t-test statistical tests reveal that the change in the taxation regime was unlikely to act as an incentive to reduce business mileage. This finding is consistent with the descriptive statistics analysis of responses to question 7 of the questionnaire with 90% of respondents indicating that annual business mileage for the forthcoming year will remain approximately the same. The most probable explanation for business mileage not significantly reducing (despite taxation incentives being withdrawn which may have encouraged drivers of company cars to maximise business mileage beyond thresholds of 2,500 miles and 18,000 miles to minimise their individual tax burden) is that annual business mileage covered is an essential part of the job and has not, in the vast majority of cases, been artificially inflated to benefit from an advantageous tax position.

Pearce (1991), in a discussion of abatement costs associated with environmental taxes, suggested that varying rates of pollution abatement will come about because of individuals' costs of abatement being different. In so doing, Pearce acknowledged that individuals would consider levels of taxation in any decision affecting the extent of pollution caused by the individual's actions with the underlying elasticity for energy being crucial. Pearson & Smith (1990) suggested an increase in the marginal cost of road transport would reduce the aggregate distance travelled. In the case of company car drivers, the removal of the previous incentive would increase the cost of the company car for those drivers above the threshold points of 2,500 miles and 18,000 miles.

However, the findings for this research, which refer to the converse of individuals' costs of abatement; that is incentives (previously) for individuals to drive more miles than necessary, has not in the past been capitalised on by company car drivers, as 90% of company car drivers' business mileage will remain the same post-taxation reform. Whilst company car drivers would not be subjected to an increase in the marginal cost of a company car, they would be affected by a step increase in costs at the two mileage threshold points referred to earlier. Based upon the literature, one may expect a greater reduction in mileage, particularly from those respondents whose mileage was marginally above a threshold point previously, than observed from the data.

This may be explained by noting that Pearson & Smith were specifically referring to marginal cost increases arising from fuel price rises. Fuel price increases would result in consumers (generally) purchasing less fuel, because of price sensitivity and travelling fewer miles by road. However, it is recognised that the majority of company car drivers have little control over the number of business miles that are driven, nor do they have to pay personally for fuel for business mileage. For this group of motorists business mileage appears to be inelastic.

The latter deduction is corroborated by responses to question 7, which revealed that only 1% of respondents' annual business mileage would reduce because there is no longer a tax incentive to drive more miles than necessary. The total number of respondents who anticipated a reduction in business mileage because of 'other factors' and a reduction because high mileage 'is no longer a tax incentive' amounts to only 6% (5% + 1%) of the sample. In addition, the total number of respondents' mileage data which had reduced below the threshold points of 2,500 miles and 18,000 miles for the 'forthcoming year' was 10 (9 + 1). Such a small proportion of the sample provides additional evidence that the reductions in the levels of CO_2 emissions in the population of company car drivers as a whole, as a consequence of reduced business mileage are not significant. This is confirmed by the statistical tests for Hypothesis 1.

However, the withdrawal of Benefit in Kind (BIK) reductions for the mileage threshold discussed above does result in an increase in the tax burden, based upon existing company car. In isolation, this part of the tax reform may not be considered revenue-neutral by company car drivers. For an individual's tax burden to remain approximately the same, they would have to downsize their choice of next company car immediately (Hypothesis 2) to a vehicle producing less CO_2. This would mitigate some of the increase in taxation borne by 'high'-mileage company car drivers caused by the withdrawal of the BIK threshold reductions. For example, a company car driver, selected from the sample data, driving a Ford Mondeo 1.8 LX (1,798cc, 185g/km CO_2 emissions), covering in excess of 18,000 miles would have previously incurred a BIK charge as shown in Figure 56.

Figure 56   Determination of Benefit in Kind (BIK): previous system

2001/02
Ford Mondeo 1.8 LX list price: **£14,580**
Percentage of list price (based upon mileage): **15%**
Benefit in Kind: (15% x £14,580) = **£2,187pa**
∴ Benefit in Kind Total over 3 years: (3 x £2,187) = **£6,561**

Under the 'new' system of taxation, with the favourable 'high-mileage' treatment removed, the increase in tax charge for the first three years are shown in Figure 57.

Figure 57   Determination of Benefit in Kind (BIK): revised system

2002/03
Ford Mondeo 1.8 LX list price: **£14,580**
Percentage of list price 2002/03 (based upon 185g/km CO_2): **21%**
Percentage of list price 2003/04 (based upon 185g/km CO_2): **23%**
Percentage of list price 2004/05 (based upon 185g/km CO_2): **25%**
∴ Benefit in Kind Total over 3 years: (**£3,061.80 + £3,353.40 + £3,645**) = **£10,060.20**

The difference in BIK of (£10,060.20 - £6,561.00) £3,499.20 for a basic rate taxpayer would be equivalent to an extra £769.82 in income tax, and for a higher-rate taxpayer an extra £1,399.68 in income tax. This rise in taxation may only be mitigated in part by selection of a lower CO_2 emission vehicle as the lowest rate of emission for 2002/03 is 165g/km, attracting a percentage of list price for taxation as BIK of 15% (the same as under the previous system). This level of emission falls to 155 g/km for 2003/04 and 145 g/km for 2004/05. A vehicle with a lower list price would also have to be selected.

Assuming the lowest rate of emission for 2002/03 of 165g/km (as above), the list price of the replacement car would also have to fall to (£6,561 ÷ (15% + 17% + 19%)) £12,864.71 for the taxation charge to be at an equivalent level to that pre-taxation reform. For some 'high-mileage' company car drivers this approach would be unrealistic, as the high-mileage company car driver with a mean level of CO_2 emissions (based upon the sample data) would have to (for example) select a vehicle with 11% less CO_2 emissions and 13% lower list price to be tax-neutral post-taxation reform.

The most probable explanation for business mileage not significantly reducing, despite taxation incentives being withdrawn as discussed earlier, is that annual business mileage covered is an essential part of the job. The example given above (taken as an average case from the sample data) illustrates the likely emphasis on lower CO_2 emissions by company car drivers when selecting their next car. This was tested in sub-problem 2 (Hypothesis 2).

The very small number of threshold changes (at 2,500 miles and 18,000 miles) would also provide additional evidence that the reforms to the taxation arrangements for company car drivers to no longer take into account business miles travelled, has had no significant impact on individuals' business miles travelled and provides additional assurance for the parametric tests inability to reject the null hypothesis.

In terms of the significance of the results and the generalisability of the findings, the analysis has revealed that taxation changes where previous incentives are withdrawn do not have a significant effect on company car drivers' polluting behaviour from business mileage. The majority of individuals are not in control of the decision to travel (pollute) or otherwise. The implication of this for ecological taxation is that if raising revenue is paramount then this type of taxation modification is effective. However, if increasing the burden of taxation to individuals is to discourage polluting behaviour from business mileage, such a change is unlikely to achieve its objective. The removal of the previous incentives, or conversely the introduction of a punitive system of taxation based upon mileage, which could also include road pricing where the individual has to pay the charge or a proportion of the charge, is unlikely to significantly alter the number of business miles travelled by an individual, nor make a significant contribution to the Kyoto Target for CO_2 reductions as the opportunity to mitigate the number of business miles travelled appears very limited.

Whilst the number of business miles covered by company car drivers remained largely unchanged for individuals, the total number of business miles travelled would be affected by the numbers of company car drivers. The Inland Revenue estimated the number of company cars had been stable at 1.6 million cars up to 2001. However, since the taxation reforms there had been a decrease of approximately 250,000 company cars up to 2003 (Inland Revenue 2004). This decrease in company cars may be because of the increasing popularity of employees opting out of company car schemes, instead preferring cash alternatives to use towards personal contract leasing. More employees preferring to take alternative cash incentives and make their own car arrangements could result in cars chosen with higher emissions as individuals will not be penalised personally by the sliding scale tax increases in the reforms. The increasing popularity of Personal Contract Purchase (PCP) together with other cash incentives towards travel make it problematic to reach firm conclusions as to whether total business miles covered, as opposed to individual business mileage covered by company car drivers, has increased or declined.

However, due to the inelasticity of business miles travelled and the actuality that all company car drivers are employed and their earnings are sufficiently high to pay taxation, there should be minimal impact on the poorest households as a result of this tax modification. The distributional effects of such a change in the taxation regime are unlikely to be strongly adverse. It follows that the opportunity to raise taxation generally or specifically to contribute to environmental repair from this tax modification is good. The efficacy of tax earmarking or tax hypothecation for this purpose should be borne in mind.

HYPOTHESIS 2

H_0: *There is no significant difference between the anticipated mean level of CO_2 emission and anticipated mean CO_2 emission, based upon a proposed replacement company car.*

The number of individual company car intended choices resulting in a lower g/km CO_2 emission on their own may indicate that the reforms to the taxation arrangements for company car drivers to take into account levels of CO_2 emission on a g/km basis could have had an impact on individuals' vehicle choice. Furthermore, the outcomes of the difference between means and paired t-test statistical tests, for the purpose of testing the above hypothesis, reveal a rejection of the null hypothesis and hence the acceptance of an alternative hypothesis; H_1 using the parametric tests. This permits the conclusion that the change in the taxation regime was likely to act as an incentive to choose lower CO_2 emission vehicles than an individual was currently driving.

Using the parametric tests described in Chapter 3 provides additional assurance that the observed differences in this experiment are wholly attributable to changed conditions and could not have occurred purely by chance. Indeed, these findings may also be corroborated by the survey data which revealed that 56% of respondents indicated they would try to choose a car with a low g/km of CO_2 emission to reduce the taxation burden (question 9). This increased to 75% of respondents indicating they would try to choose a car with a low g/km of CO_2 emission to reduce the taxation burden if the taxation burden were to be doubled for CO_2 emission (question 10). This analysis provides some evidence that company car drivers are price sensitive to environmental taxation, where they may have some influence on the outcome.

The responses to question 8 indicated that 93% of respondents were able to exercise some choice over the next company car when the current vehicle was due for replacement. This confirms that, unlike the results for Hypothesis 1, the majority of individuals did have some opportunity to mitigate, at least in part, the effect of BIK taxation by selecting a vehicle from the choice available, with a lower CO_2 emission than the existing vehicle. Pearson & Smith (1990) observed the previous system of company car taxation encouraged large cars. The authors concluded that 'as a result of this [now previous] system of charging, the largest tax "perk" is achieved by giving a car towards the top of each engine size category' (Pearson & Smith 1990:34). They concluded that to discourage such an incentive to choose larger cars, it would be necessary to introduce progressive scale charges, which this part of the taxation reform attempts to do.

A change with the potential to reduce CO_2 emission may be more attractive from a distributive point of view than increasing petrol prices (Pearson & Smith 1990) to achieve the same aim. Whether such a change affecting company car drivers will curtail this incentive to choose cars with higher CO_2 emissions is verified by Hypothesis 2, by confirming company car drivers' price sensitivity, to a certain extent, to environmental (emissions) taxation in so far as they are able or prepared to moderate their choice of car from those available to them. However, it is acknowledged that this choice was restricted not only by the variety of vehicles available to the individual, but also the purpose for which the company car was used in the course of business.

As discussed earlier for Hypothesis 1, the actuality is that all company car drivers are employed and their earnings are sufficiently high to pay taxation; there should be minimal impact on the poorest households as a result of this tax modification. The distributional effects of such a change in the taxation regime are again unlikely to be strongly adverse. It follows that the opportunity to raise taxation generally or specifically to contribute to environmental repair from this tax modification is good. The efficacy of tax earmarking or tax hypothecation for this purpose remains a possibility.

The change to BIK calculations based upon the CO_2 emissions is not a carbon tax as it would be traditionally considered, in that the carbon content of the fuel is not being assessed for the basis of the taxation. An important observation to make is that whilst both Pearson & Smith (1990) and Manne & Richels (1993) claim that carbon taxes would lower the consumption of carbon-intensive fuels and hence have the possibility to reduce CO_2 emissions, such taxes may not dampen total energy consumption. The possibility of fuel substitution exists. In their discussion of price elasticity, Manne & Richels concluded that 'carbon taxes [in their traditional form] create incentives for fuel switching away from carbon intensive fuels'. (Manne & Richels 1993:5) This observation is consistent with the findings of the study, in that whilst total CO_2 emissions have declined, this was primarily as a result of company car drivers switching to diesel car alternatives as opposed to downsizing to smaller-sized cars or lower-performance cars that tend to pollute less. From the sample data, the switch from petrol cars to diesel cars does result in an overall reduction in CO_2 emission of 228,570,518g. Indeed, from the sample data collected, the proportion of diesel-powered cars for the existing vehicle was 11.3%. However, the expressed choice of company car drivers for a replacement vehicle highlighted a change in these proportions to 37.6% diesel engines, demonstrating a significant shift to diesel models, over a short period of time. This data is not inconsistent with diesel penetration of 36% for the new car market for 2004 (SMMT 2005).

Moreover, this 26.3% (37.6% - 11.3%) increase in the choice of diesel cars overall in the sample, results in a 21% reduction in CO_2 emission for such drivers. The increase in diesel penetration of the UK car market has been an important aspect of the improving average CO_2 emission rates (SMMT 2005). Such a year on year increase in diesel cars as preferred choice by company car drivers in the sample data is not inconsistent with SMMT statistics, which revealed a 23% increase in diesel fleet cars between 2003 and 2004 (SMMT 2005).

The corroborated findings reveal that the substitution for diesel cars does bring about significant reductions in CO_2 emissions and the changes to company car taxation encouraged company car drivers to substitute their petrol vehicle for a diesel one. SMMT (2005) highlighted Government policy, including company car taxation, as a key determinant in diesel penetration levels in the UK.

Despite attempts to mitigate the increase in company car taxation by those company car drivers in the sample who expressed an intention to downsize by choosing a lower CO_2 emissions car and selecting a diesel alternative; a comparison of the BIK for the first three years of the changes for the 'existing scheme' and 'new scheme' reveals an overall increase in BIK of £519,078 and an average BIK increase of £3,821 per company car driver (based upon existing car) and an overall increase of £271,921 and an average increase of £1,999 per company car driver (based upon selection of a diesel alternative). The financial penalty of this change in taxation is not entirely mitigated by this choice, but is approximately halved (47.6%).

Notwithstanding the benefits of Euro IV compliant diesel engines, there would, as a result of this switch, be a rise in other pollutants including dangerous particulates known to be linked to respiratory diseases. These other gases would have an environmental impact, but may not be as significant as carbon emissions for global warming. The switch to less carbon-intensive forms of transport (currently with these undesirable side effects) may be less of a concern if company car drivers were able to embrace alternative technology cars such as hybrid/electric cars, which produce less total emissions. However, the survey results revealed considerable reluctance to do this with 88% of the survey respondents ruling out choosing hybrid/electric cars with very low/zero emissions, on the basis of poor range (28%), poor performance (23%) and other reasons (37%).

As discussed in the previous chapter, at the time of the survey there were only two mass-produced cars that fell into this category (Honda and Toyota). Other manufacturers are, for example, researching into stop-start technology as a variant to hybrid, regenerative breaking and, significantly, hydrogen cell power. The introduction of, and in some cases the maturity of, alternative fuel technologies and their acceptance, precipitated by taxation reform, may promote substitution and mitigate the level of carbon emissions from company cars.

Such emission reductions arising from alternative technologies are difficult to assess at this stage. Such cars are unlikely to populate company car fleets given the limited numbers of these types of cars available and their relatively high list prices (in an attempt to recoup high research and development costs) and the reluctance, at this point, of company car drivers to switch from conventionally (fossil fuel) powered cars to other sources. Uncertainty concerning availability of power/fuel supply and also the residual values for alternative fuel cars would also be problematic for fleet managers in determining viability and lifecycle costs for the same.

Implications for CO_2 Reductions

The implications for CO_2 reductions arising from the conclusions drawn from Hypothesis tests 1 and 2 are firstly irrespective of the changes to the taxation system affecting company car drivers. The withdrawal of incentives to travel more business miles or the punitive abolition of a reduction in taxation for 'high' business mileage does not yield statistically significant results; the distance travelled and the CO_2 produced from distance travelled remains largely unchanged, so as not to be statistically significant. This indicates that employees, using company cars, in the normal course of their business were unable to affect the number of miles travelled. The inelasticity of business mileage travelled provides little opportunity for reduction in CO_2 emissions. Secondly, CO_2 emissions would be reduced as a result of company car drivers intending to select a lower emission next car. The overall reduction of CO_2 at the sample mean vehicle emission (for intended choice) to 174g/km is equivalent to a reduction of 782,168 miles or an average of 1,574 miles per company car driver.

Whilst it may be concluded that the selection of a lower-emission car is likely to provide far greater CO_2 reductions compared to reductions in business mileage which were negligible, it should also be contemplated that the removal of possible incentives to travel further distances than may have been necessary could have contributed to a lowering of CO_2 emissions by a more prudent selection of car than would otherwise have been made. This could point to company car drivers considering their overall tax position with respect to BIK for company car taxation, thus permitting the inelasticity of business mileage, coupled with a less-favourable tax treatment than was previously available for the same, to influence the make and model selection with respect to g/km CO_2 emissions. This would be in an attempt to mitigate overall increases in taxation to compensate for the loss of the formerly more generous taxation treatment for this category of company car driver.

This assertion is supported by the sample data, where the 'high' business mileage drivers have expressed an intention to select the next car with, on average, an emission reduction of 12.19g/km (184.98g/km – 172.79g/km) compared to their existing vehicle. Whereas non-'high' business mileage drivers have expressed an intention to select cars with, on average, an emission reduction of less than half (44%) of that for 'high-mileage' drivers of 5.39 g/km (184.15g/km – 178.76g/km) compared to their existing vehicle.

Accordingly, a tax modification which in one part does not propose tax increases (that may not be mitigated because of inelasticity) is unlikely to achieve the same reductions in CO_2 emissions as one that does. The implications arising from this may be significant for further taxation reforms to curb emissions and are discussed later in this chapter.

The extrapolated reductions of CO_2 emissions for the tax modifications for the whole population of company car drivers, based upon company car population data estimates from the Inland Revenue (1.6 million cars up to 2001, with a decrease of approximately 250,000 cars up to 2003) (Inland Revenue 2004), may be estimated from the data collected. The total extrapolated CO_2 reductions are estimated in the region of 0.59 million tonnes of CO_2. Such a reduction is consistent with the Government's anticipated reductions of between 0.5 million tones of carbon (MtC) to 1.0mtc arising from this taxation change (Inland Revenue 2004). Such a reduction would make a significant contribution of towards the Kyoto Target of 12.5% below 1990 levels (required by 2012).

However, further measures of the type discussed in this research would therefore be necessary if the transport sector were to deliver CO_2 emission reductions consistent with the Government's obligations under the Kyoto Protocol. Particular emphasis may need to be given to shipping and aviation, where CO_2 emissions, particularly in the case of the latter, continue to rise unabated. It is problematic to quantify with any degree of accuracy the overall contribution that the taxation change alone could make to the overall CO_2 emission by the dates referred to above. This is as a consequence of variables such as the increase in road traffic generally over the aforementioned time periods, the European Commission's requirement for manufacturers to reduce CO_2 emissions to an average emission figure of 140 g/km by 2008 and 130 g/km by 2012 and the introduction of, for example, bio-fuels and more economical tyres with lower rolling resistance.

Implications for Taxation

Inland Revenue estimates for company car taxation reform were that 'it would be broadly revenue neutral in its first year' (Inland Revenue 2004:24). Receipts were estimated at £2,660 million, with an estimate that revenues would reduce by approximately £25 million in the following year and £75 million in the year after that (Inland Revenue 2004). A combination of a reduction in the numbers of company cars and employees selecting cars with lower than anticipated CO_2 emissions has resulted in the above estimates being 'greater than anticipated' (Inland Revenue 2004:24). The decrease in the number of company cars since the company car tax reform has increased the popularity of various types of employee ownership schemes including PCP and contract hire schemes. Such schemes have contributed to the reduction in revenue.

The tax modification was introduced as a revenue-neutral reform rather than a new earmarked tax. Therefore, it is unlikely that the proceeds from such a reform would be hypothecated towards clean-up costs in this instance; indeed, there has been no expressed intention to do so.

Taxation suffered by individuals becomes progressively greater, over the first three years of the reform, representing an increase of 4% (of list price) between 2002/03 and 2004/05. This increase is illustrated in Figure 58 with an extract from the table for rates of taxation for the 'new' system in the first three years of reform. (The full table is reproduced in Chapter 1, Figure 11). This increase, coupled with the abolition of business mileage as a factor in determining the BIK tax, has resulted in significant tax rises for many company car drivers.

Figure 58   Rates of taxation (extract) for the new tax system for the first three years of reform

Percentage of List Price (Petrol)	CO$_2$ Emissions (g/Km)			Percentage of List Price (Diesel)
	2002/03	2003/04	2004/05	
15	165	155	145	18
16	170	160	150	19
17	175	165	155	20
18	180	170	160	21
19	185	175	165	22
20	190	180	170	23
21	195	185	175	24
22	200	190	180	25
23	205	195	185	26
24	210	200	190	27

It may be demonstrated that the taxation reform works, in principle, as a mechanism to generate revenue, with a high degree of compliance and reduced CO$_2$ emission, through the selection of low-emission vehicles. The taxation at its current or proposed level yields a CO$_2$ emission reduction that is consistent with the Government's anticipated reductions of between 0.5mtc to 1.0mtc. However, it should be borne in mind that the revenue raised from the revised taxation system may be insufficient at its present or anticipated taxation level to cover the clean-up costs for the CO$_2$ emitted. Difficulty in the quantification as part of a financial assessment of clean-up costs is a problem already alluded to earlier in this book. Clean-up costs arguably become less significant if the damage cannot be repaired. CO$_2$ clean-up also becomes problematic due to CO$_2$ ability to mix homogeneously globally, requiring a global, rather than a local (country-based) response to such a problem.

Moreover, it may also be observed that where taxation modifications on their own do not appear to yield desired benefits (in this case lower pollution arising from less distance travelled) the modification itself may still lead to desirable outcomes (lower CO$_2$ emissions overall) when combined and linked with other taxation reforms. The combined taxation change effects and the opportunity to mitigate any increase in the BIK charge to the individual in one tax with another tax may have important implications for future environmental tax reform. Specific reforms may result in inelastic outcomes, which may be initially judged as of little environmental benefit in terms of reducing the polluting behaviour (but may raise additional revenue which could be used towards clean-up costs). However, when combined with other reforms, they provide an opportunity for individual choice to be made to lower the overall taxation burden and reduce the amount of pollution also. Individuals may look at total or overall taxation burden within a category, as long as the policies appear to be related (for example, company car taxation relating to mileage and CO_2 emissions are still both related to the company car driver) rather than a piecemeal taxation burden according to individual tax policies.

The principle applied in BIK for determining a theoretical valuation to add to a taxpayer's income provides a useful mechanism for evaluating an individual's responsibility for carbon emissions. Such an application of a theoretical valuation for environmental damage permits ecological taxation to be introduced without a wholesale realignment of prices of goods and services to take into account environmental impact. Instead, each individual will have the costs of certain polluting activities adjusted according to their marginal rate of taxation, as BIK is linked to a sliding scale within the overall system of personal taxation, which reflects an individual's ability to pay. Accordingly, individuals with higher personal income who choose to engage in higher carbon emissions through choice (personal benefit) would suffer a higher financial penalty. The principle applied in BIK within the personal taxation system offers some assurance of equity in terms of the ability to pay and is consistent with a system of progressive taxation.

Furthermore, rises in taxation may become more pertinent in an individuals' decision-making process, relating to the extent of pollution, if individuals view taxes within a category (that is, company car taxation) where one tax is out of the individual's control (that is, mileage cannot be reduced) and is inelastic. This may increase the desire/need to compensate for this further, particularly as tax concessions for higher mileage are withdrawn and if tax rates rise. This observation may also be corroborated by the quantitative data referred to earlier and to a certain extent by the descriptive statistics for questions 9, 10 and 11. This data shows a significant rise in the numbers of respondents influenced by vehicle CO_2 emission levels if the tax rate were doubled and a significant reduction in the number of respondents influenced by vehicle CO_2 emission levels if the tax rate were halved.

Further studies on similar related taxes where one tax proves to be inelastic (in this case business mileage) and the other elastic (in this case choice of company car) to observe the combined outcomes would be worth undertaking to determine whether the outcomes are consistent with this tax reform.

It should be borne in mind that if a tax has inelastic outcomes this is unlikely to result in non-compliance in a highly regulatory environment where the returns to statutory bodies are made by third parties, such as employers, and where employees are unlikely to be the poorest members of society.

Compliance

A tax system requires the cooperation of the vast majority of taxpayers if it is to function effectively, so matters pertaining to tax compliance (the extent to which taxpayers comply with the law) are worthy of mention here. James & Nobes (2000) concluded that the motives of the tax payer are paramount, having given consideration to the possibility of detection together with the consequences of non-compliance (the carrot and stick approach) as well as activities intended to encourage voluntary compliance (the responsible citizen approach) that regard the view of the revenue authorities and the State as important matters.

In the case of the specific taxation reforms considered, there has been no suggestion of tax hypothecation by the Government in this case to carbon emission matters, notably clean-up or carbon capture schemes. However, the possibility of the application of a specific environmental taxation to curb emissions, by reducing the demand for high CO_2 emission cars, is explicit in the reform and has been tested and confirmed as part of this research.

There was little evidence from the descriptive statistics to suggest there would be widespread opposition to the change, even though a tax which had a 'green' basis was not promoted exclusively for clean-up purposes or even for its green credentials. The application of this specific environmental taxation to '...reduce CO_2 emissions, which contribute to global warming' (survey instrument: q13) is explicit in the reform (and was explicit in the questionnaire). The responses to question 9 of the survey instrument indicated an influence on the procurement decision by the majority, suggesting a readiness to comply. The responses to question 13 also indicate that the majority of respondents (77%) have some agreement (with a caveat that low CO_2 emission cars are available as a choice) with the change so as not to be considered opposed to the revised system. The opportunities for non-compliance with the tax could be considered minimal. The information to determine a company car driver's BIK is provided to the Inland Revenue by the employer, not the employee, via an existing system (form P11D) for determining all benefits paid to an employee over and above an employees' salary. Such BIKs are added to an individual's gross salary, to determine the tax to be deducted by the employer and paid directly to the Inland Revenue. Compliance is likely to be maximised where an existing system is used which is monitored and controlled by the employer and must be adhered to as part of the employer's statutory obligations. In this way, the information required to determine the taxation to an individual via BIK is provided by a third party rather than the tax payer. In addition, reliance on an existing, albeit modified system for compliance, results in a reduction in costs for this activity. Indeed, the Inland Revenue estimate a reduction in on-going compliance costs of approximately £35 million (Inland Revenue 2004).

Pearce (1991) concluded of taxes relating to carbon emissions that countries are more likely to implement politically 'soft' measures before accepting carbon taxes. Pearce was suggesting such measures as energy-saving campaigns as an example. However, the change in company car taxation could also be viewed as a 'soft' measure as the introduction of the taxation has been undertaken on a 'revenue-neutral basis' providing little emphasis for matters relating to carbon emissions.

The opportunities to mitigate the taxation burden for an individual also exist through choice of vehicle with a level of CO_2 emission consistent with the tax that an individual would have suffered previously. This arguably does little to heighten awareness of the significance of the damage arising from CO_2 emissions or the costs of repairing the same through an increase in taxation for activities that result in significant carbon emissions. The likelihood of compliance is enhanced if there is little or no net increase in cost to an individual.

Other Implications

In addition to the implications discussed earlier in this chapter, there are additional repercussions of the taxation reform which are worthy of mention here.

An awareness of the new company car tax arrangements for employees is likely to have an impact on the makes and models of cars available. This in turn will have implications for fleet managers in developing their procurement strategy for new cars.

The annual market for the replacement cars for companies was in the region of 450,000 cars and approximately 50% of all new cars were provided to companies (SMMT 2005). Therefore, any change in procurement policy is likely to be actively responded to by manufacturers. Such matters as car size, engine size, type of transmission, car weight, economy and availability of diesel and hybrid variants have an impact on the level of CO_2 emissions. Emissions may become increasingly important for new cars at the expense of other features of the type outlined in question 16 of the survey instrument. This in turn will have an effect on the used car market and the types of vehicle available to the private used-car buyer.

The numbers of company cars may continue to decline, due to increasing numbers of company car drivers opting out of company schemes, particularly if the system becomes more punitive in an attempt to reduce emissions further. This may necessitate a review of employee car ownership schemes and the authorised mileage allowance payments systems to implement measures similar to company car taxation reforms. In this case, the generalisability of the findings of this research takes on a greater significance.

Generalisability of Findings

The generalisability of these findings may be pertinent for other ecological taxation opportunities in the transport sector and indeed other sectors in pursuance of the CO_2 emissions reduction target as the method and principles employed in the taxation reform may be able to be applied elsewhere to good effect.

The alteration to the basis on which tax is charged for company cars, together with the taxation rate becoming increasingly greater in each tax year, despite delivering reductions consistent with the Government's target for this reform, may be insufficient to achieve overall environmental goals for CO_2 emission for the transport sector, either through clean-up or prevention, to attain the Kyoto Target. The unabated rise in aviation CO_2 emissions within the transport sector poses a significant problem for CO_2 target attainment overall for the transport sector as a whole.

The descriptive statistics supported the outcome of the hypothesis tests that higher taxation would result in lower environmental impact. In order that an individual has appropriate incentive to reduce polluting behaviour, it may be necessary to ensure that revenue neutrality is only achieved where reasonable and feasible reductions in emissions pollution are made (that is, the status quo is not maintained). Question 11 from the survey revealed that where the taxation burden was hypothetically reduced, many respondents no longer gave CO_2 emissions the same priority as under the 'existing' system.

The opportunities for opting out of any taxation through careful tax planning/avoidance should be considered and minimised where possible. In the case of company car drivers, approximately 250,000 employees chose to do this which may have consequences in terms of lower tax revenue and the likelihood of these drivers selecting higher emission cars.

One of the reasons identified for company car drivers choosing low CO_2 emission vehicles was the need to mitigate the change in BIK rules and hence taxation for 'high-mileage' company car drivers. This illustrated that individuals did not view business mileage and CO_2 emission in isolation, but rather a part of an overall tax burden, as both components counted toward the BIK calculation which was ultimately subject to income tax at the prevailing rate according to overall levels of income. The way tax is charged and how it is perceived is paramount to its success. The use of some form of BIK measure for environmental taxation is likely to be very significant. Rather than applying a flat rate of taxation to emissions, where all consumers suffer the same tax burden,, BIK has a significant advantage in that it is added to other income to determine the overall taxation position and may be adjusted to take into account specific circumstances. Utilising the principle of BIK for ecological taxation may also be consistent with a system of progressive taxation. However, it is acknowledged that the term 'Benefit in Kind' may be misleading as the extent of pollution by an individual may be regarded a benefit.

The characteristics of the tax which have led to the partial accomplishment of its stated objectives may be contemplated alongside the four 'canons' of taxation proposed by Smith (1776) in an attempt to determine which principle is pertinent to the particular aspect of the reform and to identify those aspects of the reform that are consistent with the literature and those that arise from the study in pursuance of a generalisable model which may be used for future taxation developments. Figure 59 provides a table which cross references the important characteristics of the taxation reform to the four 'canons' of taxation.

Figure 59   Characteristics of taxation reform and the four 'canons' of taxation

Taxation Reform		Four 'Canons' of Taxation			
Source	Characteristics	Equity*	Certainty**	Convenience†	Efficiency‡
Literature	Prior anticipation of tax change		✓ *(Taxpayer aware of how tax calculated)*	✓ *(Taxpayer aware of how tax paid)*	
Literature	Specific group of existing taxpayers		✓ *(High degree of regulation)*		✓ *(Collection via existing system)*
Study	Compulsory taxation component	✓ *(Recognises a benefit)*	✓ *(High degree of regulation)*		
Study	Sliding scale of taxation	✓ *(Higher polluters pay more)*	✓ *(Given by sliding scale)*		
Study	Utilisation of 'Benefit In Kind'	✓ *(Progressive tax)*	✓ *(PAYE calculation)*	✓ *(PAYE deduction)*	✓ *(Not distortionary)*
Literature	Based upon existing system (with high degree of compliance)			✓ *(PAYE deduction)*	✓ *(No major collection system changes)*
Literature	Lower compliance costs			✓ *(Existing PAYE system)*	✓ *(Lower collection costs envisaged)*
Literature	Revenue-neutral reform	✓ *(Not intended to increase overall tax burden)*			
Study	Significant tax increases (for high mileage drivers)	✓ *(Higher polluters pay more)*			
Study	Opportunity to reduce tax paid (through choice)	✓ *(Taxpayer may mitigate tax)*	✓ *(BIK determined easily)*		

*   equity – the fairness of the tax, taking into account the relative contributions of different individuals.
**   certainty – the certainty (not arbitrariness) of tax liabilities.
†   convenience – the consideration of the way the tax can be paid and the timing of the same.
‡   efficiency – the cost of collection of the tax should be a small proportion of revenue raised. Distortionary effects on the taxpayer should also be avoided.

The taxation reforms may also be appraised with respect to James & Nobes (2000) four criteria for contemplating an economic perspective for appraising tax systems. These reforms may be carried out with a view to discriminating between potentially worthwhile and inappropriate reforms in order that the outcome may contribute to a generalisable model which may be used to inform future taxation developments.

Efficiency – *How could a particular tax proposal impact on the efficiency of the economy? (For example, would a particular tax cause distortions in the price mechanism that would affect the actions of producers and consumers.)*

Polluting behaviour is an economic distortion in that the costs of the same are not addressed by the price mechanism. Such a tax reform is likely to have some impact on the price mechanism and would contribute towards addressing this distortion (depending on the severity of the taxation and the alternative choices available to the consumer). Evidence from the research study shows that company car drivers' behaviour will change as they are likely to choose cars that produce lower CO_2 emissions as a result of the reform providing a sliding scale of tax based upon CO_2 emissions coupled with an element of choice of emissions efficiency by the individual taxpayer. Company car drivers would also have a heightened awareness of CO_2 emissions generally which may provide benefits for other environmental policies or taxation reforms. Car manufacturers are likely to produce lower-emission vehicles to respond to this demand.

Incentives – *To what extent would the tax impact on the behavioural influences of an individual's desire to:*

a)   *work or undertake certain types of work?*

b)   *save and take advantage of investment opportunities?*

c)   *tolerate economic risks associated with business enterprise?*

The taxation change may have an influence on whether individuals choose to have a company car, where a choice exists. At the current level of taxation, it is unlikely that individuals would choose not to undertake work associated with a company car. However, it is acknowledged that for 'high'-mileage drivers, there are significant rises in taxation.

Any increase in taxation will reduce the amount of disposable income which may be utilised, amongst other things, for savings and investment. For 'high'-mileage drivers, increases in taxation as the previously favourable treatment for such drivers is withdrawn, that cannot entirely be mitigated by a choice of lower CO_2 emissions car, will result in a reduction in disposable income.

The economic risks associated with business enterprise are likely to remain unchanged, as any increase in taxation burden is borne by the individual (employee), rather than the organisation (employer). It is anticipated that compliance costs will be reduced, which may be of some benefit to organisations.

> Macroeconomic considerations – *Are there any implications for the levels of employment in the economy?*

The taxation reform is intended to be revenue-neutral. There are no anticipated implications for the levels of employment in the economy. The sliding scale for tax based upon emissions does provide an opportunity for low CO_2 emission vehicles to be chosen. Such cars provide greater economy and lower fuel consumption generally. Taxation changes of the type discussed in this study result in greater economy in the consumption of carbon-emitting fossil fuels. This may have implications for companies that supply fossil fuels and for levels of employment within those organisations.

> Equity – *The principle of horizontal equity suggests 'that similar people in similar circumstances should be treated similarly' (James & Nobes 2000:17).*

The taxation reform will treat all company car drivers similarly, in that there is a compulsory tax component for driving a company car and a variable component based upon CO_2 emissions. The latter will affect individuals differently depending upon the car driven, which to a certain extent is dependent upon choice. Whether the tax is fair requires a certain amount of subjective judgement as to how to interpret 'similar circumstances'. Where this relates to vehicle choice, based upon a sliding scale of emissions taxation, or the overall taxation position based upon the principle of BIK contributing to overall income for taxation purposes at the prevailing rates, '…similar people in similar circumstances [are] treated similarly' (James & Nobes 2000:17). However, where this relates to all personal circumstances affecting the individual, the tax modification is sufficiently small, in so far as it maintains many of the principles of the existing system, so as to have little impact on this.

The incidence of taxation may be significant in understanding the role for ecological taxation in that the incidence of the majority of taxes are shared with several parties. This is likely to have implications for the ability of a tax to impact on an individuals' behaviour and actions and may reduce an individual tax's effectiveness in achieving specific environmental aims. Kay & King (1991) argued that the effectiveness of a tax could be improved if it was more discriminatory, for example, being imposed on a single manufacturer or in this case a single individual. In such circumstances the manufacturer may shift to a less-adversely taxed business or in this case a less-adversely treated form of transport (for example, diesel or hybrid car) and thereby demonstrate the opportunity for taxation reform to modify individuals' behaviour and actions, where alternatives exist to the rising costs of continuing with the actions.

Underlying Theory

The conceptual framework for this study lies in the connection between the necessity to preserve natural capital and the efficacy of an ecological taxation to contribute towards preservation of it. Such taxation could either discourage its consumption and pollution and/or use the additional tax revenue raised directly from polluters to offer the possibility of repair or clean-up. The primary theoretical contribution of this research was the consideration and development of concepts and methodologies for the internalisation of environmental costs into accounting and pricing mechanisms, and to study and identify characteristics which contribute to the efficacy of the same specifically through the use of taxation to achieve a specific environmental objective – the reduction of CO_2 emission.

Economic theory is pertinent to the study in so far as the modifications to the arrangements for company car taxation, which could be considered an ecological tax reform, provided an opportunity to study the price sensitivity of a category of mandatory car users and the effect such price sensitivity has on company car drivers' intentions for car procurement decisions and distance travelled. Both of these factors have consequences for the level of pollution generally and CO_2 emissions in particular. The research study demonstrated the price sensitivity of individuals to taxation linked to carbon emissions. The results demonstrated that the modification of an existing taxation affecting an existing group of taxpayers is capable of achieving reductions in carbon emissions consistent with the objectives. This contributes to a more comprehensive understanding of the role that resource pricing can take for specific forms of (non-substitutable) natural capital by internalising, through the application of ecological tax reform, previously disregarded externalities.

The conceptual model diagram in Figure 60 introduces the significant components identified from the study. These may be combined and are, potentially, applicable generally to develop similar taxes which could contribute to environmental aims in general (through lower consumption of fossil fuels and the resulting lower emissions). This is discussed in the context of a company car, but the model is also discussed with respect to a hypothetical property tax (to replace council tax) to illustrate the broader applicability of the model.

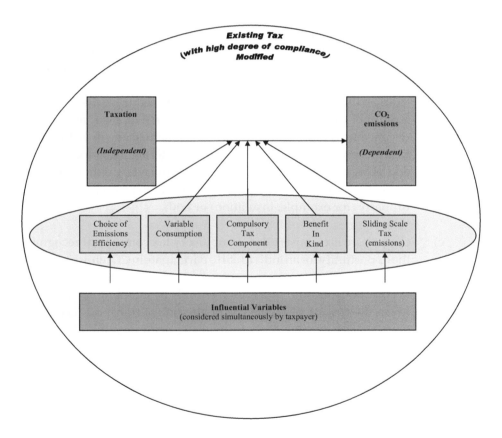

Figure 60   Conceptual model diagram for taxes which contribute to environmental aims in general and emission obligations in particular

The diagram highlights taxation as an independent variable and CO_2 emissions as a dependent variable, the level of emissions dependent on the severity of the ecological taxation, this is subject to the following influential variables:

a)   *Choice of emissions efficiency:* The taxpayer may influence the amount of taxation payable by choice of emissions efficiency. Greater emissions efficiency would lead to lower taxes and lower CO_2 emissions. In the case of company cars this would represent the g/km CO_2 emissions. In the case of a property tax this could represent (say) the g/m² CO_2 emissions for a house, or an energy rating band for the property to indicate the general level of energy efficiency.

b)   *Variable consumption:* The choice of emissions efficiency will influence the rate of consumption of fossil fuel, but this is dependent, in the case of a car, on the distance travelled to determine the overall fuel consumed; or in the case of a property, the amount of heat and power consumed. Taxation on the fossil fuel permits the taxpayer to affect the amount of taxation payable by reducing the amount of fossil fuel consumption either by, in the case of a car, altering the distance travelled or choice of emissions efficiency or both. In the case of a property, this would represent altering the amount of heat and power consumed, which could be reduced by either acquiring a smaller property or additional energy saving measures within a property (for example, insulation) or both.

c)   *Compulsory tax component:* A compulsory tax component recognises the opportunity for an individual to participate in CO_2 emissions from a particular decision to procure a car (or property). A compulsory tax component could be avoided entirely by avoiding procurement by, in the case of a car, the use of alternative transport. Ecological taxes replace existing taxes for revenue neutrality and also to rely on an existing regulatory environment for enforcement.

In so doing, when the original tax is withdrawn and replaced by an ecological tax, the consequence of continuing the status quo of environmental impact should be an increase in taxation, in order that individuals reconsider their environmental obligations to mitigate any rise in taxation.

d)   *Benefit in Kind (BIK):* The principle of BIK permits a 'benefit' to be valued and this notional value added to the taxpayer's income for tax to be paid according to the prevailing rate for an individual in a progressive income tax system. Polluting the environment cannot be considered a benefit, but the principle of BIK provides an appropriate mechanism for the inclusion of the quantified (and taxed) effects of the polluting activity into an individual's personal tax position in a progressive taxation system.

e)   *Sliding scale tax*: It is recognised that certain activities will inevitably cause some environmental damage, but are difficult to avoid completely. However, other activities cause excessive environmental damage for little or no appreciable benefit, for example the use of very high-emission Sports Utility Vehicles (SUVs) as regular transport. Sliding scale taxation may be very punitive indeed for ultra-high emissions and minimally penalising for ultra-low emissions, for example hybrid cars to encourage the latter. Property may also be evaluated according to occupancy and size (m²).

The taxpayer should consider all of these influential variables simultaneously to facilitate a personal tax level that the individual is prepared to bear. Each influential variable may be adjusted independently or simultaneously to achieve a tolerable taxation level alongside a desired emissions pathway. Government should ensure that the overall emissions pathway is consistent with emissions targets set and that taxation revenue required for public spending is attainable.

Conclusion

This chapter provided further scrutiny of the results of the research in the form of a discussion and critical review of the significance of the findings from the study with due regard to the literature considered in Chapter 2 and the theoretical underpinning introduced in Chapter 1. The change in the taxation regime is likely to act as an incentive to choose lower CO_2 emission vehicles than an individual is currently driving. The possibility of fuel substitution exists. There was a significant switch from petrol cars to diesel cars resulting in an overall reduction for CO_2 emission. The findings reached analogous conclusions to studies carried out by the SMMT and the Inland Revenue, although neither used a similar methodology to this study. The estimated CO_2 reductions arising from this taxation change are consistent with the Government's anticipated reductions arising from this reform.

It was demonstrated that the taxation reform overall works in principle, as a mechanism to generate revenue, with a high degree of compliance and to discourage CO_2 emission, through the selection of low-emission vehicles. The opportunities for non-compliance with the tax were considered minimal.

The withdrawal of BIK reductions for the mileage threshold did result in an increase in tax revenue, based upon existing company car. The financial penalty of this change in taxation is not entirely mitigated by intended car choice but is approximately halved. This, coupled with the abolition of business mileage as a factor in determining the BIK tax, has resulted in significant tax rises for many 'high'-mileage company car drivers. The taxation change where a previous incentive is withdrawn does not have a significant effect on company car drivers' polluting behaviour from business mileage, where the majority of individuals are not in control of the decision to travel (pollute).

The distributional effects of such a change in the taxation regime are unlikely to be strongly adverse. The inelasticity of business miles travelled and the actuality that all company car drivers are employed and their earnings are sufficiently high to pay taxation indicates that the opportunity to raise taxation generally or specifically to contribute to environmental repair from this tax modification is good.

A tax predicated upon inelastic activities may still make a contribution to reducing emissions overall, even though for the particular tax in question the contribution is not significant. Individuals may look at total or overall taxation burden within a category, as long as the policies appear to be related (for example, company car taxation relating to mileage and CO_2 emissions are still both related to the company car driver). This permits the inelasticity of business mileage coupled with a less favourable tax treatment than was previously available for the same, to impact on car make and model selection with respect to g/km CO_2 emissions. This is in an attempt to mitigate overall increases in taxation to compensate for the loss of the formerly more generous taxation treatment for this category of company car driver.

Ecological taxes would be best introduced to modify an existing tax (with a high degree of compliance). The rate of taxation should be sufficiently punitive to have an impact on the level of CO_2 emissions. The rate of taxation should comprise a compulsory tax component, a sliding scale of tax for emissions, and permit the amount of consumption and level of emissions efficiency to impact on the amount of tax paid using the principles of BIK.

6

Working Towards a Low-Carbon Society

This book has deliberately adopted a more pragmatic approach (as opposed to a mainly philosophical approach) to the study of the efficacy of emissions-related taxation regimes and the reform of the UK company car taxation regime provided an opportunity for such a study. In adopting a more pragmatic paradigm for the research, it is acknowledged that some of the conclusions and recommendations could be considered sub-optimal as they emphasise piecemeal reforms as opposed to tackling the underlying problems arising from the conceptual framework underpinning a less than perfect economic model. However, piecemeal reforms still offer the opportunity for significant improvement and, given the immediacy of the timescales, it is recognised that action must be taken to curb the excess of our polluting behaviour sooner rather than later.

This chapter provides recommendations arising from the findings from the study with due regard to the literature considered in Chapter 2 and the theoretical underpinning introduced in Chapter 1, in order to conclude the study within an appropriate academic framework and also make recommendations pertinent to the research carried out. The chapter also provides an opportunity to give emphasis to the significant matters emerging from the book.

Contribution of the Research

This research, through its concern with matters affecting the environment, attempted to address issues of sustainability, at least in part, by contributing to a more comprehensive understanding of ecological fiscal reform in the pursuit of a credible taxation model which may exist within the current economic framework. The research, in considering the efficacy of emissions-related motor taxation, provides an opportunity to contribute to a more comprehensive understanding of whether such changes to a principle and method in the UK taxation regime is likely to: firstly, contribute to lowering Carbon Dioxide (CO_2) emissions and secondly, be potentially applicable generally for ecological taxation.

The research problem was concerned with the consideration of concepts and methodologies, for the internalisation of environmental costs into accounting and pricing mechanisms, in an attempt to reduce environmental damage. The taxation reform studied would permit internalisation of some (but not all) previously unaccounted costs, in that previously ignored costs which can be quantified may be represented and imputed by the level of taxation imposed on a particular polluting activity. This reform may also provide incentive to pollute less because of price elasticity for tax rises, which in turn offers the opportunity of hypothecation of tax revenues to repair environmental damage. Accordingly, the concepts and theories underpinning the study were identified in an attempt to explain the current situation and to provide an opportunity for further conceptualising of theory once conclusions were drawn from the study. Moreover, the strategies and characteristics of ecological taxation were reviewed. In particular, those aspects that may contribute to its efficacy and may also contribute to the development of a framework for ecological taxation relating to emissions were considered.

In pursuit of the objectives, the research has discussed scientific, economic, public policy and behavioural matters that must underpin any strategy for environmental improvement. The scientific matters relate to the validation as to the causes for environmental concern, the effects of the same together with CO_2 and other pollution abatement strategies. Such matters were discussed in Chapter 1. The economic issues relate to the contemplation of the possibilities for quantification and inclusion of the negative environmental effects of Greenhouse Gases (GHGs). The theory relating to externalities is also pertinent here as it may contribute to an approach which offers some significant environmental improvement, or pollution curtailment, albeit disaggregated or piecemeal. Such an approach must be within the context of the existing economic framework (that is, the status quo). These matters were introduced in Chapter 1 and further discussed in the literature review in Chapter 2. The public policy matters relate largely to issues and implications of implementation of fiscal policy in the form of taxation arising from the desire to recognise and reduce or eliminate externalities, in pursuit of both a more efficient allocation of resources, from an economic point of view, and a more sustainable position from an environmental perspective. Such matters were discussed as part of the literature review in Chapter 2 and further contemplated with the results of the study carried out in Chapters 4 and 5. The behavioural matters relate to how the implementation of a tax with an environmental emphasis could change an individual's decision behaviour, even if existing behaviour demonstrates an emotional, rather than rational response. The results of the study in Chapter 4 and the discussion of the same in Chapter 5 permit conclusions to be drawn concerning this matter.

Limitations of the Research

The research was carried out through the use of hypothesis testing on quantitative (survey) data. Such tests appraised whether perceived environmental benefits of lower CO_2 emissions were achievable through lesser business mileage or lower car CO_2 emission choice, or a combination of both as a result of a specific taxation reform affecting company car drivers.

The analysis yielded results which were not inconsistent with other sources, notably the Inland Revenue (2004) and the SMMT (2005). However, no specific prior research of the type carried out could be identified to corroborate the principal findings. The research was not a longitudinal study. The opinions expressed by respondents may only have been valid at the time of measurement and may have subsequently changed post-implementation. The use of questionnaires provided a sufficient sample size of data for analysis. However, there was no opportunity to supplement questions later, once the responses received had been considered. This did not provide the author with the opportunity to investigate issues in greater depth, perhaps from interview, which may have been valuable in determining the likelihood of expressed intentions changing over time. The research was not carried out in an experimental environment, but in a real-world setting. Responses may have been affected by external influences not known to the researcher. Such influences could distort the research, but it may also be argued that the inclusion of such influences make the outcomes more meaningful.

Despite assurances offered in Chapter 4, it cannot be confirmed with complete certainty that the sample data is representative of the population as a whole. This is inherent of a random sampling approach of the type undertaken for this study. The predictive capacity of sample data may be limited. Accordingly, the use of such data for extrapolation to reach conclusions concerning CO_2 emissions for all company car drivers may not be appropriate. However, despite these misgivings where such analysis was carried out, it was shown to be broadly consistent with data from other bodies. Notwithstanding the adequacy of the sample sizes and the robustness of the methods applied, it may be worthwhile carrying out further replication studies to confirm the findings of this research. Such studies would now be carried out post-implementation and it may also be useful to examine the differences between actual choices and intended choices. Given the heightened environmental awareness since the study was carried out, it may be worthwhile to observe the changes in behaviour arising from this, which was not possible at the time of the original survey.

It is possible that some significant variables were excluded from the research. For example, any consideration of price elasticity may be influenced by levels of income. The survey instrument deliberately omitted questions relating to income, due to the reluctance of many to provide such details and the unreliability of the data obtained for this in the pilot study. This was as a consequence of a reluctance to answer such questions honestly and partially due to bonus/commission structures for sales staff in particular and the difficulty of predicting their annual income. However, it is acknowledged that where such data could be obtained and verified, this may provide an opportunity for further richness of analysis.

Key Findings

Ecological taxation in the form of a CO_2 emission tax was broadly supported by company car drivers, despite advantageous 'high-mileage' thresholds being abolished, but with a caveat that choice should be available in the form of low-emission cars to mitigate any increase in company car taxation for individuals. The research did not reveal widespread opposition to the changes in taxation affecting company car drivers, despite the taxation becoming progressively greater in the early years of operation. The taxation reform works in principle as a mechanism to generate revenue. The environment is highly regulatory and relies on existing tried and tested systems and procedures. There is little opportunity for non-compliance. The reform is not considered to be regressive.

The taxation reform may yield a CO_2 emission reduction that is consistent with the Government's anticipated reductions of between 0.5mtc to 1.0mtc. The implementation of this tax will make a contribution towards achieving the Kyoto Target for CO_2 emission reduction in line with the Government's expectations.

The role that Benefit in Kind (BIK) plays in the personal taxation system is acknowledged. BIK provides a quantifiable basis that may be used for evaluating an individual's responsibility for carbon emission. BIK is also linked to a sliding scale within the overall system of personal taxation which reflects an individual's ability to pay. It provides some assurance of equity in terms of the ability to pay and is consistent with a system of progressive taxation. The distributional effects of the tax reform are unlikely to be strongly adverse and are more palatable than increasing fuel prices.

There is heightened awareness generally of the potential damage that CO_2 emission may have on the environment in general and climate in particular. Notwithstanding this, the majority of company car drivers were unlikely to make any attempt to reduce CO_2 emissions without ecological tax reform.

The underlying theoretical propositions relating to price elasticity arising from economic theory combined with the analysis carried out would suggest that company car drivers are price sensitive (price elasticity) to environmental taxation, of the type they are now subjected to, in so far as they can mitigate their behaviour, to minimise individual personal taxation. A more punitive rate of taxation would yield greater reductions in CO_2 emissions brought about by the selection of lower-emission cars.

The research revealed that the change in taxation would not have a significant effect on the levels of CO_2 produced from the number of business miles travelled. Most business miles covered were mandatory and cannot be reduced by an individual. This proved to be the case despite the previous incentive to travel more miles than perhaps necessary being withdrawn.

A tax predicated upon inelastic business mileage may still make a contribution to reducing emissions overall, even though for the specific part of the tax in question, the contribution is not significant. If the policies appear to be related (for example, company car taxation relating to mileage and CO_2 emissions are still both related to the company car driver) this permits the inelasticity of business mileage coupled with a less favourable tax treatment than was previously available for the same, to impact on make and model selection with respect to g/km CO_2 emissions. This is in an attempt to mitigate overall increases in taxation to compensate for the loss of the formerly more generous taxation treatment for this category of company car driver.

An increase in taxation for one component part of the taxation does have implications for abatement costs for another component part. This was borne out by formerly non-'high' business mileage drivers expressing an intention to select cars with on average an emission reduction of less than half of that for 'high-mileage' drivers.

Most company car drivers do have some choice in the selection of their next company car. The change in taxation does have a significant effect on the levels of CO_2 produced from the selection of next company car. Material CO_2 reductions were achieved through greater fuel efficiency, some of which could be attributed to ongoing technological development, some as a consequence of the downsizing of engine size, but the greatest reductions were obtained because of fuel substitution, with petrol engines substituted for diesel engines. The latter offers greater fuel efficiency and lower CO_2 emissions. Such a substitution to an alternative fossil fuel may not be entirely desirable (particularly as they both arise from crude oil). Those individuals who were likely to suffer the greatest increase in financial penalty arising from the taxation change chose the lowest CO_2 emission cars, in particular diesel cars.

It is acknowledged that the selection of a company car may be made on the basis of both behavioural and economic factors which are likely to influence individuals differently. However, the findings did reveal that greater emphasis is given to economic considerations as the tax rate rises. Equally, should the rate of taxation fall, economic considerations are less significant. Instead, behavioural considerations become more prominent with the latter possibly at the expense of higher emissions. These findings suggest that ecological taxation (or some similar method of imputing costs) is necessary to modify individuals' decision behaviour to achieve environmental aims.

Despite attempts to alleviate tax increases by individuals through intended car choice, the financial penalty was not entirely mitigated, but on average approximately halved. The taxation burden has, on average, increased for individuals.

The change in taxation arrangements has not acted as a catalyst for demand for alternative technology vehicles. The greatest change has been from petrol to equivalent diesel models. Greater incentives, both social and economic, are needed to encourage alternative technology vehicles such as hybrid (petrol/ electric) coupled with a maturity of low-emission technologies to result in lower asset lifecycle costs.

Contribution to Theoretical Development

The difficulty in developing a theoretical framework for the recognition and valuation of externalities, particularly with regard to the environment, is acknowledged. However, quantification and monetisation of emissions is paramount to be recognised alongside economic activity. It is only then can such an activity be internalised into accounting and pricing mechanisms. Such internalisation would permit ecological recognition throughout a value chain and would heighten awareness of environmental matters amongst corporate and private decision makers. The market would then be able to give proper status to environmental matters. The internalisation of an activity's effect on the environment is central to sustainable accountability for business and private citizens.

It is not contested that the pursuit of the 'holy grail' of 'true cost' is unrealistic. However, it is feasible to recognise costs and benefits that may be determined through research along the way and to consider where optimal environmental policy, a balance between the costs of pollution and the costs of controlling this may lie. Pollution should be curbed to this point.

Such evaluation of marginal damage costs versus Marginal Abatement Costs (MAC) is likely to prove valuable in providing some broad economic indication of the direction that taxation and fiscal policy should be heading in to achieve environmental objectives.

Tax reforms arising from such analysis must be predicated upon the four canons of taxation. Changes should be 'imposed gradually and with long term prior anticipation' (Ekins 1994:577) together with a caveat that such taxes permit individuals to mitigate taxation and that such taxes are progressive in nature. The latter may result in some juxtaposition in taxation setting and result in sub-optimal tax policy. Such a policy may allow individual taxpayers through their actions to place too much emphasis on abatement or repair.

The reclassification of taxation is necessary to move from existing traditional headings of (say) corporation tax, income tax, council tax and so on, to being more interspersed within activities that cause or promote environmental damage as costs that (through the use of taxation) may be internalised into many more activities, but at a level to simultaneously broadly achieve revenue neutrality and emissions reduction targets. Such a reclassification would require further evaluation, in all but the most carbon-intensive environments, where significant carbon emission reductions and fuel substitution may not be possible, to confirm that a revenue-neutral taxation reform is unlikely to undermine competitiveness or result in a level of taxation which may be prohibitive to conform with.

The key findings of the research, coupled with existing theory, has led to the development of a conceptual model (framework) which may be of use when considering the extension of ecological taxes to other areas of the economy, where the dual benefits of lower environmental damage and availability of revenue for hypothecation to clean-up costs are desirable. The model is generalisable in that marginal damage costs and MACs may not be the same for all circumstances considered.

The research undertaken demonstrates that CO_2 emissions may be influenced by the level of taxation confirming the economic price elasticity where choice may be exercised according to economic and social influences and inelasticity where an activity is mandatory. The model illustrated in Figure 60 in the previous chapter recognises this and suggests that there are a number of influential variables which will impact on the efficacy of the tax to reduce emissions as follows:

- choice of emissions efficiency;

- variable consumption;

- compulsory tax component;

- BIK; and

- sliding scale tax (emissions).

The significance of the model is that it provides the individual a similar opportunity usually only afforded to organisations, in that there are opportunities to consider both economic and social factors and mitigate the amount of taxation according to the environmental significance of the activity under consideration. This, coupled with a progressive system of taxation with varying rates of taxation according to an individual's ability to pay, provides an opportunity for some of the characteristics identified in the reforms of company car taxation to reduce CO_2 emissions, to be generalised elsewhere.

Generalised Implications of the Research

GOVERNMENT

The UK Government have proposed a long-term target of reducing CO_2 emissions by 60% by 2050 (DTI 2003). Moreover, there are specific environmental obligations arising from international agreements, which will have to be translated into short- and medium-term objectives. Such objectives must result in plans and strategies which will deliver CO_2 reductions consistent with these obligations. A change in the taxation regime for company car drivers is likely to deliver CO_2 reductions from company car drivers of the magnitude anticipated by such a change. For this reason, Government would consider this change effective. However, a caveat should be added that since the taxation reforms have been introduced, there has been a decrease of approximately 250,000 company cars up to 2003 (Inland Revenue 2004). This decrease in company cars may be because of the increasing popularity of employees opting out of company car schemes as a consequence of the increasingly punitive company car taxation regime, instead preferring cash alternatives to use towards personal contract leasing. This may result in cars chosen with higher emissions as individuals will not be penalised personally by the sliding scale tax increases in the reforms, nor the cost of fuel which would be borne by the employer for business mileage. The increasing switch to Personal Contract Purchase (PCP) together with other cash incentives towards travel make it problematic to reach firm conclusions as to the precise extent of CO_2 reductions delivered by the reforms. Moreover, if the trend of such cash alternatives continues, this may undermine the whole system of company car taxation.

Notwithstanding these observations, consideration should be given to extending this type of reform to other areas where CO_2 emissions reductions are also feasible. Those areas producing the highest carbon emissions, where there is an existing taxation regulatory environment and a high degree of compliance, should be considered first for reform as they have the potential to produce the greatest reductions in emissions for minimal cost and also maximum environmental benefit. It is for these reasons that property tax reform should be given priority.

Details of the outcomes of such reforms should be studied and disseminated. The application of a conceptual model of the type discussed briefly in this chapter and introduced in Chapter 5 for other areas of the economy may also prove effective in reducing CO_2 emissions elsewhere.

ORGANISATIONS

The removal of the previously advantageous 'high-mileage' thresholds did not significantly reduce business mileage, providing no cost savings to organisations. The compliance costs of the new tax are also not dissimilar to the old system. The taxation reform provides no incentive for companies to assist employees to reduce business mileage, through job evaluation, improvements in logistics and so on. Raising fuel prices would provide such an incentive, but has far-reaching distributional effects for the whole economy, affecting low-income groups disproportionately.

The increase in taxation suffered by 'high-mileage' drivers despite attempts to mitigate this through choice of a lower-emission car, may ultimately result in higher salary costs as employees attempt to recoup some of this cost in annual salary negotiations.

INDIVIDUALS

Company car drivers are prepared to take steps to mitigate their tax burden. Intended choice is influenced by a number of factors including: availability of choice of car, CO_2 emissions of the car, rate of taxation for the individual from both a CO_2 g/km and personal taxation point of view, functionality of the car and a status and emotional dimension in the choice.

The increasing rates of tax arising from the reducing baseline emission (from 15% to 35% per 5g/km) of CO_2 for the first three years of this tax reform result in more punitive taxation rates for the future. This increase in taxation is foreseeable and provides some prior anticipation for individuals when making a future car choice.

The motives for tax rises are often treated with some scepticism by individuals. Individuals may expect a reduction in taxation elsewhere, or some tangible environmental benefits, possibly through tax hypothecation, for further tax rises to be acceptable. Without this, tax rises are likely to prove politically unpalatable. Notwithstanding that, if similar ecological taxes are introduced using a framework similar to that discussed in the previous chapter, individuals are likely to consider environmental issues more central to their decision behaviour, irrespective of whether they have environmental concerns.

Non-company car drivers purchasing used cars will, in the future, benefit from an increase in supply of low-emission ex-company cars also. Given that approximately 50% of new cars are company cars, these cars will ultimately form a significant part of the used car stock.

FLEET MANAGERS

A fleet manager's primary objective is to provide the lowest-cost fleet of company cars that is fit for purpose. In determining the overall asset lifecycle costs of a car, the following factors are taken into account: purchase cost, repairs and maintenance costs, fuel consumption, insurance, Vehicle Excise Duty (VED) costs and, finally, the estimated residual value at the end of the asset life. Secondary considerations would include preferences of individual company car drivers, but this is only likely to be of overriding importance where recruitment incentives are an issue.

Low-emission vehicles provide for greater fuel economy and are likely to be more desirable in the second-hand car market at the end of the asset life, boosting the residual values for such cars and thus reducing asset lifecycle costs for fleet managers.

Currently, the reforms penalise company car drivers only, as opposed to employers for the selection of high CO_2 emission vehicles. However, company car drivers are only able to choose a company car from the available selection and for some the choice is limited. The discussion earlier concerning increasing rates of tax from 15% to 35% of list price per 5g/km increase of CO_2 for the first three years of this tax reform are also relevant here. This foreseeable tax increase, coupled with the recognition that high CO_2 emission cars will prove to be more expensive for employees year on year, is likely to place increasing pressure on fleet managers to make available low-emission cars for employees to choose, including the possibility of innovative alternative technology cars.

The taxation change has served to focus attention on CO_2 emissions from cars and provides companies an opportunity to consider their Corporate Social Responsibilities (CSR) with respect to the company car, either proactively or reactively. This could influence fleet managers to offer a greater choice of low-emission cars and in turn provide organisations an opportunity to disclose the same as part of its annual report.

MANUFACTURERS

The research study revealed that company car drivers were likely to select lower-emission cars in response to the tax reform. Given that approximately 50% of new cars are company cars, the demand for low-emission vehicles from employees, via fleet managers, is likely to intensify competition between manufacturers to provide such cars. The voluntary agreements reached with manufacturers for lowering CO_2 emissions, together with an anticipation that increasing rates of tax from 15% to 35% of list price per 5 g/km increase of CO_2 for the first three years of this tax reform may continue, is likely to provide an increased emphasis for manufacturers to innovate to employ cleaner and more efficient technologies to achieve lower emissions. There is evidence of this already taking place. Engines are becoming more efficient, through superior and more prudent mapping of Electronic Control Units (ECUs). Alternative/dual fuel (bio fuel) engines are increasingly available. Alternative technologies, incorporating regenerative braking, are becoming more widespread. Hydrogen and hydrogen cell-powered cars are being developed, although this technology will require additional infrastructure. Manufacturers are also incorporating alternative materials such as aluminium and carbon fibre as a part of vehicle construction in an attempt to reduce vehicle weight, which has an impact on CO_2 emission. The use of 'stop-start' technology is also increasing in an attempt to improve overall efficiency.

A positive trend is that the car manufacturers are also promoting explicit disclosure of CO_2 emission of a vehicle as part of any marketing campaign, targeting company car drivers in particular, but in the process creating heightened awareness for all prospective car buyers.

Manufacturers providing lower-emission cars may also capitalise on this from a CSR perspective as it provides a valuable disclosure opportunity for the companies to demonstrate active engagement with their social responsibilities.

Conclusions and Recommendations

Specific ecological tax reforms can contribute to CO_2 emissions targets whilst maintaining revenue neutrality. Ecological taxes, when appropriately targeted, are effective for reducing carbon emissions. Such taxes may also demonstrate efficiency in that reductions are attainable using existing fiscal infrastructure. It is important to consider elasticity and the distributional effects of tax changes, particularly with respect to low-income groups. Innovative application of the principles of BIK could serve to heighten interest in such reforms whilst simultaneously preventing strongly adverse outcomes. The use of a compulsory tax component, coupled with a sliding scale for CO_2 emissions using bands, appears to demonstrate efficacy. Ecological taxation has the potential to provide consistency in revenue-raising capability and may substitute for existing taxes, for example taxes on labour and profits. The internalisation of previously disregarded externalities also becomes feasible through the use of taxation. Costs and prices may be realigned using taxation without the need for a paradigm shift in our economic model. International taxation reforms offer the opportunity to act as a catalyst for low-carbon technologies worldwide, rather than merely encourage geographical substitutions with respect to carbon.

In the course of this book, a number of matters that are worthy of note have emerged, some of which lead to the recommendations made. These arose from the literature, some from the analysis of the data, which were considered alongside existing theory and also other matters which could be considered as reflections on the research based upon an enhanced understanding of the subject.

GENERAL RECOMMENDATIONS

- Ecological taxation reform for CO_2 emissions should be considered to modify tax policy for society. The absence of an agreed conceptual framework for ecological taxation does not preclude its implementation. Such modifications would be piecemeal, gradual and incremental, as piecemeal reform is more likely to be carried through. However, it is acknowledged that such an approach to this problem is unlikely to eliminate CO_2 emissions externalities for the environment.

- There must be long-term prior anticipation of such reforms, together with a clear and unambiguous rationale as to why such reforms are essential for sustainability. This is paramount to persuade those of the need for taxation reform and this requires a strategic planning approach.

- Taxation reform should be punitive for those that make no reductions in their levels of emissions, but also provide individuals and organisations the opportunity to mitigate some part of the taxation, using sliding scales, in return for polluting less. The taxation should also be progressive, utilising differing rates of taxation for total income.

- The opportunity to lower labour taxes should be taken as ecological taxation is given greater emphasis. On the whole, such reforms should be revenue-neutral to begin to encourage acceptance, however, heavy polluters and also those who make no change in their levels of pollution should be penalised with net increases in taxation to discourage such activities.

- The absence of a widely accepted theoretical framework, for sustainability, places greater burden on existing frameworks and mechanisms and the need to modify these to achieve the desired environmental objectives. The modification of the economic 'status quo' will inevitably result in some realignment of costs and prices.

- The role that the principle behind BIK within the personal taxation system can play in such reforms, as a mechanism to charge to tax an amount different to that present in costing and pricing systems should be evaluated. The use of BIK in this way provides an opportunity for costs and prices to be weighted according to environmental significance and provides a buffer between the monetisation and internalisation of an adverse environmental activity and the ability to pay according to the prevailing tax rate for the individual, which of course is affected by total earnings. Unlike direct taxation, the utilisation of the principle of BIK would allow all to pay taxation according to environmental damage, but the amount paid influenced by the ability to pay, based upon total earnings and the prevailing tax rate for the same. This goes some way towards satisfying the Pearce et al. (1989) requirement of monetising the environmental implications of economic activity, classified by Bebbington et al. (2001) as 'full privatisation approach' and may also provide a catalyst for individuals and organisations to take more interest in their own taxation matters.

- An ecological taxation regime may provide opportunities for individuals and organisations to evaluate their individual taxation position, with the opportunity to mitigate tax increases through reductions in environmental impact. This would require a programme of education for taxation reforms, public information for environmental matters and prominence for the consequences of certain types of polluting behaviour. This is consistent with the classification by Bebbington et al. (2001) of 'the democratic/ accountability approach'.

- A proportion of tax revenue from ecological taxes should be hypothecated towards environmental clean-up and environmental education. That proportion should be at least equivalent to any net increase in taxation revenue arising from the reform.

- Greater emphasis should be given to environmental matters, simultaneously to taxation reforms, particularly CO_2 emissions, by way of an explanation of the problems and the consequences so as to influence those who make economic choices (arguably more rational choices) and those who make emotional choices (arguably less rational choices) into a decision which provides the least environmental harm.

- Organisations should be required to disclose more environmental information, in particular the quantification of the effects of actions. This would require consistency in reporting arising from conceptual theory development for the quantification of negative environmental effects to provide the basis for quantification and standard methods for disclosure. Such theory should take into account that taxation on goods and services permits the internalisation of environmental costs into accounting and pricing mechanisms and this component can be identified as part of the accounting and reporting process (in the same way as Value Added Tax (VAT) is identified).

- The contribution that any new ecological tax makes toward achieving a specific environmental objective should be measured. The efficacy of such a particular taxation revision should be periodically evaluated along with fuel substitution opportunities and the effects of the same. Such evaluation should be published and disseminated as widely as possible.

- An ecological taxation framework should form the basis for a common tax approach for all Kyoto parties and is a rational step in developing the treaty beyond obligations with targets, towards a common tax policy.

SPECIFIC RECOMMENDATIONS

The problem of carbon emissions from cars must be addressed from both a supply side (manufacturers) and a demand side (customers) to provide maximum opportunity for CO_2 emission reduction. However, it is acknowledged that the catalyst for this is likely to arise from the demand side with the reforms to company car taxation and increases in both VED and fuel prices.

- The possibility to influence demand primarily through taxation is acknowledged and the following specific recommendations are made.

- The removal of previously advantageous high-mileage thresholds did not have any significant effect on business mileage travelled, as it was considered that business mileage was mandatory. Notwithstanding the possibility of raising fuel prices, which would affect all stakeholders in society, consideration should be given to other measures to increase the cost per mile, such as the introduction of a road pricing scheme for employers of company car drivers based upon distance. This would encourage employers to place additional emphasis on reducing business mileage. This would prove beneficial from both an emissions and congestion point of view.

- The reduction in the qualifying level of CO_2 emissions designed to reflect the anticipated improvements in the fuel efficiency of new cars should be continued to be increased for the foreseeable future. The rates of tax from 15% to 35% per 5g/km increase of CO_2 should be continued, in order that the punitive increases in tax continue to influence company car choice in the manner demonstrated in the study, rather than the ecological benefits from this reform being a one-off for the early years of implementation. Further ultra-low emission bands below the 10% band introduced in 2008/09 should also be considered.

- The highest rate of taxation should be increased from 35% of list price to 50% of list price in 1% intervals for each increase of 5g/km CO_2 emission beyond the current maximum of 235g/km (2008/09–2011/12) to reflect the very high levels of emissions produced by some cars. The 3% diesel supplement should apply for all levels of emission and not be capped at the highest level for petrol. Such measures will provide a degree of 'equity' (Smith 1776) between all polluters. This would overcome the situation (from the sample data) where a company car driver with a car emitting 245g/km will suffer an increase in taxation of 4% of list price over the first three years of the reform, whereas a company car driver with a higher-emission car of (say) 265g/km will suffer no increase year on year.

- The use of grants or enhanced capital allowances for organisations should be considered for ultra-low emission cars as none of these cars featured in the sample data (pre- or post-taxation reform) indicating some reluctance on the part of companies to offer such cars.

- Car manufacturers should be encouraged, by the extension of voluntary agreements for lowering car CO_2 emission, discussed in Chapter 1, to produce even lower-emission cars which are desired by consumers. In this way, any economic incentive, via ecological taxation to acquire a low-emission car which was demonstrated in the study, is supplemented by an emotional desire to procure, because of other features or desirable factors.

OTHER RECOMMENDATIONS

The other recommendations which could be considered as reflections on the research which are worthy of note are as follows:

- To encourage all purchasers to choose lower-emission cars, a similar sliding scale of an increase of 1% in tax for each 5g/km increase in CO_2 emissions (commencing at the same threshold as company car taxation) could also be applied to the purchase price of new cars through (say) VAT for new cars. This would result in higher-emission cars becoming significantly more expensive for individuals and organisations to procure at the outset. This may also be fairer in the sense that it does not increase the tax burden during ownership, but affects the replacement cost.

- To encourage companies to offer low-emission cars to employees, an additional taxation for employers, based upon the company car tax for employees should be considered. Tax increases to employers for such reforms may be mitigated at least in part by reductions to business taxation elsewhere, either through (say) the reduction of corporation tax, or a reduction in employers' National Insurance (NI) contributions. Such reductions would permit companies to achieve a tax revenue-neutral position, provided that lower emissions were achieved, thus not adversely affecting business profitability.

- Graduated VED rates should be increased significantly as g/km CO_2 rises and should not be capped at the current maximum 255g/km (2008/09–2010/11), but should adopt a g/km CO_2 scale consistent with that used for company car taxation to increase the asset lifecycle costs of high-emission cars. These measures will deter fleet managers from offering high-emission vehicles and encourage employers to be more discriminatory in the choice of vehicles they offer in each class, where emissions can vary significantly between similar vehicles in the same class.

- In addition, such an increase in VED would encourage private buyers to choose low-emission cars which in turn will depress used car values for high CO_2 emission cars. An adverse effect on used car values for high-emission cars will have the effect of lowering residual values of such fleet cars, which in turn will result in higher asset lifecycle costs for the fleet manager and hence discouraging the employer from offering such cars. The first year VED rate introduced in 2010/11 applying to new car purchases (reverting to the standard rate in subsequent years) applying each time the car is purchased would act as an additional incentive to private buyers to choose low-emission cars.

- Lower residual values for higher-emission cars are likely to make such used cars a more attractive purchase for lower-income groups. It may therefore be necessary for the first year (higher) VED rate introduced in 2010/11 applying to new car purchases (reverting to the standard rate in subsequent years) to apply each time the car is purchased. In addition, modest rises in fuel prices could also be introduced, to affect such demand. The latter measure would prove unpopular, without tax reductions or increases in incomes elsewhere.

- As part of CSR obligations, organisations should declare the amount of CO_2 emission that has arisen from company cars within the financial statements and provide a five-year summary of the same. Such disclosure could also require the publication of steps taken to compensate for CO_2 emissions arising from this category (for example, carbon offset measures such as tree planting).

Further Research

The research study undertaken has also served to identify further research which may be worth undertaking to provide a better understanding of the problem domain in general. In particular there is some merit in repeating the survey, post-taxation reform implementation. New cars today offer lower CO_2 emissions than those available at the time of the original survey. It would be valuable to research the effects of such cars on overall emissions together with the preferences expressed by company car drivers for higher or lower CO_2 emission company cars post-taxation reforms to determine whether actual decisions were similar to expressed preferences at the time of the survey.

Company car choice exercised by individuals may only be made within the available choices offered by fleet managers. Fleet management is fundamental to the levels of emissions of CO_2 by company car drivers. Research into the types of cars offered by fleet managers, the levels of CO_2 from the same and the rationale for selecting certain makes and models of car may yield some interesting findings which would complement the study discussed in this book.

The recommendations with respect to VED for higher-polluting cars could also be evaluated, in terms of attitudes of individuals (private buyers) and fleet managers. The effect of such a change on residual values could also be reviewed.

Finally, the frameworks introduced in this book could be useful to appraise ecological taxes as they are introduced in the future to consider the efficacy of these taxes also.

Concluding Remarks

The purpose of this book is to permit discourse of many of the theoretical matters associated with ecological taxation, within the existing economic model, whilst pragmatically examining a specific tax reform with some ecological basis. This in turn would provide conclusions and recommendations that would be consistent with theoretical conjecture and could be comprehended within the existing economic framework in order that it would be feasible for environmental benefits to be harvested.

It is recognised that measuring and quantifying some of the recommendations made in this book may be problematic, because it is always difficult to attribute success or otherwise to a single reform, introduced as part of a package of measures in a world that is constantly changing in any case. Notwithstanding that, the recommendations, underpinned by theory, are consistent with measures that have already yielded positive results, so whilst measurement may prove challenging, the outcome should be consistent with desired intentions of the reforms. However, additional assurance can be offered as general recommendations that are proposed place reliance on literature from peer-reviewed authors, who have made a significant contribution to the debate. It is intended that the study itself adds value to the existing body of knowledge, but moreover, provides context which proves valuable for understanding the implications of reforms. This also permits an opportunity to reiterate, re-emphasise and offer a perspective for a different way forward.

As discussed at the beginning of this chapter and earlier in the book, this is in contrast to an arguably more complete (and philosophical) approach to environmental issues which may require a paradigm shift for the realisation of benefits. It is this pragmatic realisation of the necessity, to a large extent, to work within what already exists, coupled with a desire to make a contribution to the debate and policy that has led the author to pursue a work of this type.

As an accountant, the author understands the paramount importance and the necessity of operating within existing economic frameworks and the requirements for sometimes less than perfect frameworks and standards to do this. In so doing, it is recognised that adjustments and modifications to existing frameworks and standards can yield significant benefits and this may be realised without fundamental changes to the economic status quo, the latter being unachievable in all, but in the very long term.

Through scrutinising the material in this book, it is hoped that the reader will develop a better understanding of the issues surrounding quantification and valuation for environmental matters and how these may be best recognised by society in order to modify unsustainable practices. In so doing, the difficulties of externality recognition, valuation and internalisation of the same should be realised.

The publication of this book is timely, with increasing international concern over carbon emissions and global warming and the measures necessary to combat the adverse consequences of the same through significant emissions reductions. It is hoped that once the book is in circulation it will make a contribution to our understanding of the efficacy of the measures available generally and of taxation in particular, in working towards a low-carbon society.

Appendix:
Questionnaire for Company Car Drivers Affected by the Changes in Taxation Arrangements Commencing April 2002

Aim of the Survey

The aim of this survey is to determine the degree to which forthcoming changes in the taxation arrangements for company cars may influence your future choice of company car and whether these new tax arrangements will encourage individuals to choose cars which cause less pollution to the environment.

Non-response to Questions

If you do not feel able to answer any questions, please leave them blank or insert a comment such as 'N/A' or 'Don't know'. If you wish to make additional comments at any point, please feel free to do so using the space provided.

Feedback

If you would like to receive a copy of the report of the findings based on responses to this questionnaire, please tick this box ☐

Your cooperation in the completion of this questionnaire is appreciated.

David Russell
Department of Accounting & Finance
Postgraduate Business School
De Montfort University
The Gateway
Leicester LE1 9BH
Tel: (0116) 2577217
Fax: (0116) 2506329
Email: drussell@dmu.ac.uk

Questions for company car drivers

Please tick the box that applies or if you are completing this form on-screen, please place a cross in the box.

1. Do you currently drive a company car?

☐ Yes.

☐ No (Please go to question 15).

2. Please state:

Car Make: _____ Model: _____ Engine cc: _____

3. Approximately, how many miles do you currently drive on company business?

_____ miles per annum.

4. Are you aware of the changes to company car taxation affecting individuals that will be implemented in April 2002?

☐ Yes.

☐ No (Please go to question 6).

5. How did you find out about the changes to company car taxation affecting individuals?

☐ Employer.

☐ Media.

☐ Motor car manufacturer.

☐ Other.

From April 2002, company car taxation for individuals will no longer be based solely upon the list price of the car. Instead it will be based upon the percentage of a car's list price graduated according to its CO_2 emissions. Therefore, drivers of cars that produce more grammes of CO_2 per km will pay more company car taxation. Company car taxation will no longer take into account the number of business miles driven.

6. From April 2002, company car taxation will no longer take into account the number of business miles driven. With this knowledge, please estimate your annual business mileage for next year

_____ miles per annum

7. Comparing your estimate of business mileage for next year (question 6) with your estimate of current business mileage (question 3).

☐ My annual business mileage will reduce because there is no longer a tax incentive in driving more miles than necessary.

☐ My annual business mileage will reduce because of other factors affecting my job.

☐ My annual business mileage will increase because of other factors affecting my job.

☐ My annual business mileage will remain approximately the same.

8. To what extent do you have a choice of vehicle, when your current car is due for replacement?

☐ Extensive choice (wide variety of makes/models and engine sizes to choose).

☐ Good choice (variety of make/models, but engine size choice limited).

☐ Some choice (choice of up to 3 make/models, engine size choice limited).

☐ No choice (make and model specified by employer – go to question 12).

9. From April 2002, company car taxation will take into account the amounts of grammes of CO_2 emitted per km. Will this taxation change have an influence on your choice of your next company car?

☐ Yes – I will try to choose a car with a low g/km of CO_2 emission, to reduce my tax burden.

☐ No – I will choose a car based upon other features.

☐ Don't know – I do not fully understand how this change is likely to affect me personally.

10. If the amount of company car taxation were doubled, would such a taxation increase *have an influence on your choice of your next company car?*

☐ Yes – I will try to choose a car with a low g/km of CO_2 emission.

☐ No – I will choose a car based upon other features.

☐ Don't know – I do not fully understand how this change is likely to affect me personally.

11. If the amount of company car taxation were halved, would such a taxation decrease *have an influence on your choice of your next company car?*

☐ Yes – I would consider a car with a higher g/km of CO_2 emission.

☐ Yes – I will try to choose a car with a low g/km of CO_2 emission.

☐ No – I will choose a car based upon other features.

☐ Don't know – I do not fully understand how this change is likely to affect me personally.

12. If you already have a vehicle in mind for your next company car, please give details: (or if you have no choice, please give details of the car specified by your employer)

Car Make: _____ Model: _____ Engine cc: _____

13. Do you think the forthcoming change in company car taxation is a good idea, as it may reduce CO_2 emissions, which contribute to global warming?

☐ Yes.

☐ Yes – Provided that low-emission vehicles are available for me to choose, in order that I may pay less company car taxation.

☐ No.

☐ Don't know.

14. Would you consider a hybrid/electric car with very low/zero CO_2 emissions if such a choice was available to you and the amount of company car taxation payable were lower than you are anticipating paying for the next year: (tick more than one box if appropriate)

☐ Yes – If the taxation burden was lower by 25%.

☐ Yes – If the taxation burden was lower by 50%.

☐ Yes – If the taxation burden was lower by 75%.

☐ No – I would not consider such a car, because the range (distance travelled before recharging/refuelling) of the car is poor compared to conventional vehicles.

☐ No – I would not consider such a car, because the performance of the car is poor compared to conventional vehicles.

☐ No – I would not consider such a car, because (please state) _____.

15. Which of the following measures are likely to reduce the number of miles driven by you per annum? (tick more than one box if appropriate)

	Business Mileage	**Private Mileage**
Increase in company car taxation relating to the number of business miles travelled.	☐	☐
Increase in the cost of car fuel.	☐	☐
Introduction of congestion charging in cities for peak traffic times.	☐	☐
Introduction of road pricing, where a charge is made for the number of miles travelled.	☐	☐

16. Please rank the following features that may be important to you in choosing your next company car.

(1= most important, 9 = least important)

☐ Performance.

☐ Image.

☐ Brand (make/model).

☐ Safety.

☐ CO_2 emissions.

☐ Accessories.

☐ Colour.

☐ Reliability.

☐ Dealer support.

Questions about you

Please provide the following information. This will only be used to enter you into the prize draw, send you a summary of the survey responses if requested, or to contact you in the event of a query about your responses and will *not* be revealed to any third parties.

Name: _____

Address: _____

Tel: _____

Email: _____

Male/Female:

☐ Male.

☐ Female.

Age group

☐ 25 or under.

☐ 26–35.

☐ 36–45.

☐ 46–55.

☐ 56 +.

It is hoped to conduct some follow-up interviews. If you would be willing to participate please tick the box. ☐

Thank you for taking the time to complete this survey. Please return it in the pre-paid envelope provided or via email to: companycarsurvey@fccafcma.freeserve.co.uk

References

Advisory Committee on Business and the Environment (1996) *Sixth Progress Report to and Response from the President of the Board of Trade and Secretary of State for the Environment.* London: Department of Trade and Industry/ Department of the Environment.

Agnolucci, P. and Ekins, P. (2004) *The Announcement Effect and Environmental Taxation* (Working Paper 53). Manchester: Tyndall Centre for Climate Change Research.

Alcamo, J. and Kreileman, E. (1996) 'Emission Scenarios and Global Climate Protection'. *Global Environmental Change* 6(4), pp. 305–334.

Anetheaume, N. (1997) *Accounting For Externalities: A Presentation of the Lessons Learnt from Trying to Evaluate the Environmental External Costs of an Industrial Process.* Proceedings of the World Congress of International Association for Accounting Education: Paris.

Arrhenius, S. (1896) 'On the Influence of Carbonic Acid in the Air Upon the Temperature of the Ground'. *Philosophical Magazine* 41(251), pp. 237–277.

Azar, C. and Rodhe, H. (1997) 'Targets for the Stabilisation of Atmospheric CO_2'. *Science* 276, pp. 1818–1819.

Baker, P., McKay, S. and Symons, E. (1990) *The Simulation of Indirect Tax Reforms: The IFS Simulation Programme For Indirect Taxation* (IFS Working Paper no. W90/11). London: Institute for Fiscal Studies.

Baranzini, A., Goldenberg, J. and Speck, S. (2000) 'A Future For Carbon Taxes'. *Ecological Economics* 32(3), pp. 395–412.

Barker, T. (2004) *Economic Theory and the Transition to Sustainability: A Comparison of General-equilibrium and Space-time-economies Approaches* (Working Paper 62). Manchester: Tyndall Centre for Climate Change Research.

Batabyal, A. and Beladi, H. (2001) *The Economics of International Trade and the Environment.* New York: CRC Press.

Baumol, W. and Oates, W. (1975) *The Theory of Environmental Policy.* New Jersey, USA: Prentice Hall.

Bebbington, J. (1993) 'The European Community Fifth Action Plan: Towards Sustainability'. *Social and Environmental Accounting* 13(1), pp. 9–11.

Bebbington, J. and Gray, R. (2001) 'An Account of Sustainability: Failure, Success and Reconceptualisation'. *Critical Perspectives on Accounting* 12(5), pp. 557–587.

Bebbington, J. and Thomson, I. (1996) *Business Conceptions of Sustainability and the Implications for Accountancy.* ACCA Research Report no. 48. London: Association of Certified Accountants.

Bebbington, J., Gray, R., Hibbitt, C. and Kirk, E. (2001) *Full Cost Accounting: An Agenda for Action.* London: Certified Accountants Educational Trust.

Beggs, C. (2002) *Energy: Management, Supply and Conservation.* Oxford: Butterworth-Heinemann.

Bennett, R. (1986) 'Meaning and Method in Management Research'. *Graduate Management Research* 3(3), pp. 4–56.

Berry, A. and Rondinelli, D. (1998) 'Proactive Environmental Management: A New Industrial Revolution'. *Academy of Management Executives* 12(2), pp. 38–50.

Bird, R. and Oldman, O. (1990) *Taxation in Developing Countries* (4th edn). Baltimore: Johns Hopkins University Press.

Blundell, R., Pashardes, P. and Weber, G. (1989) *What Do we Learn About Consumer Demand Patterns From Micro Data?* (IFS/LBS Micro to Macro Papers no.3). London: Institute for Fiscal Studies.

Boero, G., Clarke, R. and Winters, L. (1991) *The Macroeconomic Consequences of Controlling Greenhouse Gases: A Survey.* Department of the Environment. London: HMSO.

Bolin, B., Doos, B., Jager, J. and Warwick, R. (1986) *The Greenhouse Effect, Climatic Change and Ecosystems.* London: Wiley.

Bovenberg, A. and Goulder, L. (1996) 'Optimal Environmental Taxation in the Presence of Other Taxes: General-Equilibrium Analyses'. *American Economic Review* 86(4), pp. 985–1000.

Boyd, R., Krutilla, K. and Viscusi, W. (1995) 'Energy Taxation as a Policy Instrument to Reduce CO_2 Emissions: A Net Benefit Analysis'. *Journal of Environmental Economics and Management* 29(1), pp. 1–24.

Brack, D. (1998) 'Energy/Carbon Taxation, Competitiveness and Trade'. *Energy Economist* 206, pp. 7–11.

Braithwaite, J. and Drahos, P. (2000) *Global Business Regulation.* Cambridge: Cambridge University Press.

Brook, E. (2005) 'Atmospheric Science: Tiny Bubbles Tell All'. *Science* 310(5752), pp. 1285–1287.

Brownell, P. (1995) *Research Methods in Management Accounting.* Melbourne: Coopers and Lybrand.

Bryman, A. (2001) *Social Research Methods*. Oxford: Oxford University Press.

Buchanan, J. (1963) 'The Economics of Earmarked Taxes'. *Journal of Political Economy* 71(5), pp. 457–469.

Burke, M. (1997) 'Environmental Taxes Gaining Ground in Europe'. *Environmental Science & Technology News* 31(2), pp. 84–88.

Carter, N. (2001) *The Politics of The Environment: Ideas, Activism, Policy.* Cambridge: Cambridge University Press.

Cline, W.R. (1991) 'Scientific Basis for The Greenhouse Effect'. *Economic Journal* 101(407), pp. 904–919.

Cohen, L. and Manion, L. (1987) *Research Methods in Education* (2nd edn). London: Croom Helm.

Costanza, R. (1989) 'What Is Ecological Economics?' *Ecological Economics* 1(1), pp. 1–7.

Cox, P., Betts, R., Jones, C., Spall, S. and Totterdell, I. (2000) 'Acceleration of Global Warming Due to Carbon-cycle Feedbacks in a Coupled Climate Model'. *Nature* 408, pp. 184–187

Curwin, J. and Slater, R. (1996) *Quantitative Methods For Business Decisions* (4th edn). London: Thompson Business Press.

Dales, W. (1968) *Pollution Property and Prices*. Toronto: University of Toronto Press.

Daly, H. (1995) 'On Wilfred Beckerman's Critique of Sustainable Development'. *Environmental Values* 4(1), pp. 49–55.

Dasgupta, P., Heal, G. and Stiglitz, J. (1980) 'The Taxation of Exhaustable Resources' in Hughes, G. (ed.) and Heal, G. (ed.) *Public Policy and the Tax System.* London: George Allen & Unwin, pp. 150–172.

Denscombe, M. (1998) *The Good Research Guide for Small-scale Social Research Projects*. Birmingham: Open University Press.

Defra (Department for Food, Environment and Rural Affairs) (2008) 'Climate Change & Energy: Climate Change Act 2008 – Key Povisions/Milestones', retrieved February 2009 from the World Wide Web: http://www.defra.gov.uk/environment/climatechange/uk/legislation/provisions.htm.

DETR (Department of Environment, Transport and the Regions) (1999) *Sustainable Development: Sequestration of Carbon Dioxide.*

DETR (Department of Environment, Transport and the Regions) (2000) *Tackling Congestion and Pollution.*

DfT (Department for Transport) (2003) *Modelling and Forecasting using the National Transport Model.*

Dillman, D. (1978) *Mail and Telephone Surveys: The Total Design Method.* New York: John Wiley.

Drahos, P. and Braithwaite, J. (2000) *Global Business Regulation*. Cambridge: Cambridge University Press.

DTI (Department of Trade and Industry) (2003) *Our Energy Future: Creating a Low Carbon Economy* (Energy White Paper).

EC (European Commission) (2000) *Greenhouse Gas Emissions Trading With The European Union* (Green Paper). Brussels: European Commission.

Ekins, P. (1994) 'The Impact of Carbon Taxation on The UK Economy'. *Energy Policy* 22(7), pp. 571–579.

Ekins, P. (1997) 'On the Dividends From Environmental Taxation' in O'Riordan, T. (ed.), *Ecotaxation*. London: Earthscan, pp. 125–162.

Ekins, P. (1999) 'European Environmental Taxes and Charges: Recent Experience, Issues and Trends'. *Ecological Economics* 31(1), pp. 39–62.

Ekins, P. (2000a) *Beyond Green GNP: An Overview of Recent Developments in Natural Environmental Economic Accounting*. London: Forum for the Future.

Ekins, P. (2000b) *Estimating Sustainability Gaps for the UK*. London: Forum for the Future.

Elliott (2003) 'Sustainable Energy: Choices, Problems and Opportunities' in Hester, R. (ed.) and Harrison, R. (ed.) *Sustainability and Environmental Impact of Renewable Energy Sources*. Cambridge: Royal Society of Chemistry, pp. 19–48.

EEA (European Environment Agency) (1996) *Environmental Taxes: Implementation and Environmental Effectiveness*. Copenhagen: Environmental Issue Series No.1.

EU (European Union) (1992) *Fifth Action Programme, vol. II*. Brussels: European Union.

Fava, J. (1991) 'Product Lifecycle Assessment: Improving Environmental Quality'. *Integrated Environmental Management* 3, pp. 19–21.

Ferriter, J. (1997) 'The Effects of CO_2 Reduction Policies on Energy Markets' in Kaya, Y. (ed.) and Yokobori, K. (ed.) *Environment, Energy and Economy Strategies for Sustainability*. Tokyo: United Nations University Press.

Foley, J. (2003) *Tomorrow's Low Carbon Cars: Driving Innovation and Long Term Investment in Low Carbon Cars*. London: Institute for Public Policy Research.

Foley, J. and Fergusson, M. (2003) *Putting The Brakes on Climate Change: A Policy Report on Road Transport and Climate Change*. London: Institute for Public Policy Research.

Galliers, R. (1992) *Information Systems Research: Issues, Methods and Practical Guidelines*. Henley-on-Thames: Alfred Waller.

Gaskins, D. and Stram, B. (1991) *A Meta Plan: A Policy Response To Global Warming* (Discussion Paper 91–3). Cambridge, MA: Centre For Science and International Affairs.

Gosling, P. (2002) 'Environmental Accounting: Emissions Trading'. *ACCA Accounting & Business* March. London: Chartered Certified Accountants.

Goudie, A. (2005) 'But It's Cold Comfort For Our Hot Times'. *The Times Higher*, 16 December 2005.

Gray, R. (1992) 'Accounting and Environmentalism: An Exploration of The Challenge of Gently Accounting for Accountability, Transparency and Sustainability'. *Accounting Organisations and Society* 17(5), pp. 399–425.

Gray, R. and Bebbington, J. (2001) *Accounting for the Environment* (2nd edn). London: Sage Publications.

Gray, R., Bebbington, J. and Walters, D. (1993) *Accounting for the Environment*. London: PCP Publications.

Grubb, M., Vrolijk, C. and Brack, D. (1999) *The Koyoto Protocol: A Guide and Assessment*. London: The Royal Institute of International Affairs, Earthscan.

The Guardian (2nd December 2008) 'EU Reaches Compromise Deal on Car Emission Caps' retrieved February 2009 from the World Wide Web: http://www.guardian.co.uk/environment/2008/dec/02/travel-and-transport-carbon-emissions.

Gummesson, E. (1991) *Qualitative Methods in Management Research*. London: Sage Publications.

Hanisch, C. (1998) 'Taking Stock of Green Tax Reform Initiatives'. *Environmental Science & Technology News* December, pp. 540–544.

Harris, I. and Goodwin, J. (2003) *New Thinking in Macroeconomics: Social, Institutional, and Environmental Perspectives*. Cheltenham: Edward Elgar Publishing.

Hasselmann, K., Latif, M., Hooss, G., Azar, C., Edenhofer, O., Jaeger, C., Johannessen, O., Kemfert, C., Welp, M. and Wokaun, A. (2003) 'The Challenge of Long-Term Climate Change'. *Science* 302(5652), pp. 1923–1925.

Hawkes, N. (2005) 'Oceans Rise At Record Rate as Industrial Age Gathers Momentum'. *The Times* 25 November 2005.

Hill, M., McAulay, L., and Wilkinson, A. (2005) 'UK Emission Trading from 2002–2004: Corporate Responses'. *Energy & Environment* 16(6), pp. 993–1007.

Hoeller, P., Dean, A. and Nicolaisen, J. (1990) *A Survey of Studies of The Costs of Reducing Greenhouse Gas Emissions*. Organisation of Economic Co-operation and Development, Survey Papers.

Hueting, R. and Reijnders, L. (1998) 'Sustainability Is An Objective Concept'. *Ecological Economics* 27, pp. 194–213.

Hughes, J. (1997) *The Philosophy of Science*. London: Longman.

Inland Revenue (2004) *Report on The Evaluation of The Company Car Tax Reform*. Inland Revenue April 2004.

IPCC (Intergovernmental Panel on Climate Change) (2001) *Climate Change 2001: The Scientific Basis. Intergovernmental Panel on Climate Change.* Cambridge: Cambridge University Press.

IPCC (Intergovernmental Panel on Climate Change) (2002) *Climate Change 2001: Intergovernmental Panel on Climate Change.* Cambridge: Cambridge University Press.

Internal Revenue Service (1991) *Compliance 2000: Report To The Commissioner of Internal Revenues.* Washington DC: IRS.

International Federation of Accountants (IFA) (1998) *Environmental Management in Organisations: The Role Of Management Accounting.* New York: International Federation of Accountants.

Jaccard, M. (2006) 'The King Has Not Left The Building'. *The Times Higher* 13 January 2006.

James, S. and Nobes, C. (2000) *The Economics of Taxation* (7th edn). Essex: Financial Times, Prentice Hall.

Johansson, P. (1990) 'Valuing Environmental Damage'. *Oxford Review of Economic Policy* 6(1), pp. 34–50.

Jung, C. (1995) *Memories, Dreams, Reflections.* London: Fontana

Kaplan, R. and Johnson, H. (1991) *Relevance Lost: The Rise and Fall of Management Accounting.* Boston, MA: Harvard Business School Press.

Kaufmann, R. (1991) 'Limits on The Effectiveness of a Carbon Tax'. *The Energy Journal* 12(4), pp. 139–144.

Kay, J. and King, M. (1991) *The British Tax System* (5th edn). Oxford: Oxford University Press.

Kirby, J., O'Keefe, P. and Timberlake, L. (1995) *Earthscan Reader in Sustainable Development.* London: Earthscan Publications.

Leady, P. (1989) *Practical Research Planning and Design.* New York: Macmillian.

Lehmann, D. (1989) *Marketing Research Analysis* (3rd edn). Boston, MA: Irwin.

Lucey, T. (2002) *Quantitative Techniques* (6th edn). London: Continuum.

Macve, R. (1997) *Accounting For Environmental Cost in the Industrial Green Game.* Washington: National Academy Press.

Mahlman, J. (1997) 'Uncertainties in Projections of Human-caused Climate Warming'. *Science* 278, pp. 1416–1417.

Manne, A. and Richels, R. (1990) 'The Costs of Reducing U.S. CO_2 Emissions – Further Sensitivity Analysis'. *The Energy Journal* 11(4), pp. 69–79.

Manne, A. and Richels, R. (1993) 'The EC Proposal for Combining Carbon and Energy Taxes'. *Energy Policy* January 1993, pp. 5–10.

Marland, G., Boden, T. and Andres, R. (2006) 'Global, Regional, and National Fossil Fuel CO_2 Emissions' in *Trends: A Compendium of Data on Global Change.*

Oakridge, TN: Carbon Dioxide Information Analysis Center, Oak Ridge National Laboratory, U.S. Department of Energy.

Marsh, C. (1989) *Exploring Data: An Introduction To Data Analysis for Social Scientists*. Oxford: Blackwell.

McKibbin, W., Shackleton, R. and Wilcoxen, P. (1999) 'What to Expect from an International System of Tradeable Permits for Carbon Emissions'. *Resource and Energy Economics* 21(3), pp. 319–347.

McKinney, L. and Schoch, R. (2003) *Environmental Science*. Boston, MA: Jones and Bartlett Publishers.

Meade, J. (1973) *The Theory of Economic Externalities*. Leiden: Leiden University Press.

Meinshausen, M. (2006) 'What Does a 2°C Target Mean for Greenhouse Concentrations? A Brief Analysis Based on Multi-gas Emission Pathways and Several Climate Sensitivity Uncertainty Estimates' in Schellnhuber, H. et al. (eds) (2006) *Avoiding Dangerous Climate Change*. Cambridge: Cambridge University Press, pp. 265–280.

Mill, J. (1874) *A System of Logic*. New York: Harper.

Mohr, E. (1990) *EC Fiscal Harmonisation, Environmental Taxes and Charges; Theory and Policy*. Keil: Keil Institute of World Economics.

Musgrave, R. (1959) *The Theory of Public Finance*. London: McGraw-Hill.

Neumayer, E. (1999) *Weak versus Strong Sustainability: Exploring the Limits of Two Opposing Paradigms*. Cheltenham: Edward Elgar.

Newbery, D. (1980) 'Externalities: The Theory of Environmental Policy' in Hughes, G. (ed.) and Heal, G. (ed.) *Public Policy and The Tax System*. London: George Allen & Unwin, pp. 133–139.

Nordhaus, W. (1975) 'The Political Business Cycle'. *Review of Economic Studies* 42(130), pp. 169–191.

Nordhaus, W. (1991) 'To Slow or Not To Slow: The Economics of The Greenhouse Effect'. *The Economic Journal* 101(407), pp. 920–937.

Nordhaus, W. (ed.) (1998) *Economics and Policy Issues in Climate Change*. Washington DC: Resources for the Future.

Nordhaus, W. and Yohe, G. (1983) *Future Carbon Dioxide Emissions From Fossil Fuels. Changing Climate. National Research Council*. Washington DC: National Academy Press.

Nordhaus, W. and Yang, Z. (1996) 'A Regional Dynamic General-Equilibrium Model of Alternative Climate-Change Strategies'. *American Economic Review* 86(4), pp. 741–765.

OECD (Organisation for Economic Co-operation and Development) (1976) *Revenue Statistics Paris Part II*.

OECD (Organisation for Economic Co-operation and Development) (1999) *National Climate Policies and the Kyoto Protocol.*

Oppenheim, A. (1966) *Questionnaire Design and Attitude Measurement.* New York: Gower.

Pearce, D. (1991) 'The Role of Carbon Taxes in Adjusting to Global Warming'. *The Economic Journal* 101(407), pp. 938–948.

Pearce, D., Markandya, A. and Barbier, E. (1989) *Blueprint for a Green Economy.* London: Earthscan.

Pearson, M. and Smith, S. (1990) *Taxation and Environmental Policy Some Initial Evidence* (IFS Commentary no.19). London: The Institute for Fiscal Studies.

Pigou, A. (1912) *Wealth and Welfare.* London. Macmillian

Popoff, F. and Buzzelli, D. (1993) 'Full Cost Accounting'. *Chemical and Engineering News* 71(2), pp. 8–10.

Popper, K. (1959) *The Logic of Scientific Discovery.* London: Hutchinson.

Quinn, J. (1998) *Strategies for Change: Logical Incrementalism.* Homewood, IL: Irwin.

Remenyi, D., Williams, B., Money, A. and Swartz, E. (1998) *Doing Research in Business and Management: An Introduction to Process and Method.* London: Sage Publications.

Retallack, S. (2005) *Setting a Long-Term Climate Objective.* London: International Climate Change Taskforce. Institute for Public Policy Research.

Rosenthal, R. and Rosnow, R. (1991) *Essentials of Behavioural Research Methods and Data Analysis* (2nd edn). New York: McGraw Hill.

Rubenstein, D. (1994) *Environmental Accounting for the Sustainable Corporation.* London: Quorum Books.

Ryan, B., Scapens, R. and Theobold, M. (2002) *Research Method and Methodology in Finance and Accounting* (2nd edn). London: Thomson.

Saunders, M., Lewis, P. and Thornhill, A. (2003) *Research Methods for Business Students.* London: Pearson.

Schmolders, G. (1970) 'Survey Research in Public Finance – A Behavioural Approach to Fiscal Theory'. *Public Finance* 25(2), pp. 300–302.

Schneider, S. and Goulder, L. (1997) 'Achieving Low-Cost Emissions Targets'. *Nature* 389, pp. 13–14.

Selltiz, C., Wrightsman, L. and Cook, S. (1981) *Research Methods In Social Relations* (4th edn.). New York: Holt Rinehart and Winston.

Smith, A. (1776) *An Inquiry Into The Nature and Causes of The Wealth of Nations.* Boston, MA: Adamat Media Corporation.

Smith, C. (2001) 'Vunerability to Climate Change and Reasons for Concern: A Synthesis' in McCarthy, J., Canziani, O., Leary, N., Dokken, D. and White, K.

(eds) *Climate Change 2001: Impacts Adaptation and Vulnerability*. Cambridge: Press Syndicate of the University of Cambridge, pp. 913–967.

Smith, M. (2003) *Research Methods in Accounting*. London: Sage Publications.

Smith, S. (1993) '"Green Taxes" – The Scope For Environmentally-Friendly Taxes' in Sandford, C. (ed), *Key Issues in Tax Reform*. Bath: Fiscal Publications, pp. 220–237.

Smith, S. (1997) *Evaluating Economic Instruments for Environmental Policy*. January 1997. Paris: Organisation for Economic Co-operation and Development.

Smith, S. (1998) 'Environmental and Public Finance Aspects of the Taxation of Energy'. *Oxford Review of Economic Policy* 14(4), pp. 64–83.

SMMT (The Society of Motor Manufacturers and Traders) (2002) *Towards Sustainability: The Automotive Sector Third Annual Report*. The Society of Motor Manufacturers and Traders.

SMMT (The Society of Motor Manufacturers and Traders) (2005) *New Car Registrations by CO_2 Performance*. The Society of Motor Manufacturers and Traders.

Stern, N. (2007) *The Economics of Climate Change: The Stern Review*. Cambridge: Cambridge University Press.

Stott, P., Stone, D. and Allen, M. (2004) 'Human Contribution to the European Heatwave of 2003'. *Nature* 432, pp. 610–614.

Swedish Environmental Protection Agency (SEPA) (1997) *Environmental Taxes in Sweden – Economic Instruments of Environmental Policy. Report 4745*. Stockholm.

Symons, E., Proops, J. and Gay, P. (1994) 'Carbon Taxes, Consumer Demand and Carbon Dioxide Emissions: A Simulation Analysis for the UK'. *Fiscal Studies* 15(2), pp. 19–43.

Taylor, M., Rubin, S. and Nemet, G. (2006) 'The Role of Technological Innovation in Meeting California's Greenhouse Gas Emission Targets' in Hanemann, W. (ed) and Farrell, A. (ed) (2006) *Managing Greenhouse Gas Emissions in California*. Berkeley, CA: California Climate Change Center, University of California.

Teja, R. and Bracewell-Milnes, B. (1991) *The Case for Earmarked Taxes: Government Spending and Public Choice*. London: Institute of Economic Affairs.

Tietenberg, T. (1985) *Emissions Trading: An Exercise in Reforming Pollution Policy*. Washington DC: Resources for The Future.

Tol, R. (2005) 'The Marginal Damage Costs of Carbon Dioxide Emissions: An Assessment of the Uncertainties'. *Energy Policy* 33(16), pp. 2064–2074.

Tulpule, V., Brown, S., Lim, J., Polidano, C., Pant, H. and Fisher, B. (1998) *An Economic Assessment of the Kyoto Protocol using the Global Trade and Environment Model*. Background Analysis for the Kyoto Protocol OECD Workshop. Paris, 17–18 September 1998.

Tuppen, C. (ed.) (1996) *Environmental Accounting in Industry: A Practical Review.* London: BT.

Tyndall, J. (1863) 'On Radiation Through the Earth's Atmosphere'. *Philosophical Magazine* 4, pp. 200–206.

UNCED (United Nations Commission on Environment and Development) (1987) *The Brundtland Report.*

UNCTAD (United Nations Conference on Trade and Development) (1996) *Self Regulation of Environmental Management: An Analysis of Guidelines Set By World Industry Associations and Their Member Firms.* Geneva: United Nations Conference on Trade and Development.

UNFCCC (United Nations Framework Convention on Climate Change) (2005b) 'Status of Ratification', retrieved June 2005 from the World Wide Web: http://unfccc.int/essential_background/kyoto_protocol/status_of_ratification/items/2613.php.

USEPA (United States Environmental Protection Agency) (1996) *Environmental Accounting Case Studies: Full Cost Accounting for Decision Making at Ontario Hydro.* Washington: USEPA.

Uzawa, H. (2003) *Economic Theory and Global Warming.* Cambridge: Cambridge University Press.

Victor, D. (2001) *The Collapse of the Kyoto Protocol and the Struggle to Slow Global Warming.* Oxford: Princeton University Press.

Wallschutzky, I. (1993) *Achieving Compliance.* Proceedings of the Australasian Tax Teachers' Association. January, Christchurch, New Zealand.

Weitzman, M. (1974) 'Prices vs. Quantities'. *Review of Economic Studies* 41(4), pp. 477–491.

Weizsacker, E. and Jesinghaus, J. (1992) *Ecological Tax Reform: A Policy Proposal for Sustainable Development.* London: Zed Books.

Weyant, J. (1998) 'The Costs of Carbon Emissions Reductions' in Nordhaus, W. (ed.) *Economics and Policy Issues in Climate Change.* Washington: Resources for the Future, pp. 204.

Wheatley, M. (1992) *Leadership and the New Science.* San Francisco: Berrett-Koeler Publishers.

Wigley, T., Richels, R. and Edmonds, J. (1996) 'Economic and Environmental Choices in the Stabilization of Atmospheric CO_2 Concentrations'. *Nature* 379, pp. 240–243.

Wilson, G., Peake, S. and Furniss, P. (2001) *Introduction to Sustainability.* Milton Keynes: Open University Press.

Wintour, P. (2006) 'Carbon Emission Targets Delayed by Government'. *The Guardian* 31 January 2006.

Wittneben, B., Haxeltine, A., Kjellen, B., Kohler, J., Turnpenny, J. and Warren, R. (2005) *A Framework for Assessing the Political Economy of Post 2012 Global Climate Regime* (Working Paper 80). Manchester: Tyndall Centre for Climate Change Research.

Yanarella, E. and Levine, R. (1992) 'Does Sustainable Development Lead To Sustainability?'. *Futures* 24(8), pp. 759–774.

Young, S. (1996) 'Survey Research in Management Accounting: A Critical Assessment' in Richardson, A. (ed) *Survey Research in Management Accounting: A Critical Assessment. Research Methods in Accounting: Issues and Debates.* Vancouver: The Canadian General Accountants Research Foundation, pp. 55–68.

Zimmerman, M. (1994) *Contesting Earth's Future: Radical Ecology and Post Modernity.* London: University of California Press.

Index

For Product Safety Concerns and Information please contact our
EU representative GPSR@taylorandfrancis.com Taylor & Francis
Verlag GmbH, Kaufingerstraße 24, 80331 München, Germany